STAGE TO
SCREEN

STAGE TO SCREEN

Theatrical Origins of Early Film:
David Garrick to D. W. Griffith

A. NICHOLAS VARDAC

A DA CAPO PAPERBACK

Library of Congress Cataloging in Publication Data

Vardac, A. Nicholas.
    Stage to screen.

    (A Da Capo paperback)
    Reprint. Originally published: Cambridge: Harvard
University Press, 1949.
    Includes index.
    1. Moving-pictures — History. 2. Moving-pictures and
theater. 3. Theater — History. I. Title.
PN1993.5.A1V3   1987   791.43'09   87-13617
ISBN 0-306-80308-9 (pbk.)

This Da Capo Press paperback edition of *Stage to Screen*
is an unabridged republication of the edition published
in Cambridge, Massachusetts in 1949. It is reprinted by
arrangement with the author.

Published by Da Capo Press, Inc.
A Subsidiary of Plenum Publishing Corporation
233 Spring Street, New York, N.Y. 10013

TO

SPYROS P. SKOURAS

PREFACE

The position of the motion picture in the evolution of the theatre of the world has yet to be determined. Much has been written in description and in critical analysis of the film. These studies spread roots like aerial plants through a fruitless vacuum. The atmosphere of nineteenth-century theatre has yet to be cleared and the proper source of cinema exposed. A new art form does not simply appear. In aesthetic as well as scientific and political areas the old dies as the new is born, the whole process being as insistent as it is gradual. The time has come to see how the film fits into the evolutionary pattern of world theatre, how the blood stream of the screen was drawn from the stage, and how, under the pressure of this withdrawal, certain stage forms died upon the boards.

ʄ The roots of a new art form are to be found in the sociological needs and tensions, in the spirit of the times, which sponsor its growth. This tension is so thoroughly woven into the cultural fabric that it can best be identified through its expression in the arts, in this case, in the related arts of theatre and of staging. In this fashion the spiritual, the sociological, and most of all, the aesthetic roots of the motion picture can be revealed through a composite study of both the early film and theatrical methods during the years leading to and surrounding its birth. ⟋

The patterns within this period of theatrical history, as yet uncharted, must be traced by direct scrutiny of the spectacular promptbooks and the revealing periodical accounts of productions appearing during these years. From this body of source material the expression as well as the motivation of the forces, the social tensions, working behind the aesthetic strivings of the popular nineteenth-century stage, the early twentieth-century popular theatre, the early twentieth-century experimental "producers' theatre," and finally the motion picture, will appear in their distinct and special relationship. A more complete and accurate understanding of stage and screen will arise.

I should like to acknowledge my gratitude to Professor Allardyce Nicoll for his inestimable support of the ideas of this study. To Dr. William VanLennep, Curator of the Harvard Theatre Collection, I am indebted for much valuable material. Untapped sources in that great collection eventually disclosed the use of cinematic devices upon the stage of the nineteenth century. To Miss Iris Barry, Curator of the Film Library of the Museum of Modern Art, may I express appreciation for courtesy and consideration in the arrangement of special showings of early American and foreign films. I am particularly grateful to Mr. Percy MacKaye, whose interest in my subject has made possible the use of material concerning the work of his father, Steele MacKaye, which otherwise might not have been available for presentation at this time. And for the careful editorial perusal of Professor Hubert C. Heffner both the reader and myself will find, I am sure, good reason for gratitude.

A. NICHOLAS VARDAC

Palo Alto, California
June 1947

CONTENTS

ILLUSTRATIONS

All the illustrations in this book were obtained from the Harvard Theatre Collection and the Museum of Modern Art Film Library, through whose kind permission they are reproduced here. In the list below, the abbreviations HTC and MMA designate the sources of the pictures.

A very interesting single source was a specimen book of theatrical cuts, dated 1869, in the Harvard Theatre Collection. The title page of this volume reads: "Specimens of Theatrical Cuts: Being Fac-similes, in miniature, of Poster Cuts: comprising colored and plain designs, suitable for Theatrical, Variety and Circus Business. . . To be had at the Ledger Job Printing Office, Public Ledger Building, Philadelphia, George W. Childs,—Proprietor." The "cut" numbers listed below refer to this book.

The end papers are from a New York City newspaper, dated "Jan. 1875 January 30" in pencil on the bottom margin, now in the Harvard Theatre Collection. The legend beneath the pictures reads: "Scenes in the Play of 'The Two Orphans,' Now Running at the Union Square Theatre."

GROUP ONE

1. Design by P. J. Loutherbourg for David Garrick's production of *The Christmas Tale,* presented at the Drury Lane Theatre, London, December 27, 1773. W. J. Lawrence has described Loutherbourg's theatrical innovations for this scene: "The fleeting effect of various colours on a landscape was produced by means of silkscreens working on pivots before concentrated light in the wings" (*Magazine of Art,* XVIII [1895], 173). HTC.

2. *Arrah-na-Pogue* (Dion Boucicault), Escape Scene (cut no. 84). HTC.

3. *Arrah-na-Pogue,* Escape Scene (cut no. 2033). HTC.

4. *David Copperfield; or, Little Emily* (Charles Dickens), Shipwreck Scene (cut no. 191). HTC.

5. *David Copperfield; or, Little Emily,* Churchyard Scene (cut no. 192). HTC.

6. *Oliver Twist* (Charles Dickens), Murder Scene (cut no. 1013). HTC.

7. *Oliver Twist,* Hanging Scene (cut no. 1012). HTC.

54. *Forty Thieves* (cut no. 120). HTC.

55. *Forty Thieves,* advertising streamer (cut no. 157). HTC.

56. *The Sleeping Beauty* (cut no. 130). HTC.

GROUP THREE

57. *Le Royaume des fées* (The Kingdom of the Fairies), a George Méliès-Star film of 1903. MMA.

58. *Le Royaume de Neptune* (The Kingdom of Neptune; or, Under the Seas), Tableau 27: Entangled in a Net. A George Méliès-Star film of 1907. MMA.

59. *L'Homme à la tête en caoutchouc* (The Man with the Rubber Head), a George Méliès-Star film of 1902. MMA.

60. *L'Homme à la tête en caoutchouc,* George Méliès-Star film of 1902. MMA.

61. *Uncle Tom's Cabin* (Harriet Beecher Stowe and G. L. Aiken), Eliza Crossing the Ice, as produced by William Brady at the Academy of Music, New York, March 1901 (Byron photograph, showing Mabel Amber as Eliza). HTC.

62. *Uncle Tom's Cabin,* Uncle Tom in Heaven, William Brady's production, March 1901 (Byron photograph, showing Wilton Lackaye as Uncle Tom). HTC.

63. *Uncle Tom's Cabin,* Eliza Crossing the Ice, from the film directed by Edwin S. Porter for the Edison Company in 1903. MMA.

64. *Uncle Tom's Cabin,* Cotton-Picking Scene, from Edwin S. Porter film of 1903. MMA.

65. *Edgar Allan Poe,* from the film directed by D. W. Griffith, February 1909 (with Linda Arvidson and Herbert Yost). MMA.

66. *Fighting Blood,* from the film directed by D. W. Griffith for the Biograph Company, June 1911 (with Blanche Sweet and Lionel Barrymore). MMA.

67. *The Count of Monte Cristo,* from the film directed by Colin Campbell for Selig in 1912 (with Hobart Bosworth). MMA.

68. *The Count of Monte Cristo,* from the film produced by Famous Players in 1913 (with James O'Neill). MMA.

69. *The Prisoner of Zenda* (Anthony Hope), from the film directed by Edwin S. Porter and Daniel Frohman for Famous Players in 1913 (with James K. Hackett and Beatrice Beckley). MMA.

INTRODUCTION

REALISM, ROMANCE, AND THE DEVELOP-
MENT OF THE MOTION PICTURE

Art in any of its many forms cannot be considered in terms of static manifestation. It must forever be viewed in the light of its dynamics, its flow, and its changing social origins. The birth of the need for the motion picture, the expression of this need in the related arts of the times, its growth, and eventually its transition from the related arts to the screen must be considered as a study in aesthetic dynamics.

The spirit which dominated the nineteenth century arose from the intellectual upheavals of the eighteenth. Through the mid-years of the 1700's realistic rebellion and intellectual inquisition were breeding. The universe was questioned and dissected and its fabric examined. The modern objective and scientific point of view was in the process of birth. Its most immediate and sensational manifestations may indeed have been in the political arena, with revolutions flaring upon two continents within a matter of decades, but the power of this new spirit, pervading the eighteenth-century horizon, found a ready reflection in aesthetic areas as well.

In the arts of the theatre this spirit, beginning with the work of David Garrick, stimulated the growth of a new realism in staging and acting. As the objective or scientific point of view dominated society, finding its outlet in the flood of scientific invention of the nineteenth century, the cycle of realistic theatrical presentation inaugurated by Garrick marched in close step. Garrick's new aesthetic departure, stated simply, was that of achieving a greater pictorial realism in staging. This intention is indicated by the many stagings made for him by P. J. de Loutherbourg, by the withdrawal of his production into the proscenium picture frame, as well as by changes in lighting and in character interpretation. He was aiming at theatrical production pictorial, thus cinematic, in conception. Can the motion picture, then, be considered as the ultimate aesthetic expression of a cycle of realistic-pictorial theatrical production which had been a part of the rebirth of the objective spirit in the middle of the eighteenth century and which was to mature through the nineteenth-century age of invention?

The theory of the persistence of vision upon which the motion picture is based is said to have been understood and demonstrated by Ptolemy in 130 A.D.[1] But the cinema was born of a different era. Is there connection between the arrival of the motion picture in the late nineteenth century (1895) and theatrical production surrounding and preceding its arrival? Is it true that the cycle of nineteenth-century stage realism stemming from Garrick was the early expression of the same aesthetic need that gave rise to the cinema? Is there, first of all, any coincidence between the course of the development of realism in staging arising with Garrick and the course of progress in the invention of the motion picture? Any study of the transition of theatrical method from stage to screen must attempt to answer these questions.

Progress in the invention of the motion picture falls into three distinct periods. The first period produced animated pictures; the second, animated photographs; and the third, the culminating phase, the continuous projection of objects photographed in motion,[2] or motion pictures.

In 1824 Peter Mark Roget presented before the Royal Society a paper entitled "The Persistence of Vision with Regard to Moving Objects." In 1829 Joseph Nicéphore Niepce joined in a pact with Louis Jacques Mandé Daguerre for the furtherance of photography. The thaumatrope had already been demonstrated in 1825. A series of devices calculated to create the illusion of motion followed, with the eventual development of the phenakistoscope by Joseph Antoine Plateau and the stroboscope by Simon Ritter von Stampfer. Thus the period 1824-1832 saw the achievement of animated pictures.

With the consummation of this preliminary goal, activity if not interest subsided and for over twenty years nothing of significance in the direction of the motion picture seems to have been precipitated. Progress came in well-defined surges. The second period started in 1853, when Baron Franz von Uchatius projected the phenakistoscopic pictures of Plateau with a magic-lantern apparatus. In 1857 a patent was issued in France to Leon Scott for a phonautograph. In 1860 Désvignes patented a zoëtrope. On numerous blades of a paddle wheel he mounted successively posed photographs. Then the wheel was spun. On February 5, 1861, a United States patent was granted to Coleman Sellers for a zoëtropic machine known as the kinematoscope. Thus with the animation of successively posed "stills," the second stage from 1853 to 1861 was completed.

In 1864 a patent is said to have been issued to Louis Arthur du Hauron anticipating the entire scheme of the motion picture. This and the combination of photography with magic-lantern projection in the phasmatrope of Henry Renno Heyl in 1870 opened the third and final period. Successively posed stills were projected. Once the relationship between photography and projection was established, progress quickened. Muybridge, working from 1872 to 1877, eventually utilized John D. Isaacs' battery of twenty-four cameras, shutters timed in succession, to photograph the movement of a galloping horse for Leland Stanford. And in 1881 Meissonier projected these stills at a private showing in Paris, using a zoöpraxiscope. In 1887 Edison joined W. E. L. Dickson in an attempt to photograph and project motion. Two years later William Friese-Greene patented photography on celluloid, and at the same time Eastman's celluloid film became available for still photography. Edison saw the possibilities and on October 6, 1889, demonstrated an Edison-Dickson kinetoscope at West Orange, New Jersey, utilizing a strip of Eastman's film with frames moving as fast as forty per second between a magnifying lens and a light source. In 1895 Thomas Armat projected an Edison kinetoscopic film upon a screen with his vitascope, and in the same year Edison, joined now with Armat, exhibited an improved form of the vitascope named, oddly enough, the kinetoscope. And so the final phase in the projection of the photography of motion was completed in the period from 1864 to 1895.

From this brief examination of the line of inventive progress, which gathered momentum through the nineteenth century and culminated, toward its end, in the motion picture, a rough over-all coincidence appears between the invention of cinema and the nineteenth-century cycle of theatrical realism stemming from Garrick. That the birth of cinema should have come at the end of a gradual process of invention running from 1824 to 1895 is, when we turn to examine conditions in the contemporaneous related arts, not surprising. The necessity for greater pictorial realism in the arts of theatre appears as the logical impetus to the invention of cinema. This necessity, an "aesthetic" tension of the nineteenth century, found its preliminary satisfaction in the theatrical forms preceding and surrounding the arrival of the film.

During the nineteenth century the related literary arts of the novel and the drama tended both toward the romantic and the realistic modes. While on one hand greater and more glamorous escape was offered, on the other we find reaction and an effort, despite the traditional rose-colored glasses of a romantic age, to view and appraise real values of the day. Paradoxical as it may appear, however, this dual character of certain nineteenth-century art forms presented but a single problem to the scenic artist. Romantic conceptions of the playwrights might become more and more exaggerated in their never-ending quest for escape, but it would never do for the scene builder to follow a similar pattern. His job was to render believable upon the stage the increasingly glamorous, unreal, and spectacular ideas of the romantic playwrights. The more romantic the subject matter the more realistic must be its presentation upon the boards, else the entire effect would be lost. The conventional staging methods, forced upon audiences and producers alike by the stage building itself, were a serious limitation to realism, but were agreeably tolerated for their capacity in pictorializing the most romantic conceptions of the age. Within the limitations of the conventions and as the century progressed, the essential goal of the scenic artist became that of providing an ever larger and more elaborate pictorial realism. Thus, strange as it may seem, the nineteenth century witnessed a union of romanticism and realism in the arts of the drama and of staging.

In the face of this combined front, the waning pseudoclassic temper of eighteenth-century staging was rapidly spent, and even before the turn of the century the new realism found increasing support. The aural productions of the pseudoclassicists gave way before the visual productions of either realist or romanticist. Charles Macklin had already played *Macbeth* in kilts. David Garrick combined his realistic reforms in staging with the pictorial, spectacular scenic conceptions of M. de Loutherbourg, fresh from the baroque staging methods of Parisian theatres. Soon came the archaeological innovations of William Capon. In the drama, similar graphic inclinations were reflected in the work of the realist-sentimentalists, Thomas Holcroft and Mrs. Inchbald, and the romanticist, George Colman, the younger. Under the influence of Kotzebue, he managed such a piece as *The Iron Chest* in 1796. The novel, too, demonstrated the growing graphic bias of the new objective spirit. Again the pictorial approach, including realistic pictures of romantic subjects and romanticized pictures of subjects from immediate life, appeared in the work of Samuel Richardson, Henry Fielding, Tobias Smollett, Samuel Johnson, Oliver Goldsmith, "Monk" Lewis, and Horace Walpole, among others. Seeds of cinema, thus found in the realistic and romantic pictorial leanings of novel, drama, and theatre, were sown even before the arrival of the nineteenth century.

The pattern of this realistic-romantic movement, with its increasing stress upon pictorial values, harmonized throughout the nineteenth century with the three phases in the invention of the motion picture. Modern theatrical realism is said to have begun with the archaeologically authentic costume production of *King John* by J. R. Planché at Covent Garden, January 19, 1824.[3]

Planché's production and Roget's paper on the persistence of vision appeared in the same year, both apparently reflections of that social tension which was bringing about an aesthetic preference for the visual, the graphic, the pictorial illusion. Looking further into the Planché-Roget coincidence, we find that a new peak in realistic-romantic activity in theatrical production occurred simultaneously with the first phase in the development of cinema. Neither Planché nor Roget was an isolated phenomenon. Chronological parallels, of course, must be viewed with care, yet it may be of certain interest that the early nineteenth-century boom in pictorial theatre, marked by the work of Charles Macready, Edmund Kean, Edwin Forrest, Madame Vestris, and Charles J. Mathews, ran concurrently with the first phase in the invention of the motion picture. In novel and drama surrounding the 1824-1832 period, great activity appeared in the same pictorial direction. J. S. Knowles's *Virginius* appeared in 1820, and *The Hunchback* in 1832. Hugo's *Hernani* (1830) was translated into English for private production in 1831. Shelley's *Cenci* appeared in 1819. Miss Mitford moved into the scene of the twenties, Scribe filled the twenties and thirties, and Browning the thirties. Byron's *Sardanapalus* and *Marino Faliero* came in 1821, and his *Werner* in 1823. The *Waverley Novels* appeared from 1814 to 1831, and the work of James Fenimore Cooper, highly cinematic in conception and execution, was concentrated in the years from 1821 to 1826. Activity in these arts, to be sure, was of a continuous nature, yet the grouping within this period is sufficiently marked to justify consideration. It is not at all strange that the first phase in the development of the motion picture, the achievement of animated drawings, was begun and completed in the years from 1824 to 1832, for during the same period social tensions and the resultant aesthetic preferences sponsored a boom in pictorialism, both romantic and realistic, in these related arts. This concentration of activity directed toward a pictorial aesthetic expression offers the first indication in the century of that necessity which pointed to the invention of cinema.

With the completion of the initial stage in the invention of the motion picture, activity subsided while success was assimilated. Meanwhile, the graphic proclivities of this realistic-romantic trend in theatrical arts continued in an unbroken line until, with the work of Charles Kean, a second peak in activity and achievement was reached. Kean entered the Princess' Theatre in 1850. The success of his authentic pictorial productions continued into the next decade. Surrounding him in the theatre of London were such luminaries as Samuel Phelps at Sadler's Wells and Charles Fechter at the Lyceum. A younger Booth, Edwin, a more restrained and realistic performer than his forebear, made his debut in Boston in 1849 in *Richard III*. In the same decade Thackeray became firmly established. Darwin's *Origin of Species* was published in 1859. Dumas *père* built his own Théâtre Historique in Paris in 1847, and the design of this theatre, a sharp break from contemporary practice, reveals again the growing interest in staging realism. George Boker and the Philadelphia romanticists flourished through the fifties. Thus the decade of the fifties appears as a second period of achievement in the upward cycle of realism and romanticism.

Again coincidence is to be noted, for during the years from 1853 to 1861 the second phase in the invention of cinema, animated photographs, was completed. This coincidence carries a certain significance, for it would indicate that both the need for cinema and for greater pictorial realism in the theatre came in response to a single stimulus, a similar aesthetic, or, as Waldemar Kaempffert has applied the term, "social tension."[4] Two apparently independent developments, both sponsoring a greater pictorial realism for the arts of theatre, appeared simultaneously. The relationship so well demonstrated by Kaempffert to exist between the "social tension" of an age and its scientific progress also holds for its aesthetic growth. Progress in the invention of cinema came when the need for pictorial realism in the theatre was at a peak. Thus, while the second phase in its development did not provide the projection of motion pictures, such advance as did occur was so closely allied with the social tensions and aesthetic preferences of the times that there would seem to have been an impulse to supply, through scientific progress, a greater pictorial realism for the arts of the theatre.

The final phase in the invention of cinema and the final phase in the progress of the realistic-romantic theatrical cycle which had been going forward during the century were both inaugurated at about the same time, the former in 1864 and the latter in 1865. In 1864 M. du Hauron was issued a patent covering the scheme of cinema. In 1865 the Bancrofts' production of *Society* was given at the Prince of Wales's. With these two events began the final surge in the two related developments.

In staging method, the ultimate in nineteenth-century pictorial realism came with the productions of the Bancrofts and

Henry Irving in England, of Augustin Daly, Steele MacKaye, and David Belasco in America, and with the Saxe-Meiningen group, the Théâtre-Libre of Antoine, and the Moscow Art Theatre as vanguard on the Continent. The Bancrofts may have used genuine falling leaves to complete a realistic picture, but Antoine included beeves fresh from the slaughterhouse for his stage butcher shop, and Steele MacKaye in America used real ships on real water. A parallel expression can be seen in the novel among such realists as George Eliot, George Meredith, Henry James, and Thomas Hardy, and such romanticists as Robert Louis Stevenson, A. Conan Doyle, H. Rider Haggard, Rudyard Kipling, and James M. Barrie. In the drama, Ibsen, Chekhov, and Strindberg are the outstanding figures of the cycle, surrounded by a multitude of lesser lights— Hauptmann, Masefield, Zola, Brieux, Augier, Robertson, Bernstein, Jones, Pinero, Granville-Barker, Houghton, and Galsworthy. Boucicault, Herne, Belasco, Stephen Phillips, and Maeterlinck supply a colorful romantic counterpoint, while the Irish playwrights are both realistic and romantic. Thus, at the moment of the arrival of the motion picture, pictorial realism and romanticism in these related arts had attained a pinnacle. The cinema came at the very crest of the realistic-romantic cycle which had been introduced a century before by Garrick. In marking time with this cycle, the invention of cinema seemed to have come in response to that same need for greater pictorial realism born with Garrick. When it finally did arrive, the cinema, as shall be seen, challenged the realistic-pictorial stage producers and took over the creations of the romantic authors.

The arrival of the motion picture cannot be looked upon as an isolated and haphazard expression of scientific progress. Two fundamental relationships now appear which indicate that the arrival of cinema, viewed in the light of growing social tensions and changing aesthetic preferences, came at a most logical phase in the evolutionary pattern of world theatre. The first relationship is simply the over-all coincidence between the realistic-romantic theatrical cycle in the nineteenth century and the invention of the motion picture. Both were devoted to the creation of visual or pictorial illusion, and both ran a similar course from 1824 to 1895, coinciding nearly to the year. Secondly, to cement this over-all similarity, the three separate stages in the development of cinema —animated pictures, animated photographs, and the projection of photographed motion—each coincided with three peaks in realistic-romantic activity in the related arts of the novel, drama, and theatre. Progress in the cinematic direction and progress in this pictorial cycle moved in response to a similar audience need. When, however, realism and romanticism had, toward the end of the century, attained real leaves, beeves, and ships, the stage could go no further. But the need for pictorial realism on an ever greater scale remained. Only the motion picture with its reproduction of reality could carry on the cycle.

In the face of such a theatrical presentation as Alexander Black's *Miss Jerry*[5] on October 10, 1894, the arrival of cinema would appear to have been preordained. The time was fully ripe and waited only upon the proper combination of technical knowledge and skill. *Miss Jerry* was a strange kind of play, a "picture-play." Current staging methods were apparently failing to satisfy the full pictorial preference of the late nineteenth-century audience. The play itself had now become less important than the realism of its pictorial aspects, for it was read by Black in a darkened hall. On a screen at one end were projected more than three hundred photographs taken from life. These pictures, shown in about two hours at a rate somewhat above two per minute, imparted life, vitality, and probably even imaginative motion to the play. The need for pictorial realism was apparently so great that, lacking motion pictures, a succession of "stills" was substituted.

That the motion picture finally made its appearance in response to the insistence of social pressure for a greater pictorial realism in the theatre is indicated still further by the manner of its arrival. This pressure was so great and so diversified that if Edison had not been available others would have pioneered. From a variety of quarters, almost simultaneously, the cinema sprang. In 1890 William Friese-Greene developed and printed successfully the first moving picture photographed on celluloid. In 1891 C. Francis Jenkins perfected a motion-picture machine complete with cogs, gears, and lenses, and in 1894 projected a film called *Annabelle the Dancer*. This machine, improved by Armat, was refused a patent in 1895. Jenkins bought out Armat for $2500. In 1895 and 1896 Jenkins, now sponsored by Edison, exhibited the machine as the Edison vitascope. In France the Lumière brothers patented a projection machine in 1895. In the same year in London, Robert Paul exhibited a machine along other lines. The times rather than the men controlled the ultimate arrival of the motion picture, for at just the point beyond which stage realism would have broken down and in many instances did, the cinema came to meet the need for a greater pictorial realism. By coming at the very peak of the nineteenth-century cycle of realism, it upset normal expectations in the theatre itself. For in accordance with the principle of organic change which is regularly found in theatrical art, one might have expected, in the early twentieth century, the rapid development of newer experimental forms with the consequent breakdown of both the realistic and the spectacular styles. Just at the time, however, that such a change might have been expected, the regular development of theatrical forms was checked and thwarted by the appearance of the motion picture. Naturally, in these early years, the film and the stage were hardly differentiated from one another; the cinema frequently borrowed from the theatre, while the theatre, in an attempt to counter the new attraction, in its turn borrowed from the film. From the beginning the cinema was recognized as a highly realistic and representational medium with, paradoxically, the means of proceeding in the romantic direction many degrees beyond the stage. The result was that the two styles which defined the nineteenth-century theatre, realism and romanticism, and which most probably would have seen alteration in the early years of the twentieth century, were given a new lease on life.

Did the cinema take over the audience of the nineteenth-century pictorial stage? Did this pictorial stage disappear? How did early twentieth-century theatrical producers combat the encroachment of the film? Was there a change in style? How do the sporadic reactionary experiments of the "producers' theatre" in the early 1900's fit into the picture? These and other questions evaluating stage and screen during the years of their aesthetic merger may be elaborated and clarified by this study. The roots of the cinema will be examined, and a better understanding of the relationship between stage and screen today will eventually appear.

STAGE TO
SCREEN

ONE

THEATRES, STAGING METHODS, AND THE BREAKDOWN OF NINETEENTH-CENTURY CONVENTIONS

 "The history of the motion picture—how it took over the old melodrama . . . is a story which needs to be told."[1] The old melodrama formed one of the largest and most significant parts of nineteenth-century theatrical fare. Any attempt to investigate the contribution of the nineteenth-century stage to the screen, either in general terms of the preparation and consolidation of an audience, or in the matter of specific dramatic techniques, must be prefaced with a look into the productional facilities by which this melodrama was presented. An examination of the production scripts themselves might reveal cinematic concepts embodied in this romanticized dramatic form, but a preliminary survey of productional facilities and methods could expose certain technical factors which would enable the melodrama of the screen to replace that of the stage.

Conventional staging methods of the nineteenth century have already been thoroughly considered and discussed. It is not my desire to duplicate this work. A review of the facilities and the methods used for the production of melodrama upon the stage, conducted with a critical bias governed by the new realism which arose in the last part of the century, in the years surrounding the arrival of the motion picture, may clarify conditions of breakdown within these methods which undermined the popularity of this dramatic form.

The melodrama of the last half of the nineteenth century found its greatest audience among the lower classes of the larger cities and, with the growth of the railroads, in provincial manufacturing towns and country-wide agricultural centers. Hence, "it is this theatre which is a more integral part of the theatre of yesterday."[2] The provincial "opera house," endeavoring, with its limited technical facilities, to entertain the bulk of the melodrama audience, was eventually to bear the brunt of the competitive force of screen melodrama. It is this stage, this "more integral part of the theatre of yesterday," the theatre of the "town that could only boast a thousand inhabitants," that must be reviewed.

The system of staging used in such theatres, as well as in the theatres of the metropolitan centers, was essentially the same at the time of the cinema's arrival as it had been at mid-century. There had been quantitative changes and elaborations, of course, but the over-all, basic pattern remained the same. Niblo's Theatre, rebuilt in New York after the fire of May 6, 1872, from the plans of architect F. Schmidt, depended upon the conventional system of wings, grooves, bridges, traps, and flies, and retained a twelve-foot apron and a sloped-stage floor.

The dimensions of the present stage are as follows: 75 feet in width, 62 feet in depth, 103 feet in height, from gridiron to sub-cellar... There are, properly speaking, seven grooves or entrances, all of which are utilized, though the scenery itself is only set to the fifth groove... It is particularly rich in traps. Of these contrivances, the ordinary theatrical average is five, but Niblo's boasts fifteen. There are also five working "bridges" connected with the stage... The machinery of the stage floor is technically divided into thirty-two sections—"cuts," as they are called.[3]

These various appliances were devised to control two-dimensional side wings or cut-outs which, arranged in sequence at either side of the playing space, offered a perspective pictorial illusion. Painted cloth drops lowered from the flies, or wooden-frame canvas flats called "shutters" run in to the center from the sides, could be used to close the rear of such a scene. Such drops or shutters might also be introduced in the foreground as painted background for a forestage scene while wings and properties, thus concealed, could be changed.

The stage floor in this system became an elaborate mechanism. "In ordinary stages the traps are floored over, and before they can be used a portion of the floor of the stage has to be removed. This is done by releasing a lever and letting the section of the floor drop into a groove and slide under the immovable parts at the side of the stage. The opening left in the stage is filled by the floor of the ascending trap."[4] This trap might be used for an exit or an entrance, or a bridge might be introduced into it "to raise bodily any heavy scene, furniture, or a group of figures, but it only raises its load level with the stage."[5] In addition to the trap-and-bridge system, the stage floor included a device known as the "cut." According to A. A. Hopkins' description, narrow strips of the floor were made to slide horizontally, right and left, beneath the fixed section at the sides.[6] A windlass on the mezzanine level below the stage controlled their movement, and when both slides were withdrawn the open space in the floor and the space below became the cut. Into the cut was placed flat scenery to be raised to stage level. Such was the conventional system of staging during the last half of the nineteenth and early twentieth centuries. With side wings, overhead borders, back flats or shutters, cloth drops, bridges, traps, and all the counterweight and windlass apparatus necessary for their control, it sought to create a perspective pictorial illusion through the proper arrangement of its painted two-dimensional scenic pieces.

For the propitious use of this conventional stage machine, theatre architect Walter Emden suggested in 1883 certain requisite proportions for the stage building.

The height of the proscenium from the stage should be more than the width of the opening, which I have taken at thirty feet, say about thirty-five in height. . . With regard to the stage, the width of the site being sixty-three feet, and the opening of the proscenium thirty feet, there would be on either side, exclusive of walls, a space of about fifteen feet . . . where the space is less, it will be found that the difficulty of working scenery is proportionately increased.[7]

These dimensions and proportions, with their implied considerations for the working of scenery, would limit the tour of a stock melodrama using two-dimensional scenic effects in the season of 1897-1898, just after the arrival of the film, to the large provincial centers. In cities the size of Boston, Philadelphia, Chicago, or Cleveland, staging facilities would be adequate to handle the conventional set built for a typical New York stage.

For example, at the Euclid Avenue Opera House, Cleveland (population 366,000), we would have found a stage in 1897 with the following specifications.[8]

> Proscenium width .... 36'
>   height .... 37'
> Stage depth from footlights .... 45'
>   depth apron .... 5'
>   width, wall to wall .... 76'
>   depth below stage .... 12'
>   height floor to grooves .... 20'
>   height floor to rigging loft ...... 66'
> Complete set of traps
> Three bridges

Grooves set at twenty feet would have allowed the use of standard-height wings, and hence the original scenery could have been used. Loft, wing, and trap areas were all ample for the storage and shifting of stock sets. There were three theatres in Pittsburgh, the Alvin, the Bijou, and the New Grand Opera House, all well equipped to compete, along the conventional lines, with early film melodrama. But if the original production had been designed for a New York playhouse such as the People's Theatre, which boasted a series of ten grooves, ten traps, four bridges, a trap area sixteen feet deep, and a stage a hundred feet wide,[9] it is entirely possible that considerable staging difficulty would have been encountered in the most commodious of provincial theatres. An impairment of even the conventional scenic illusion would have resulted.

If our hypothetical itinerary included provincial cities with populations of a few thousand, staging limitations would have been excessive. Both the scale and the variety of the stage pictures would have to be geared to the facilities of the smallest overnight stand. A road show originating in New York would require stringent scenic alterations for such a town as Garrett, Indiana (population

3,500), where Wagner's Opera House[10] had a proscenium twenty feet wide and thirteen feet high. The full depth of the stage, including the apron, was twenty-one feet. There were no traps, bridges, or counterweight system, and illumination was provided by gas. In the same year, 1897, Starkville, Mississippi (population 2,000), possessed an opera house[11] with somewhat better equipment. Here the proscenium was twenty feet by twelve, the stage forty-five feet wide and twenty-two feet deep. These proportions satisfy Emden's basic specifications. There were five grooves on either side and a single trap which opened into an area three feet deep. The grooves were set ten feet above the stage floor, thus preventing the use of standard twenty-foot wings. But this could hardly have been a sacrifice where the proscenium itself was only twelve feet high.

Limitations such as these existed in the majority of the provincial stages toward the end of the century. Road shows were often required to travel simply with their drops, using them in outlandish combinations with whatever wings and borders were available at each stand. According to Garrett H. Leverton, this "incongruity of wings and drops was vouched for by an old actor, George Bertram, who had played in minor rôles in many of the smaller theatres of the country during the 1880's with a traveling company of *Uncle Tom's Cabin.* He said that they carried drops for the various scenes with them but not the wings. In many theatres, he explained, the southern mansion and the ice scene were played in 'palace wings.' "[12] This kind of scenic absurdity marked the beginnings of the breakdown of conventional staging methods.

In Gloucester, Massachusetts (population 28,500), facilities were slightly better than at Starkville. The stage at the City Hall,[13] used by traveling companies, offered a proscenium twenty-seven feet wide but with only two feet at either side for working the wings. The rigging loft was twenty-one feet above the stage, and a single trap opened into a four-foot cellar. Illumination was supplied by either gas or electricity. In the same year on the West Coast, at Bieber, California (population 800), the Town Hall stage was still illuminated by oil.[14] At Pulaski, Virginia (population 4,000), the Pulaski Opera House, with its eighteen- by ten-foot proscenium, was still using kerosene lamps.[15] In Ayer, Massachusetts (population 2,000 in 1897), Page's Hall still used oil for lighting.[16] But at Pasadena, California (population 12,000), gas had been installed by 1897.[17] Stages in other provincial theatres varied in size and equipment. Coal Creek, Tennessee (population 2,500), boasted Weldon Opera House, where ten-foot wings might be used within a proscenium eighteen by fourteen feet.[18] The Opera House at Franklin, Pennsylvania (population 9,000), had better proportions and equipment.[19] Here the proscenium measured twenty-eight by twenty-three feet and the stage, including the apron, had a depth of thirty-six feet. Wing space on either side extended seventeen feet, more than the requisite half of the width of the proscenium opening. There were six sets of grooves and these were adjustable in height. The floor included four traps, one bridge, and a trap area nine feet deep.

These instances can be multiplied. They provide a cross section of theatre facilities available to road companies in this country at the turn of the century. Without reviewing, for the moment, the artificiality of the staging conventions themselves, it seems that at about the time of the arrival of the cinema most towns and cities with a population below ten thousand possessed inadequate equipment for the presentation of road shows which might compete, even along conventional lines, with the realism and the sensationalism of the motion-picture melodrama.

What was most detrimental to the successful production of stage melodrama, however, was not the general inadequacy of staging facilities but the very artificiality of their conventions. Consider, for instance, in an era since heralded for the realism of its theatrical reforms, the persistence of staging methods hailing from Serlio, Sabbatini, and the Italian Renaissance. The great scenic innovations of the seventeenth century became the dead wood of the nineteenth century. Theatrical illusion in the playhouses of the smaller cities and towns catering to the larger proportion of the national audience depended, at the time of the arrival of the motion picture, upon the acceptance of two-dimensional wings painted to counterfeit, and arranged to fake, a three-dimensional stage picture. The excesses introduced in the name of this convention ex-

tended to the mixture of real with painted actors and even to the
continuation of the traditional baroque sloped-stage floor. A. A.
Hopkins spoke in 1897 of nineteenth-century stage floors which
"fall three-eighths to one-half inch in a foot, from the back to the
front,"[20] and architect Walter Emden wrote, in 1883, that "the
height of the stage from the floor of the pit is usually four feet and
six inches, and as the stage should rise from the footlights at the
rate of one-half inch in the foot, everyone on the floor of the pit
obtains a good view."[21]

The stage apron, running mate of the sloped-stage floor, persisted in the provinces throughout the century. At the Starkville,
Mississippi, Opera House, in 1897, a stage depth of twenty-two
feet included an apron of four feet.[22] At Creston, Iowa, a seven-
foot apron was used.[23] The New Castle Square Theatre opened in
Boston on November 19, 1894, with a seven-foot apron.[24] The
Bijou Theatre in Milwaukee had one of the same size.[25] At
Helena, Arkansas, a seven-foot apron jutted into a house whose
capacity was only 915.[26] The Marysville Theatre, Marysville, California (capacity 800), used an eight and one-half foot apron with
only twenty-four and a half feet behind the proscenium.[27] The
apron here was over a third as deep as the stage itself and, in all
likelihood, about a half as deep as most settings. At Nevada City,
California,[28] the local theatre used a six-foot apron and a stage
twenty-two feet deep. Such dimensions, instances of which can
readily be expanded, indicate that, at the time of the arrival of the
motion picture, theatres of this country employed an apron jutting
into the auditorium from one-third to one-sixth of the depth of the
stage itself. The significance of such a condition lies in its contribution toward the over-all counterfeit of the conventional productions. An apron in front of a raked stage, surrounded by two-
dimensional wings and drops, all arranged parallel to the footlights, made it inevitable that the actors leave the setting and come
down to the apron to play to the audience. Realism could hardly
prevail in the face of this presentational style of production. It
was this kind of staging fraud which marked the breakdown of the
conventional methods and which made stage melodrama particularly vulnerable to the motion picture.

The incongruity between wings and backdrops, characteristic of provincial theatres because of the inadequacy of equipment, may have been unsatisfactory but was undoubtedly preferable to the dull repetition which resulted when only local stock sets were used. William Crane, an actor of this period, has written of production in the late seventies: "For exteriors there was always a rocky mountain pass, a dark wood, and a light landscape; flats did service for interiors; these were classified as a center door, chamber sets, throne rooms of palaces, kitchen sets, and possibly a prison scene or interior of some such sombre outline, rounded out the adequate supply."[29] These settings comprised the total of stage pictures that the typical theatregoer in any but metropolitan centers might be offered. Is it any wonder that he tolerated the fraud of the ice scene in *Uncle Tom's Cabin* played in palace wings as long as the touring company provided a new backdrop of the frozen river and riverbank? The use of stock settings produced either scenic repetition or scenic incongruity, and the marked inadequacy and artificiality of these settings added to the eventual dissatisfaction with the methods of the nineteenth-century theatre.

But in stage lighting is to be found the greatest single reason for the discontinuation of the traditional manner of theatrical production upon the arrival of the cinema. The principal method for lighting the stage in the years prior to the motion picture depended upon gas; calcium lights were used for special effects. Some of the larger metropolitan theatres, using three-dimensional settings, had been equipped with electricity for several years. The Lyceum Theatre of Steele MacKaye in New York opened on April 6, 1885, "lighted by electricity for the first time."[30] The Madison Square Theatre, hailed on February 4, 1880, as an advanced piece of theatrical design, did not use electricity but boasted, instead, gas lights which "do not draw oxygen from the air of the theatre, but are boxed in individual lanterns and breathe the outer air."[31] Electricity for the stage had been unsuccessfully attempted at the California Theatre, San Francisco, on February 21, 1879;[32] and at Nashville, Tennessee, the Masonic Theatre was still paying "$6.50 per night to the Gas Company" in 1874.[33] Generally speaking, gas was installed in the provincial theatres of this country from about 1850 to 1870[34] and electricity in the metropolitan theatres during the eighties. This delay in the widespread introduction of electricity for stage lighting had a favorable effect on the realism of the illusion offered by the traditional two-dimensional wing-and-groove settings. The persistence of these methods during a period otherwise noted for its realistic reforms was, in considerable part, due to the contribution of gas and oil lighting. At the end of the century the great turn to electricity suddenly threw the obvious frauds of conventional scenic practices into focus. Two-dimentional settings, deprived of the soft lights and mysterious shadows of gas lighting, lost all semblance of reality in the garish glow of the incandescent bulbs.

Again it was the conventional factor in the method of lighting which brought the electrical-light source into direct conflict with scenic realism. Footlights, overhead light borders, vertical wing-and-tormentor borders provided arbitrary and distorted lighting which may have been tolerable with oil- or gas-light sources but which, with the bright, directional rays of the electric bulb, served to expose and destroy the illusion of the two-dimensional scenery. Changes in the lighting system came slowly. By 1917 Belasco had managed to eliminate the distortion of footlighting.[35] But the screen melodrama, in the meantime, had already put its stage counterpart out of business, and the popular stage had been forced by the competition of the screen into a more thorough and three-dimensional realism.

The artificiality of the conventional pattern for lighting the stage was matched by the obvious hokum of special effects. Moonlight provides an interesting example. In the downstage acting area "a calcium light [was] thrown through a green glass"; for the scenery at the rear, " 'green mediums'—lamps with green shades" could be placed both as wing or overhead borders.[36] Into this bath of calcium and gas green light the moon itself was often injected. In the better-equipped theatres of the period the moon might be "about eighteen inches in diameter . . . made of porcelain or milk glass and oval in form. Within are six incandescent lamps of sixteen candle-power, connected with a rheostat."[37] Usually, there were three red and three white lamps, and the operator, by controlling the volume of either the red or the white light, or both, could vary the color of the moon. The intention, here, is that of pictorial naturalism. But to the critical mind of the nineties, as, indeed, by our own standards, the effect was the height of naïveté. It is small wonder that D. W. Griffith's successful experiments with realistic lighting effects upon the screen found such ready approval.

Lightning effects, of course, provided sensational if conventional spectacle. Magnesium, burned in the proportion of "three parts of magnesium powder and one part of potassium chlorate,"[38] could be used. In theatres electrically equipped, two large files connected to ends of an electrical circuit could be rubbed over each other to "produce a series of brilliant flashes."[39] Or, as Franklin Fyles suggested, one end might be a carbon stick.[40] The latter method, whether employing carbon or steel file, or both, created the garish luminosity of a flashing carbon arc. But the best lightning, according to Olive Logan, was "produced by an electric light, which, throwing a rapid flash upon a scene prepared beforehand with a vein to the effect, is simply blinding in its naturalism."[41] Another method utilized projections of lightning and cloud effects painted on rotating pieces of glass, where "the operator revolves the disks one over the other, and the forked lightning seems to shoot across the heavens."[42] All of these stock devices strove to present the picture of nature in action. All achieved a certain measure of success but none could match the naturalism of the motion picture.

When the ensuing thunderbolt literally struck down the object upon which the lightning had been projected, the effect was more childish than spectacular.

When a thunderbolt is to strike an object, a wire is run from the flies to the object which is to be struck. A rider runs on the wire. The rider consists of a section of iron pipe. Around it is secured asbestos by means of wire. The asbestos is soaked with alcohol, and is lighted just at the instant it is to be projected upon the object. It is usually held by a string, which is cut. It rushes flaming through the air, and produces the effect of a ball of fire striking the object.[43]

Thunder effects also depended upon stock techniques: the thunder sheet, the drum, the cart, or the "venetian blind."[44] Fire, of course, was always pure convention. The method of the fire effects used for Boucicault's *The Octoroon,* at the Howard Athenaeum (Boston, 1863), is marked into the Henry Willard promptbook[45] and indicates the general usage: "Two firepans, with red-fire, ready to be lighted." Red fire was a chemical preparation included in the stage manager's kit. The Owen Fawcett promptbook[46] of the Philadelphia production of the same play (April 1876) directs that "all hurry off to ship,—alarm bell rings—loud shouts; a hatch in the deck is opened—a glare of red." In this case, the profile cut-out steamer had been lying at the pier bathed in the conventional green glow of moonlight. With the fire scene came the spectacular change from green to red light, possibly accompanied by steam which was often "used to represent the smoke."[47] Such artificial effects, whether of fire, thunder, or lightning, practiced, it seems, more for their own sake than for their illusion of reality, had lost conviction for all but the most remote provincial audiences by the time of the appearance of the motion picture.

Water and sea effects had undergone small change since the time of Sabbatini (1638). Here we find the traditional sea cloths, wave cut-outs, and wave cylinders. A pebble-box was used for the sound effect. When into such a counterfeit sea a flesh-and-blood actor plunged, illusion must have strained to the point of breaking. At the same time, however, it must be noted that this very combination of the real and unreal gave rise to a sensational effect. Herein may be found some of the reasons for the continuance of an outworn, conventional staging method into the days of the early film.

In this nineteenth-century stage of stereotypes all manner of natural phenomena were represented. Rain was managed in a number of ways. When it was not necessary for the audience to see the rain, the sound effect was created by the customary rain machine placed high in the flies. "A hollow wooden cylinder five feet in circumference and four feet in length is provided. Upon the inside are placed rows of small wooden teeth. A quantity of dried peas are placed in the cylinder, and a belt is run around one end of it and down to the prompter's desk."[48] When rain had to be seen by the audience, the appearance of falling rain was "caused by suspending many fine, polished wires and vibrating them in strong light. That is an excellent illusion for a moment, but betrays itself if continued for too long."[49] Behind a door or a window this effect may have been satisfactory. Real water, however, was preferable, and in theatres sufficiently well equipped it was sometimes used. The many theatrical reforms advanced by Steele Mac-Kaye included a simple device: "Rain was provided for by a series of perforated pipes connected with a water supply, so that a gentle rain or a hard shower could be produced."[50] When this kind of device was used, a metal or canvas trough sunk below the level of the stage carried off the falling water. Such attempts to provide a more thorough graphic realism often brought about startling inconsistencies. In the quest for greater and more authentic pictorial illusion, the real was often combined with the unreal. How, in a scene of this sort, could illusion be maintained when the actors in the rainstorm remained dry? When the foreground rain never fell on the actors within the set? When the rain ran off in a neatly arranged trough behind the footlights, never touching the canvas of the set? Such incongruity exemplifies the final stage in the progressive breakdown of the nineteenth-century staging methods. As realistic as this particular device might appear, it was still artificial. Yet anything beyond this would have been impracticable and would, at best, have been available only to a small segment of the national audience. The motion picture fell natural heir to this entire pictorially minded theatre.

Snow effects often combined a number of techniques. The storm itself might be represented by confetti-like paper showered down by men in the flies.[51] The "coats and hats of the actors who are supposed to be out in the snow are generally well dusted with flour."[52] Flour "snow," of course, would not melt, so that in the best productions actors were sprinkled "with soapsuds by means of a birch broom before they appear upon the scene."[53] This, too, had its limitations, for "in the case of rich costumes it is impossible to use soapsuds, so that bone shavings or ground corn are used instead."[54] These methods, even in the case of soapsuds, which had its own special problems when a large group entered out of the snow or in the matter of control of its melting speed, were unsatisfactory. Wind effects, in such snowstorms, were created with the customary paddle wheel, "the paddles scraping against a piece of ribbed silk drawn over the upper part of the wheel."[55] Belasco, Irving, or Steele MacKaye, in their metropolitan productions employed wind-driven salt or cereals controlled by huge fans, but that great audience of the provincial theatres, whose support was later to establish the film as theatrical entertainment, was gulled with these sham, toylike devices. It is small wonder that a simple topical film, *Bucking the Blizzard,* claimed box-office appeal in 1899. People could at last see the real thing inside the theatre.

Dramatic authors of the period did not appreciate the dangers of relying upon these staging conventions. Their oversize pictorial demands and the emphasis on external effects in their dramatic conceptions drew attention to the inadequacy of the traditional practices, hence often undermined the success of their plays, and subsequently hastened the breakdown of these methods. Gunplay is an interesting case in point. Single shots by gun or pistol need not be counterfeit. What happened, however, when the playwright called for great volleys of musketry or booming barrages of cannon? Large explosions of gunpowder backstage were dangerous, but even where this may have been possible, "the smoke of gunpowder proved objectionable, as it obscured the scene and choked the audience." Consequently, in a large proportion of the productions showing in this country at any one time during this period, it was altogether likely that "a blow on a bass drum represented the discharge of a cannon, and rapid strokes with rattans on a dried calf-skin, a volley of rifles."[56] Theatregoing seems to have been a boys' game in these pre-cinema days; how else explain this obviously fake imitation of muskets firing and bullets whistling through the air to strike a target? It is impossible, of course, to say where the original fault lay, but it can be seen that the vicious circle involving playwright, producer, and audience had, by this time, attained a giddy and tenuous extension.

Gunplay had always been a difficult effect, and special devices were sometimes built. According to A. A. Hopkins, a French pyrotechnist, M. Philippi, attempted to duplicate the effect of the explosion of guns, complete with noise, flash, and smoke.

The charge consists of a small quantity of fulminate prepared so as to give a red fire and a light smoke which quickly clears away, leaving no disagreeable odor, and not affecting the throat. The preparation is held in a cavity formed in a small cork which is introduced into the extremity of the gun barrel. The firing pin passes through the barrel ... causing the charge to explode through a simple blow.[57]

It is extremely doubtful if this effect provided a totally realistic illusion. Certainly such a contrivance, limited in the matter of control, and burdened with the requirement of a special preparation and a special fitting in the hands of one trained in its method, could hardly have been in general use.

In the staging of battle scenes great pains were taken. Shells to explode on-stage were ingeniously devised.

A *papier maché* shell is formed of separate pieces glued together. This contains the quantity of powder sufficient to separate the pieces and produce the bursting. In the powder there is an electric primer which is ignited by a current. *The primer is connected by wires which go back of the scene.* At one of the sides of the stage, out of sight of the spectator, there is a charge which is also ignited by electricity at the same time that the bomb is exploded. At the proper moment a man throws the shell and touches the button, the bomb bursts, and the spectators, hearing the loud report of the cannon at the same instant, imagine that the harmless paper bomb is the cause of the formidable explosion.[58]

Theatre, in its greed for spectacular pictures, had descended to circus level. The hunger for this type of pictorial drama must have been great indeed for an adult audience to accept as real a paper shell, dangling with wires, which popped in the center of the stage while the detonation was heard off in the wings and a few actors staggered about to die a battered death among the ruins on the floor. And, as we have already noted, cannon fire in such battle scenes, according to Franklin Fyles, dramatic editor of the *New York Sun,* writing as late as April of 1900, was often produced by a blow on a bass drum. These effects, appropriate to cinema, fraudulently presented on the stage, became, because of this inadequacy, prime mover of an audience for the motion picture.

As if this hokum were not enough, the "crash machine" was

used simultaneously to portray the damages arising from the explosion of such a "bomb." This machine epitomizes conventional practices of the period. "It consists of a wheel with paddles set at an angle of about forty-five degrees. Upon the top of the wheel one end of a stout piece of wood is placed down by fastening the other end to a portion of the framework. When the wheel is turned, the slats passing under the stationary piece produce a rattling crash."[59] Both the representation of musketry by the striking of taut leather—the sound of rattans on dried calfskin—and the use of this huge rattle to create the effect of destruction by cannonading summarize the nineteenth-century conventional approach to staging. In the search for sensation and spectacle, counterfeit was acceptable, and truth or naturalism found its refuge with the reformers. This kind of pictorial theatre, stirring uneasily toward the ideal of the motion picture, was lashed for the greater part of the century to the artifices of the conventional methods.

We have, to this point, attempted to suggest some of the artificialities and weaknesses in the kind of dramatic show which formed the theatrical fare of the small but nevertheless significant playhouses of the late nineteenth century. In a period since proclaimed for the birth of naturalism, there must have been many reasons for the continuation of the wing-border-drop system beyond the time when more realistic pictorial methods had been seen in the popular theatre. It must be remembered that the first box set appeared in England, according to Leo Waitzkin, "at the Olympic, on November third, 1832. By 1837 it was in use at the Covent Garden and Haymarket theatres. The walls of Vestris's box sets were not thin, shaky flats, but solidly constructed, papered, and decorated . . . Ceilings, too, were substantial affairs: they were arched or painted . . . and chandeliers burned brightly."[60] Madame Vestris, of the London Olympic, came to New York, opening at the Park Theatre on September 17, 1838, and it is altogether likely that she either used or discussed the use of this interior box set. The Bancrofts at the Prince of Wales's in London, of course, prospered by their exploitation of practical, three-dimensional scenery. Bancroft himself said of the first production of Tom Robertson's *Caste,* which opened on April 6, 1867, at the Prince of

Wales's: "It was in 'Caste' that we made a distinct stride towards realistic scenery. The rooms, for the first time, had ceilings, while such details as locks to doors, and similar matters, had never before been seen upon the stage."[61] John H. McDowell quotes E. W. Mammen's statement that the Boston Museum first used a box set in November 1862,[62] and further states that the first box set on the New York stage was designed by Charles W. Witham for the Booth production of *Hamlet* in December 1869.[63] A box set was apparently used in New York seventeen years previous to 1869. The promptbook marked by prompter and stage manager John Moore for the production of *The Corsican Brothers* at the Bowery Theatre, New York, on April 21, 1852, includes a sketch of what appears to be a box set used in the opening scene.[64] The reasons, then, for the retention of the traditional system of staging beyond the time of the introduction of newer and more realistic methods are to be found elsewhere, probably in more urgent staging requirements of pre-cinema melodrama. For, while theatrical realism had continually been sought and improved since the time of Garrick, a romantic form such as the melodrama made other demands upon staging.

Many of the reasons for the continuation of the conventions were of a negative nature, undesirable, but forced by the facilities of existing theatre buildings. This was particularly true of provincial stages. Changes in theatrical architecture and stage design are gradual and expensive processes, so that the staging system still in use about 1897 had not changed, as has been noted, in over fifty years. Despite its many shortcomings, it offered a positive and distinctive contribution toward the realization upon the stage of the theatrical values of the melodrama and the spectacle-drama of the period. These values will be presented in detail in the chapters devoted to these dramatic forms; hence, for the present, a hasty glance at the technical advantages of the traditional staging methods will suffice.

First of all, they offered the facility of speed in the scenic production, rapid change from one locale to another. Without the necessity of even a curtain drop, stage lights could be lowered, and fresh wings, borders, rear shutters, or practical pieces automatically or manually shoved, raised, or lowered into position. When the gas was turned up the new locale gradually and mystically appeared. This technique was often specified as a "wand change," suggesting a "presto-chango," magical, sensational effect. Or very simply, a drop might be lowered in the front part of the stage, changing locale on the apron with its representational, perspective painting; and with action proceeding in front of it, the scenery behind it might be altered and subsequently revealed. Or a pair of shutters might be used to close a wing-and-border set, say at the third wings. Scenery behind the shutters, in wings four, five, and six, could be altered and arranged to reveal such an effect as the popular "vision" sequence, the pictorial presentation of action proceeding within the mind of one of the characters on stage. Speed in scene changes was more the essence of nineteenth-century melodrama than the realism of its many pictures.

In the provinces, where expense was as much a consideration as speed, stock methods provided the greatest possible scenic speed at the minimum of expense. The Masonic Theatre, Nashville, Tennessee, in 1879 paid its scene shifters only three dollars a day.[65] Three-dimensional box sets and practicable units, offering the same pictorial coverage as wing, border, drop, and shutter settings, would have both hampered speed and multiplied expense.

High speed and low cost were not the only attributes of the system. Settings on tour depended upon the stock of wings and borders available in the provincial theatres. Acceptance of this practice made it possible for road shows to travel with only a supply of backdrops and special cut-out effects. Hence traveling companies were able to utilize the graphic appeal of a large series of representationally painted perspective backdrops and special visual effects. The willingness of audiences to accept stereotyped wings and borders afforded, in return, a large measure of pictorial variety in addition to the quality of scenic speed. Within the two-dimensional pattern there were few limits. Railroad trains, horse races, boat races were as feasible as burning steamers, erupting volcanoes, ocean grottoes, or shipwrecks. It was this sort of pictorial sensationalism which enabled traditional staging to persist through a period otherwise marked by the rebirth of theatrical realism.

As the century advanced, certain liberties were taken, even in provincial theatres, with the two-dimensional conventions in the interests of pictorial realism. The trap-and-bridge system, occasionally hydraulic in metropolitan but manual in provincial theatres, allowed the introduction of solid, three-dimensional set-pieces with a fair degree of speed and ease. Without restricting speed this enhanced the variety and the realism of the stage pictures. Such a tendency, it is to be noted, marked the growing disfavor of the purely conventional techniques and at the same time committed a dangerous error. The addition of the real to the obviously counterfeit oftentimes provided such an incongruity that the illusion of the whole stage picture was destroyed. This practice not only demonstrated weaknesses of the stock methods but at the same time hastened their breakdown. But that such liberties were taken at all would indicate the continued interest in the pictorial drama combined with the desire to purge its artificialities—in other words, evidence of the growing need for the motion picture.

This examination of staging conventions and theatrical facilities of the nineteenth century has focused attention upon the fraudulent scenic practices in vogue during the period. David Belasco and Steele MacKaye may have achieved remarkable three-dimensional productions in the metropolitan and large provincial theatres, but those playhouses in the majority of cities and towns which provided theatrical fare for the American audience at large found few alternatives to the conventional ideas prior to the film. While these methods were in the process of breakdown, their continuation in the provinces clearly indicates the need for the motion picture, for their significant attributes were similar to those of the film.

The conventions of two-dimensional scenery persisted into the days of the early film partly because the romantic drama of the times demanded an excessive pictorial spectacularism and partly because of the physical limitations of the majority of the stagehouses themselves. The pictorial bias of the period revealed the inadequacy of technical facilities. The traditional scenic methods attempted to meet the requirements of the plays in three ways:

speed in the change from one locale to another, variety and quantity in the choice of locale, and a stereotyped kind of pictorial verisimilitude in the treatment of its flat scenic pieces. Three-dimensional execution of similar spectacular scenic conceptions would have been prevented by the limitations of the stages themselves, for the large number of stages could hardly handle two-dimensional scenery and would have been utterly inadequate for a three-dimensional version of the current romantic melodrama. The stage constantly endeavored to create artificially what constituted the very essence of the cinema: pictures in motion. This problem, of course, could be finally solved only by the screen.

The achievements of such producers as Belasco, Irving, or Mac-Kaye, whose work epitomized the requirements of the romantic drama and emphasized the glaring inadequacies of the stock practices, have been left for later consideration. Here, the concern has been simply with that theatre of the countless towns of less than a thousand population whose shifting support established the success of the cinema and at the same time closed the book on the conventional two-dimensional pictorial staging methods.

It has been pointed out that the growing disfavor with the system resulted in attempts to compromise it. These attempts may have indicated the need for the film but fail to reform the artificialities of the traditions, for the combination of solid scenic effects with flat scenery either caused, by its incongruity, the destruction of pictorial illusion or deprived the production of the chief benefits to be derived from the conventional methods, that is speed, quantity, and variety in change and choice of setting. Nevertheless, the progressive breakdown of the conventions saw more and more of such compromise. But while theatres were equipped for two-dimensional settings, and romantic playwrights continued their excessive pictorial demands, and audiences continued to enjoy and require pictorial sensations in the theatre, any attempt at compromise fell short. Reform in these theatrical arts became an "all-or-none" affair. In this case, it was achieved on the nation-wide basis by the motion-picture camera.

TWO

THE MELODRAMA:
CINEMATIC CONCEPTIONS AND
SCREEN TECHNIQUES

The most popular single expression of the combined romantic and realistic theatrical modes of the nineteenth century is to be found in the melodrama. Writers of nineteenth-century melodrama were essentially men of the theatre, professionally aware of the physical potentialities of the stage for which they wrote. Their success as playwrights was measured by the degree to which they exploited these capacities. Such an author was W. J. Thompson whose play, *A Race for Life,* typical melodrama of the period, was produced on August 27, 1883.[1] Despite the popularity of the play, his fame has been no more widespread than that of the ordinary Hollywood "conference writer" whose western, race-track, or crime-melodrama-thriller pictures have ever catered to a similar audience. To judge from the explicit directions for the stage settings and for the action and business of this play, he was both close to the theatre and interested in exploiting this stage machine for its physical effects. His script suggests production in cities with a population of not less than ten thousand.

The story, briefly, is the trite one of Widow Farrand whose home is mortgaged to the villain, Gaspard, who is lasciviously interested in Louise, sweetheart of the hero, Jacques Farrand. The necessary $6,000 arrives from the wealthy uncle. The villain steals it and kills the widow. A witness, Rob, threatened by Gaspard, tells nothing of the deed and is imprisoned along with the hero. Gaspard now has both the $6,000 and the widow's house. Rob and

Jacques escape from prison with the aid of a trusty Irishman, Brady O'Doyle, and soon justice triumphs and the villain is foiled. Audiences were naturally less interested in these obvious and well-known plot developments than in the sensational production. This hinged entirely upon the pictorial aspects of setting.

The opening scene of the 1883 production script used the following setting:

Double Set House R.H. with apartments above and below, coming well out to C. of stage. Upper part facing audience covered with gauze so all action can be seen above and below. Side of house facing center of stage has door and window above door, both to be used. Ladder behind house long enough to reach this window. Have window on hinges to open in and up stage. Sofa, table and chair in upper apartment. This apartment strong enough to hold three persons. In lower apartment have table, chairs, etc., two lamps lighted. R.U.E. bridge across stage from R. to L. with return Piece coming down C. Picket fence front of bridge. Railing on bridge and down return piece. Well three foot square L.H. with well pole seven foot long in it. Set barn L.H. with practical door.

These directions, at first glance, indicate the use of a fairly realistic, three-dimensional setting. A more careful examination of the production book reveals, first of all, that the conventions were not sacrificed, that the entire setting was of a two-dimensional quality, that tree-and-foliage wings and borders were used in the lower grooves, and a conventional country backdrop closed the scene at the rear. The house itself, apparently practical, was nevertheless hardly more than relief depth, a window's width, and so built that it might be lowered on one, or at most, two bridges. Action within the house was limited to movement in two dimensions. In other words, the stage picture, striving at realism, was actually conventional.

At the same time, the setting was devised for the specific sensational effects which might arise from the physical aspects of the picture. Three distinct playing areas are shown: downstairs in the house, upstairs, and outside. Action proceeded simultaneously in each of these areas with the story line cutting across from one to the other. The first-act climax grew out of this technique. The villain, Gaspard, arrives just in time to see the package of money being delivered.

Gaspard hides in Barn—Madame Farrand appears in the upper apartment—sits at table with package [containing the $6,000 draft which Louise had just received at the front door]. Patty enters from house with dog . . . (after her exit Gaspard comes out of hiding). Gaspard the villain gets ladder from behind house. Places it over door against window, ascends and peeps in at Madame Farrand (she discovers him). Gaspard slides down ladder quickly and hides with ladder behind house. Mad. F. peeps out of window, Louise enters lower apartment. Sits at table with lamp . . . Madame F. gets lamp, puts it on table, sits on sofa. Gaspard takes off his coat, puts Jacques' coat on which lies on fence. Places ladder back again to window. Mad. F. puts package under her head, lays down on sofa. Gaspard draws knife, feels edge as he is about to ascend ladder. Is stopped by Rob . . . Gaspard ascends ladder cautiously. Blows out lamps. Madame Farrand starts. Rob follows him cautiously. When Gaspard gets in window he closes it quickly. Rob on ladder tries to open it but fails. After Gaspard has killed Widow Farrand, Rob slides down ladder and hides behind well watching Gaspard . . . Gaspard feels cautiously for money, touches Mad. Farrand who wakes. He seizes her by throat . . . she thinks it is Jacques . . . stabs Madame F. who screams faintly and falls . . . Gaspard comes quickly down ladder. . . replaces ladder . . . runs up on Bridge and off R. followed by Rob. Brady and Louise appear in upper part of house.

This climactic scene has been written as if for a silent motion picture. Little, if any, value is attached to dialogue. The entire development is presented visually through stage movement and sensational business.

Secondly, the dramatic value of the scene depends a good deal upon suspense. Three lines of action proceed simultaneously in three scenic areas of the set. The story line develops its suspense by cutting across from significant action in one area to significant action in another. Louise is going about her business downstairs, the Widow prepares for bed upstairs, and the villain prepares for his villainy outside the house. The money is delivered. We see Gaspard as he reacts in recognition. Then the scene cuts across to the Widow upstairs untying the package; cutback now to Gaspard as he peers through the window; then a few frames of Louise, who is meanwhile making tea downstairs. From this sequence the story moves once again to the outside where Rob remonstrates with Gaspard. Upon Patty's arrival they both hide. Upstairs, in the meantime, the Widow Farrand has been happily and unwittingly counting the money. A cutback to Gaspard shows him on the ladder drawing his knife, then once again to the Widow, and so on. On the stage these three lines of action were presented simultaneously, and the emphasis cleverly controlled and shifted from one to the other. E. S. Porter would find that this style of playwriting was particularly suited to the screen. In the film all lines of action need not be staged simultaneously. Episodes could be photographed separately for later editorial combination. Problems of the control and shift of dramatic emphasis would disappear in the film where no distractive episode need be shown, and the duration and position of each requisite episode could be adjusted in the cutting room. Porter's development of film structure, we shall see, was rooted firmly in this successful stage-melodrama formula. It is equally clear from the productional approach of Thompson's promptbook that the screen might provide such material a more realistic pictorial treatment as well as a more fluid dramatic development than was possible to the stage.

While the dramatic scheme of the first act of *A Race for Life* employed a cross-cutting development within a simultaneous setting, the second act specified straightforward pictorial continuity. It is three years later at the prison quarry, where Rob and Jacques are prisoners. The first scene, the interior of the quarry office, comprising conventional wings, borders, and shutter, changes in full view of the audience to reveal the exterior of the quarry.

Prison Quarry. Full Stage. Horizon wings R. and L. with set rocks masking them halfway. These Rocks to draw off at Cue. Sea cloth down on stage from R. to L. of first Entrance and across stage a foreground "Rocky" 3 or 4 inches high to mask in sea cloth while it is working at back of stage. Flats represent Exterior of Prison with doors below and windows above. In centre between the two flats and coming up flush to front of them is the Revolving Tower or Light House. Before change it represents a continuation of flats, that is, Exterior of Prison, only instead of painted windows above, it is open about 5 foot square so that action can be seen. This is a double set, and at a given cue when Rocks draw off, so do Flats leaving this apartment alone. Then it revolves and comes down the stage and represents an Old Light House in the middle of the ocean forming two distinct sets. First the prison Quarry. Second an Old Light House in mid-ocean. The revolving Light House is about 5 or 5½ feet square with platform inside halfway up strong enough to hold one person. On the Light House side when it revolves is a window to open—Rope 16 feet long in the Light House—4 shovels—4 picks—2 wheelbarrows and old stone used in Quarry scene. Also chain and ball.

The production was devised to tell the story by means of a series of pictures. The action moves instantaneously as Quarry Office Interior dissolves to Quarry Yard. Here again, without benefit of written dialogue,

Officers Fire. Convicts rush on, struggle with officers. Shots outside; Gaspard seizes Jacques—is thrown off. Officer seizes Jacques he throws him off when Holmes struggles off with Brady R.H. Men and officers struggle off R. and L. when all clear
Sound Change Bell
Rocks drawn off R. and L. Prison double set center revolves to old Light House and comes down stage. Jacques and Brady come on in boat. Men work sea cloth. Patty throws rope from Light House window. Brady catches it. Picture. Slow curtain.

Climaxes in this kind of picture play rarely required speech. As in the early film, every episode in the story line was shown on the stage, and the attempt was made to dissolve one set into the next with the conventional techniques. There is clear indication here of a highly cinematic conception being limited and debased in its production by the traditional staging devices.

These limitations were recognized by Thompson, and he made certain attempts to overcome them by the introduction of such real properties as animals. Into the artificiality of the first-act setting a real dog accompanied Patty. A real horse is stabled at Doyle's Roost, Jacques' third-act hideout. When Jacques is threatened with capture, he "rushes into stable, mounts horse, rides across and off L. through Gate." Every effort was made to improve the realism of the stage pictures.

The production of this typical nineteenth-century melodrama, intended primarily for presentation in cities of as little as ten thousand population, suggests specific characteristics of the motion picture. Whatever dramaturgy may have been embodied in such a script depended upon two filmic devices: (1) cross-cutting between two or more lines of action visually presented, and (2) straightforward storytelling with a series of episodes all pictorially presented. While these were obviously cinematic conceptions, their production was conventional. Attempts which were made to compensate for the artificiality of these methods through the introduction of practical properties and live animals become prime indication of certain dissatisfaction with the conventional methods during the last quarter of the nineteenth century.

Of the playwright-producers of the popular theatre of this period none was more successful than Dion Boucicault. His work began mid-century and retained its popularity to the time of the film. His contribution to the motion picture was both direct and indirect, for not only were certain of his plays made into the earliest feature films, but his over-all theatrical approach, highly suggestive of the camera, can be identified with early motion-picture syntax. The many productions of *Arrah-na-Pogue,* which began in Dublin in June, 1864, and continued to appear in England and this country throughout the remainder of the century, emphasize this similarity and at the same time provide an interesting reference to the fading appeal of the stock staging techniques upon which he, too, relied.

Boucicault's popularity stemmed from his pictorial sensations, which, whether begged, borrowed, or stolen, never failed to impress his audiences. The DeWitt version of *Arrah-na-Pogue*[2] describes in some detail the management of the spectacular escape scene, third-act climax, and culmination of three parallel branches of the story line. The act opens at the Secretary of State's office, where O'Grady obtains pardon for the hero, Shaun, and rushes out to the prison to stop the execution. From this branch the action cuts across to a second branch, with a forestage scene of Shaun's sweetheart, Arrah, singing on the Rocky Mountainside above Shaun's prison. This is a quick "take" on the apron while the next picture in the main story line, Shaun in his Cell, Prison Interior, is moved into place and revealed, while Arrah, moving off stage, continues her song. A stone falls into Shaun's fireplace, and when he looks up, Arrah's singing comes in louder. Inspired, he plans to escape by scaling the prison wall which rises precipitously out of the sea. He "shoves grating and stone through," and the stage manager strikes "the sheet of metal several times, fainter and fainter, as of stone bounding downwards," as Shaun exclaims, "Whisht! I hear it thunderin' down the wall (splash), it's in the waves below." Then out the hole he goes.

Up to this point the development has come by cross-cutting between three simultaneous lines of action. Boucicault now drops the two tributary lines and concentrates upon showing all phases in the progress of the main line, the escape. As Shaun leaves the Prison Interior, the setting dissolves into a fresh angle of the same scene as we catch him on the outside crawling out of the hole and onto the ivy. "Sink table and close trap. Draw in side sets L. and R. Discover the frame set and set wall with Shaun halfway up." Now, to show Shaun scaling the wall, a vertical "tracking" shot was staged. The wall was designed to pass down across the proscenium opening, fresh sections coming in from the flies and disappearing through the stage floor. Shaun works his way up the wall and Arrah's voice continues.

Wall descends. Shaun climbs up as wall descends, and by the ledge reaches the 2^d flat of the wall. Climbs up it as it descends, and upon the set platform of room, when the soldier (coming on and going off R) has his back turned toward him. Shaun goes up to the cannon, climbs on it and out of the gap. Soldier comes on, looks off front, down the wall, while Shaun climbs through the gap. Soldier exits R. Shaun is seen at back of 4th groove flat, climbing along wall to exit R. All is worked down. Gas up and
Scene last: Arrah is discovered on set back R. singing as before.

Shaun has gone down just below the stage level with the last flat while lights were dimmed, and subsequently comes up through the open trap into the next scene with Arrah on the bank above the prison.

But at the moment that Shaun disappears through the floor the whistling is interrupted and, as the prison wall scene fades out, the villain, Feeny, is heard accosting Arrah. The Rocky Mountainside is quickly moved in with the lowering of the lights. When the gas is turned up the new scene "fades in" and Feeny is revealed forcing attentions upon Arrah. It now turns into a "chase" sequence, with suspense arising out of whether Shaun will get there in time to save the girl. Needless to say, he does. Feeny discovers Shaun in the trap climbing the wall. He picks up a stone to hurl at him.

Arrah struggles with [Feeny]. He is just overpowering her when Shaun's hands appear; then his head; then Shaun seizes Feeny's ankles, the stone and Feeny fall into the trap-hole. Pause. Music all through struggle, dies away, Shaun climbs up exhausted and falls full length on stage beside Arrah. Drum-beat heard below stage level.

The simultaneous development and culmination of these two lines of action provided suspense and climax. When Feeny is finished, still another line of action is introduced with the drumbeat from the prison below as the guards are mustered. O'Grady is still en route as the voices of the guards, hot on the prisoner's trail, come closer. Will O'Grady get there before the guards do? As offstage orders are issued for closing in on Shaun, O'Grady rushes on with the pardon, consummating the third simultaneous line of action and providing climax and resolution.

Throughout the play, and particularly in this last act, the effort is made to picture upon the stage every scene necessary for the development of the story, and one scene is dissolved into another, or, under cover of lights, the changes are faded out and in. Four scenes are needed in the first act, five in the second, and five, including the multiple one of the moving wall, are used for the last act. This type of staging, characteristic of nineteenth-century melodrama, goes hand in hand with episodic playwriting, and both suggest what was to become, under E. S. Porter, cinematic syntax. By flashing, dissolving, or fading from one pictorial episode into another, either in a forward line, or backward, or across in point of time, the narrative continuity is developed. But since the suspense values which might arise out of this episodic "cutting" or editorial technique are in direct proportion to the number and comparative duration of episodes as well as to the rapidity of the scene shifts, this method appears to have been better suited to the screen.

The spectacular scenic conceptions themselves were also prophetic of the motion picture. The escape scene here required, first of all, the management of a full change of scenery from the interior of the prison cell to the exterior of the wall, in place of a simple shift in camera position. Then, for a simple vertical tracking shot, an elaborate series of scenes involving counterweight systems, cuts, bridges, and covering the entire width of the stage was mechanically contrived. Although the device was clever, it was clumsy, and its

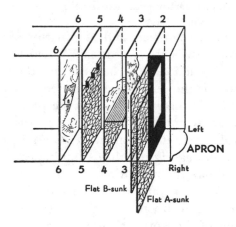

Diagram of staging method for the Escape Scene of Boucicault's
Arrah-na-Pogue *(from the DeWitt version, HTC)*

illusion was less realistic than sensational. The attempt is both suggestive of the motion picture and indicative of the limitations of the conventional staging techniques.

The use of a square inner proscenium, "painted a dead black . . . to mask the working of the changes," similar in its effect to a motion-picture screen, is disclosed in the DeWitt version. The use of this device sought to compensate for the shortcomings of the traditional staging methods by masking the working of the changes. It is significant that it should, at the same time, enhance the cinematic feeling of this production.

— 28 —

The staging of the escape scene depended upon the use of at least one bridge, traps with adequate understage area, a counterweight system, and an ample fly-loft. The production was chiefly intended for cities with a population of not less than 25,000. Production in smaller cities could hardly have met the competition of the motion pictures. The reception of such an effect, one of the most spectacular that the stage could offer, is worth probing both for indications of audience taste and for the success of the conventional method in the presentation of such a cinematic conception in some of the relatively few theatres adequate for its presentation.

The production in New York at Niblo's Theatre on July 12, 1865, met adverse criticism because of the clumsy execution, "probably because the incidents depend so much upon machinery for the scenic effects, and neither ropes nor pulleys worked well last night. The scenery of the tower and the sea, and the general effect of the escape of Shaun by climbing up the face of the tower will be good when everything works well in the carpenter's gallery."[3] On the other hand, the pictures themselves were praised, since "the valley, lake, and Round Tower of Glendalough [were] a faithful picture of that landscape."[4] The failure of this opening was due to the heavy-handed control of the conventional stage machinery rather than to the pictorial conceptions. In 1865 this audience would have accepted the traditional methods for handling the escape scene had they been more smoothly engineered.

But by 1891 audiences were more demanding. The realistic reforms of the Bancrofts had whetted the critical perception of London audiences, and at a current production of this same play at the Princess' Theatre it was noted that "the escape scene is not the only opportunity which has been lost." Specific objection was raised against the conventional method of the tower scene, "covering the whole stage as we have it now at the Princess," and it was suggested that "a veritable tower standing out by itself"[5] be erected. The practice of painting the prison tower on flats which were worked through the stage floor now appeared as the counterfeit it had always been. The conventions had broken down here, and solid, genuine scenery was demanded.

The pictorial approach, however, had not lost its popularity.

A production at the Marylebone, London, on March 3, 1888, was hailed for its "view of Glendalough by moonlight [which] opened the drama with a pretty bit of scenic illusion";[6] and at the Girard Avenue Theatre, Philadelphia, January 4, 1892, the reviewer proclaimed that "the pictures of the times drawn in the play are realistic."[7] But when it was shown at the Bowdoin Square Theatre, Boston, on January 6, 1896, a few months before the vitascope was exhibited there, the production of the escape scene was again unsatisfactory, the claim being advanced that "the stage management could be much improved, especially in the ivy-climbing scene."[8] At this time the Bowdoin Square Theatre possessed an understage depth of twelve feet and was excellently equipped with ten traps in the levels of the first four grooves and two bridges in the fifth and sixth. The rigging loft was sixty-nine feet above the stage floor. With such adequate facilities the failure of the scene can be traced to the scenic conventions which, apparently, had lost much of their conviction.

When, in the early years of the twentieth century, Andrew Mack toured the country in the role of Shaun, the pictorial effects were presented in solid, three-dimensional construction. His production with the Bishop Players, Oakland, California, used a revolving stage and there were no stock settings. "Altogether there are nine different settings in the play and each of them is being built and painted especially for next week. The last act, showing Shaun's escape over the parapet of the jail, will be one of the most novel effects ever shown, for during this scene the stage is revolved while the action of the play goes on."[9] With the abandonment of conventional wing-and-border sets, and the use of three-dimensional, built-up scenery, the number of stage pictures was cut down from the original fourteen to nine. The spectacular aspects of the original production had been compromised in favor of greater pictorial realism.

The course of this play, through its many presentations during the last half of the nineteenth and early twentieth centuries, provides certain conclusions in regard to the realistic and romantic modes of this period. The staging of the melodrama required heightened spectacular effects. These effects in general could be managed upon the stage only along the conventional lines. Thus, with the late-century increase in the taste for realism, compromise was inevitable if the stage was to continue in the production of this romantic form. Whatever may have been gained through such compromise for realism was lost for romance. Such an impasse was at the root of the waning popularity of the stage melodrama and of the booming prospects of the film melodrama; for the screen, para-doxical as it may seem, could present the most romantic conception in a realistic fashion, and by thus combining realism and romance was to fall natural heir to stage melodrama.

Adaptations of the Dickens' novels were as popular on the stage of the nineteenth and early twentieth centuries as they have been since upon the screen. *David Copperfield,* adapted and renamed *Little Emily,* was produced regularly throughout this period. In one city alone, say Boston, there are records of its production at the Selwyn (1870), the Boston Museum (1874, 1890, and again in 1892), the Bijou (1887), the Bowdoin Square (1894), and the Castle Square (1897 and 1907). It had first been staged at the Olympic in London on October 9, 1869, and in this country at Niblo's Garden, New York, on December 20 of the same year. There is a significance to be found in its continuous popularity on the legitimate stage for a thirty-year period prior to the film, its fall from stage favor at that time, and its subsequent revival in motion pictures.

The promptbook of George F. Rowe,[10] who played Micawber at the Bijou in Boston on May 23, 1887, indicates how completely this type of play was at the mercy of the conventional staging methods. For without wings and borders, traps, bridges, two-di-mensional cut-outs, and perspective backdrops, neither spectacular effects nor episodic playwriting would have been possible.

From the first scene of the first act, Sea Beach at Yarmouth, Peggotty's Ark, set up with usual side wings, borders, backdrop, and sea cloth, an instantaneous change is indicated, without bene-fit of curtain, to A View of Yarmouth. From this scene into the next, Micawber's Lodgings, again there is no indication of the use of a curtain, simply the stage manager's notation after the change has been completed, "Lights up—voices—bell." This technique of dimming the lights before the change and bringing them up after the change, in the fashion of the "fade-out" and "fade-in" of the motion picture, is used again in the third act. From scene 1, Wickfield's Office in Canterbury, to scene 2, View in Canterbury, the stage manager has noted in the margin: "Ready to darken at change scene. Lights ½ down at change, footlights down." This fade-out, fade-in device facilitated the staging of the series of episodes which identifies Dickensian drama.

Oftentimes the dissolve, without the aid of lights, was played for its own spectacular quality. The change from the View in Canterbury to The Canterbury Cathedral is managed with "Organ before change. Calcium on at change. Organ begins before change. Scene changes slowly." The intention here seems to have been that of a transformation effect. The second set gradually and visibly merges with the first until a new locale appears where the old had once stood. This kind of pictorial sensation was traditional tour de force of the conventional scenic mode.

Spectacularism was not only the aim of the manner of scene changing, but was also embodied in the scenic conceptions. Act IV, scene 1, shows The Ark Interior. A storm is raging, and every time the door opens, "Wind, rain and thunder" are sounded. Changes from this scene to Near the Beach and then to Sea in a Storm are made as dissolves without benefit of curtains but with sound effects, offstage noises, and the action itself running continuously from one scene to the next. Ham goes out of the Ark and the Near the Beach drop is lowered, while "Ham, heard within R. 'Lights, lights, boys and more ropes.' Three men return from R. crying 'Lights, Lights.' Go off and return from left with ropes and lanterns. More fishermen and their wives—enter—rush across the stage and off R.—shouting. Storm and guns till opening of next scene." The actors move through a series of stage pictures. The beach scene on the forestage lasts long enough for the setting of the Sea in a Storm behind it. Then, with actors rushing across the beach to the rescue, the forestage drop is raised to reveal "Sea in a Storm. Ship pitching among breakers. Landing stairs and wooden pier R. Steerforth seen on mast of ship . . . ship sinks." This, the most spectacular scene of all, depended upon the usual wings, borders, backdrop, sea cloths, wind and rain effects, traps, and a two-dimensional ship cut-out. Neither the dissolving scene changes nor the spectacular scenic conceptions would have been possible without these conventions. Similarly, at the end of the play, as a typical gesture to the pictorial tastes of the audience, a final tableau is shown.

> Music—shouts and change. Scene last, full stage. Peggotty on Ship with Little Emily—Micawber with glass—Mrs. M. waving pocket handkerchief—Children, Clara, Mrs. Gummidge—Emigrants all on ship—David, Agnes, Betsey and others on stage in front. Ship moves from R. to L. Chorus—"Cheer, boys, cheer." Curtain.

Dickens, with his numerous episodes all pictured upon the stage, with spectacular scenic conceptions and equally sensational transformation and tableau effects, relied entirely upon all the two-dimensional conventions. But in the last few decades of the century, audiences became dissatisfied with the traditional mounting of the scenes. When *Little Emily* was done at the Boston Museum in 1890, the *Boston Post* described the spectacular shipwreck as a "droll anti-shipwreck scene, where agitated supernumeraries rushed off at one side of the stage immediately to rush on again upon the other."[11] Another Boston paper spoke of "a very funny sea in the third [act]."[12] And so, when H. Kellet Chambers adapted the novel in 1907 for production on March 11 at the King's Theatre, Hammersmith, London, the staging of the climactic storm was omitted, and "the wreck is vividly described by Peggotty, who watches the work of the boatmen from a window."[13] With the growth and recognition of the capacities of the cinema, traditional staging methods were discarded. At the same time, its production on February 11 of the same year at the Castle Square Theatre in Boston revealed that the pictorial-episodic manner of its construction was no longer proper to the stage. "Dickens' people . . . percolate a string of episodes that are confusingly numerous taken together, and too short and scrappy taken by themselves . . . they violate every canon of play technique."[14] The two qualities, episodic construction and productional spectacle, which characterized both Dickens and this entire realistic-romantic phase of nineteenth-century theatre, were no longer effective on the legitimate stage.

The cinema, in picking up the over-all pictorial approach as well as the specific techniques of the stage, marked itself as continuer of this phase of theatrical expression.

The same values can be identified with other productions of Dickens' novels. As early as May 19, 1874, cinematic qualities of the Daly presentation of *Oliver Twist* at the Fifth Avenue Theatre were recognized. "The performance of *Oliver Twist* by Mr. Daly's Company last evening was rather a series of pictures than the representation of a complete play. There was no sequence and no coherence between the different scenes, but rather a display of dissolving views."[15] This was apparently a rapid cutting from one "graphic illustration of London Life"[16] to another. Such motion-picture staging, from its first production at the Pavilion Theatre in London in May, 1838, through the entire nineteenth century, relied upon the stock techniques of the period. Its disappearance from the boards at that time indicates, again, both the breakdown of these techniques and the recognition of a new medium better suited for its presentation. The John Moore promptbook[17] used twenty-five scenes to present a continuous pictorial development of the story. In staging, the instantaneous full-view change was used, again simulating the overlap dissolve, and attempting to achieve continuity for material which was essentially disjointed and episodic, through the quick shuffling of a series of pictures.

Within this editorial form Moore exploited every opportunity for stage pictures. When Oliver goes to sleep in the second act Parlor of the House of Mr. Brownlow, "visions appear at back disclosing pictures of his mother's reception at the workhouse and her death." The stage manager's marginal handscript describes the treatment.

The back of the scene gradually opens and discovers a snow landscape with the workhouse door R.H. A woman poorly dressed with an infant in her arms has her hand on the knocker. Oliver in his sleep: "My mother—my poor mother. Oh! Let her in—let her in." The vision closes. Reopens and discovers a pallet-bed in a plain room. A woman in a nightgown, half sitting up is giving a locket to a very old woman (old Sally) who is kneeling back to audience. Oliver in his sleep: "Mother, my poor mother. Bless me, mother, bless me." Close in slowly with next scene.

The vision effect, a nineteenth-century staging device, was the popular method for depicting the internal state of a character. Such an editorial-cutting technique, shifting the scene from what the character was doing to what he was thinking, clumsy at best upon the stage, fell naturally into the vocabulary of the film.

In the last act, two great spectacular scenes provide climax and resolution, the first being the murder of Nancy by Sikes and the second, Sikes's suicide by hanging. The murder of Nancy hardly depends upon scenery, but is significant because of John Moore's detailed handscript directions for its pantomine and business, its minimum dependence upon dialogue, and its over-all emphasis upon the stage picture.

Bill [Sikes] enters in perfect silence—stands at end of table—Looks slowly at bed—deliberately takes off his hat, coat, vest.—"She put laudanum in my drink did she."—Pause, goes to bed, calls gently "Nance," then "Nance"—knocks her feet off the bed. She wakes, "Ah, Bill is that you?" Bill: "Every word was heard!" Nancy expecting to be beat: "I never said a word agin Bill." He seizes her with both hands round the throat—she tries to speak through the strangulation: "I never did a thing agin you, Bill. I swear before the Lord I never did. Oh, Bill, you ought . . ." By a desperate effort she pushes him off— "What are you doing to me?" Rushes to window and bangs it open, "Help, Help, Watch, Police—Murder." He catches her by the hair of the head, drags her forward and swings her round so that she falls head to L.H. He falls on his knees behind her as she reaches the floor. He knocks her head on the floor still holding her by the hair, she screaming and trying to call for help as long as she can. He rises and without letting go her hair drags her off L.U.E. her feet trailing on the ground. *Music* becomes almost inaudible. Pause—a heavy dull thud is heard, followed by a scream; a second blow and a faint scream—a third blow— a short pause—a low faint groan—Pause—Bill returns scraping the wing with his back and looking off. He is still more pale and ghastly and has his hands blooded—his eyes fixed on the room L.U.E. and trying to pierce through the gloom. Backing against the furniture to feel his way out, gets C. Pauses to listen, seems spellbound—Nancy with L. side of her face a mass of blood creeps on, dragging herself at full length—She gets near Bill—Her hand touches his foot—He starts away and crouches against the wall R. Pause—Nancy faintly: "Bill, Bill, I know you are there. I hear you breathe. Light the candle and then run, Bill.—Bill, Bill. My God,—if I only knew how to pray." She dies.

This reads much like a film script for an early action-melodrama. Its pictorial murder sensation was heightened in the 1895 production. Here Nancy returns to the room, face battered and smeared with gore, holds up her bloody lips, crying, " 'Kiss me and run for your life' . . . She opens her lips but a torrent of red fluid gushes from her mouth."[18]

The hanging of Sikes caps a series of six stage scenes. The pictorial pattern of this production staged by John Moore in 1874 at Daly's Fifth Avenue was, as noted by its reviewer, both sporadic and fragmentary. The act opens on London Bridge where Fagin overhears Nancy planning to foil him. This scene is closed by a forestage drop, Dark Street 1 Groove, as Noah Claypole, hired by Fagin, "shadows" Nancy who slinks across the stage. The drop is raised to reveal the Garret of Sikes. Nancy enters and is murdered. The fourth scene returns to the Dark Street on the forestage to show Sikes wandering horror-stricken at his deed. The fifth scene cuts across to show Fagin already arrested, incarcerated in prison, and half-crazed at his impending execution. The sixth scene flashes back to Sikes eluding the police in Toby Crackitt's Garret. "A street noise in pursuit" below is marked into the script as the scene changes to show him emerging onto the Roofs of Houses where he hangs himself before the law arrives.

The pictorial-cutting technique employed here apparently anticipated the work of both Porter and Griffith. The entire act seems to have been conceived as two chase sequences, the first between Nancy and the Fagin crowd, and the second between the Fagin crowd and the law. Because of the limitations of the stage, the pattern of pictures was stiff and restricted. The last two scenes plus the indication of "street noise in pursuit" are episodes in the chase sequence between Sikes and the law. On the stage we are shown one flash of Sikes hanging himself and plunging through the trap. Even in the early Griffith pictures this sensation would have been developed by a number of separate shots interlaced to form a suspense climax. Techniques of cinema may have been in use years before the arrival of the film, but their development was stunted by the limitations of conventional staging practices.

Melodrama struggled through the century curbed by these re-

1. Design by P. J. de Loutherbourg for David Garrick's production of *The Christmas Tale* (1773).

2. Boucicault's *Arrah-na-Pogue*, Escape Scene.

3. Boucicault's *Arrah-na-Pogue,* Escape Scene.

4. *David Copperfield; or, Little Emily,* Shipwreck Scene.

5. *David Copperfield; or, Little Emily,* Churchyard Scene.

6. *Oliver Twist*, Murder Scene.

7. *Oliver Twist*, Hanging Scene.

8. Boucicault's *The Corsican Brothers*, Duel Scene, produced by Charles Kean (1852). Left to right: Stacey, G. Everet, C. Kean, Daly, Wigan, J. Vining, Rolleston.

9. Boucicault's *The Colleen Bawn*, Drowning Scene.

10. Boucicault's *The Octoroon*, Ship Explosion Scene.

11. Boucicault's *After Dark*, Drowning Scene.

12. *After Dark*, advertising streamer.

13. Daly's *Under the Gaslight,* Rescue Scene.

14. *Under the Gaslight,* advertising streamer.

15. Boucicault's *Formosa,* Boat Race Scene.

16. Boucicault's *Pauvrette,* Avalanche Scene.

17. *Peep o' Day*, Quarry Murder Scene.

18. *Our Mutual Friend*, Mill Weir Scene.

19. *Shamus O'Brien*, Betrayal Scene.

20. *Lost in London*, Coal Mine Scene.

21. *Romance of a Poor Young Man,* Tower Scene.

22. Boucicault's *The Streets of New York,* Fire Scene.

23. *Lost at Sea,* Departure Scene.

24. *Lost at Sea,* advertising streamer.

25. *Nobody's Daughter*, Tryst Scene.

26. *Rip Van Winkle*, Return Scene.

27. *Amy Robsart*, Battlement Scene.

28. *Amy Robsart*, advertising streamer.

29. *Mary Stuart,* Execution Scene.

30. *Captain Kyd,* Vision Scene.

strictions until, in the last decade, the conventions were openly greeted with disfavor. The production of May 14, 1895, at the Star Theatre, New York, with Miss Otis as Nancy, met a scathing review in the *New York Times:* "As for the other participants in the play, they imitated the scenery, and were moved with difficulty."[19] Imagine, then, if such was the quality of a New York production, how audiences scattered through the provinces must have been treated. When this same company had played Boston a few months earlier at the Grand Opera House, it was observed that "the suicide scene of the last act was more than unusually inadequate and absurd, from the old, old difficulty of trying to bring real persons in contact with unreal scenery."[20] It had become apparent to audiences of the nineties that counterfeit scenery was undermining the success of stage melodrama. Critics were bold in their censure.

The crowd of men and boys, headed by benevolent Mr. Brownlow, stand yelling in the street in despair of catching the villain on the roof, when it is evident that any one of them could step over the nearest building at a stride and without being boosted could reach the chimney, where Sikes, ridiculously out of proportion with the chimney, fits the noose and drops with a jerk to his death.[21]

This was the setting which thrilled audiences in 1874 with its authenticity, its "admirable mise-en-scene,"[22] its "powerful pictures of life."[23]

The J. Comyns Carr version of *Oliver Twist* played in the twentieth century at about the time of E. S. Porter's *The Great Train Robbery.* It employed the disjointed cutting technique of the earlier adaptation, still "strung together like a meal of pickups that must be cleared away." Further protest was raised "against the overabundant and artificial use of the limelight, that was not only disillusioning, but destroyed the effectiveness of certain situations by its artificiality."[24] The Oswald Brand production at the Grand Theatre, London, March 30, 1903, omitted the spectacular tour de force of the final act. This was not satisfactory and the complaint was raised that the opening audience "should have liked to have seen a reproduction of the celebrated scene in the novel in which Sikes surrounded by his pursuers and howled at by the mob, hangs himself accidentally from a chimney-stack. The mere mention of his capture and certain execution is insufficient . . . We advise Mr. Brand to introduce a little effective realism."[25] While stage pictures were still in demand, the conventional methods no longer satisfied and "a little effective realism" was prescribed. Recognizing the difficulty and the cost of presenting this spectacular scene realistically, this adaptor had chosen to omit it entirely.

When, as late as September 30, 1912, the J. Comyns Carr version appeared at the Plymouth Theatre in Boston, only nine scenes were used instead of John Moore's original twenty-five. At this time its cinematic characteristics were openly and formally recognized: "Whatever *Oliver Twist* on the stage may have seemed to our fathers and grandfathers, audiences of 1912 go to it as to a picture play."[26] The various stagings of this play during the entire period which saw the fusion of stage and screen reveal a production operated upon cinematic principles. The editorial technique, utilized in the film by Porter and enlarged by Griffith, had been attempted decades before by John Moore at Daly's Fifth Avenue Theatre. Its exploitation of a series of spectacular pictorial episodes relied entirely upon traditional staging methods, which collapsed under the critical theatrical awareness of late-century audiences. This breakdown began the transfer of such material from stage to screen. Thus, while the vocabulary of the early film found its original expression in nineteenth-century melodrama, its ultimate development waited upon the Porters, Griffiths, and Hitchcocks.

Similarly *The Corsican Brothers,* in both the Boucicault version made for the Charles Kean production at the Princess' Theatre, London, February 22, 1852, and another by E. Grangé and X. de Montépin, attempted the visual presentation of action occurring simultaneously in the lives of the twin brothers. The two problems which arose in this staging—that of establishing the time relationship between events in the lives of the twins and exploiting this relationship for a dramatic effect, and that of enabling the actor playing the role of the twins to be in two places at the same time—indicate the motion-picture quality of the material, for, upon the screen, they presented no problem at all.

The brothers, Louis and Fabien dei Franchi, separated, are pledged to avenge each other in the event of death at the hands of a stranger. By some supernatural means, the two are telepathically united so that incidents in the life of one, when sufficiently intense, are revealed to the mind of the other. Louis is in Paris and Fabien in Corsica. Louis is killed in a duel with a M. de Reynaud. At the end of Act I in Corsica, Fabien receives telepathic communication of this event which, taking place in Paris, is shown to him in Corsica as a vision. The story flashes immediately from Corsica to Paris, then back to Corsica, where Fabien is shown departing to avenge his brother, all in the fashion of motion pictures. The second act goes back in time to show events in Louis' life in Paris prior to the duel scene in which he was killed. At the end of the duel, shown exactly as it was at the end of the first act, locale is shifted in reverse, this time to show the vision of Fabien in Corsica. The third act shows the duel of vengeance in which M. de Reynaud is killed, and finally still another vision in which Fabien sees his brother Louis in heaven.

All of this was staged in the conventional manner of vampire traps, with a double for the actor playing the twins, and using pre-set vision scenes behind shutters subsequently withdrawn to reveal the vision. These devices are recorded in John Moore's prompt-book of the Bowery Theatre production.[27] The significance of this play, obviously of a cinematic nature, is again to be found in the changing reception accorded its production as the century progressed.

The taste for realism on the stage gradually equalled that for the romanticized pictorial sensations embodied in such a play. The resulting impasse seems to have been reflected in a growing distaste for the usual presentation of such material. The Charles Kean production was hailed in 1852 for its colorful spectacle. "The interior of the *Opera House* with the masquerade ball and carnival, was magnificently placed on the stage; scenery and accessories were perfect, bewildering in their gorgeousness and multitude."[28] But thirty years later the same scenic approach exploited in the Boucicault adaptation at Booth's in New York was censured. "An accumulation of gaudy color-effects does not make good scenery. The vast and glowing ballroom scene in *The Corsican Brothers,* was, when looked at critically, merely ludicrous." The mixture of real actors with counterfeit scenery was no longer convincing. "This scene [*Opera House*] is very badly and coarsely painted by Clare. Instead of the private boxes being built up and filled with living people, they are hideously daubed upon flat canvas."[29]

Complaint had now turned against the previously popular two-dimensional painted scenery. The methods of the fifties no longer served the eighties. The conventional vision machinery of this Booth production was "also mismanaged. Fabien is writing and goes off for a candle. His double comes on and puts the letter into an envelope, while Mr. Thorne gets upon the vampire trap. Then the double, who is heavier than Mr. Thorne, poses in terror while Mr. Thorne, as Louis, appears in the Fontainbleau at the back."[30] This scene, staged just as it had been in the original Bowery Street production, prompted by John Moore, was no longer satisfactory. Later in the play a four-poster bed was used to facilitate Thorne's change from Louis to Fabien, and the transparency of the entire business was ridiculed.

> Then Mr. Thorne got into bed; drew the curtains, jumped out on the other side, and ran to the back of the stage, while his double laid down on the bed. Enter a servant, who pulled back the bed-curtain in order to show the double. Who ever heard of a servant pulling open the curtains when he wants his master to sleep.
> The back flat then sunk and disclosed Maynard [Reynaud] in Corsica, which he had reached from Paris in precisely two minutes. Fabien says, "Welcome to Corsica!" and the curtain falls.[31]

Previously successful conventional devices had now become "transparent trickery," particularly in the final vision of Louis in the Hereafter, where

> all the previous hitches and mistakes were eclipsed by the extraordinary finale . . . The words of this final act consist of constant repetitions by Mr. Thorne [as Fabien] of the sentence, "Oh, when will the body of my poor brother Louis arrive!"
> Presto! the apparition of Louis appears in an armchair. This is well contrived. But when Mr. Thorne spreads out his dressing gown so that Louis may disappear, it is impossible not to smile.[32]

Fabien, psychically bound to his dead brother, dies with the appearance of the vision. A Corsican Funeral has been added.

The body of Louis, having thus arrived, the scene changes to a graveyard. Fabien lies dead. His mother and Emily Rigl are kneeling near the footlights. Then the whole graveyard takes a walk down the stage and swallows up Fabien, as the alligator in the masquerade scene has tried to swallow the elephant. Miss Meek and Miss Rigl come very near to being swallowed up also. The perambulatory cemetery crowds them into a corner and yawns for them.

Imagine this absurd but horrible scene.[33]

This thorough and systematic ridicule of vampire traps, doubles, and counterfeit two-dimensional stage pictures in the 1883 production reveals a *reductio ad absurdum* in the conventional pictorial strivings of the nineteenth-century theatre. When Henry Irving's production came to this country in 1895, it was noted, in spite of Irving's characteristic thoroughness in staging, that "the time is passed for taking *The Corsican Brothers* seriously."[34] What is actually meant here is that the time had passed for taking the staging of *The Corsican Brothers* seriously, for certainly the cinema has since made much of this nineteenth-century material.

The success of such plays of Dion Boucicault as *Arrah-Na-Pogue, The Colleen Bawn, The Octoroon, After Dark,* and so forth, suggests a potential motion-picture audience years before the film's arrival. Screen techniques had been used by this master of melodrama in the middle of the century. *The Colleen Bawn; or, The Brides of Garryowen* was staged for the first time in 1860 in New York, Boston, and London.[35] The construction indicated in the promptscript[36] discloses another attempt to use conventional practices for the staging of material properly in the province of the film. Its dramatic development hinges upon the technique of cutting from stage pictures of episodes in one line of action to those occurring simultaneously in another, or of proceeding directly through a series of stage pictures in a single line, or of combining the two methods into a rudimentary cinematic pattern involving flashbacks, cross-cutting, and simple pictorial continuity, and employing fourteen scenes in three acts.

Into the pictures in motion of *The Colleen Bawn* were woven great spectacular effects. Its production in 1860 at the Adelphi in London was "little short of being the first of the sensational dramas, that is to say, the first drama in which a striking mechanical effect was the principal attraction, and the first serious drama in which the actor became of secondary importance to the machinist and the scene-painter."[37] Drama depended upon mechanical scenic effects. These effects, exemplifying the romantic tendencies of the period, were generally possible upon the boards with the stock methods discussed in Chapter One. In this play, the sensation came with the water-cave scene in which Danny Mann tries to drown Eily O'Connor, who is subsequently rescued by Myles-na-Cop-paleen. The conventional setting for this scene usually consisted of a series of profile cave cut-outs arranged in perspective to give an illusion of depth. In the forestage the sea cloth could be rotated, with the necessary open trap behind it and a rock cut-out appropriately installed. Behind the trap a solid floor facilitated the working of the boat. The drowning scene pictures the intersection of parallel lines of action and, in the fashion of the cinema, suspense is developed through cross-cutting. For instance, just prior to The Water-Cave, a Front Landscape, painted on a drop, is lowered at the forestage, both to conceal the setting-up of The Water-Cave and to provide a quick picture of Myles hurrying to the cave to save Eily from Danny. The Front Landscape is flown and Myles enters The Water-Cave.

Music, low storm music. . . Myles sings without then appears U. E. R. on Rock. . . Swings across Stage by Rope. Exit U.E.L.H. Music, Boat floats on R. H. with Eily and Danny. Eily steps on to Rock C. [Danny] stepping onto the Rock the Boat floats away unseen. . . Music. Throws her into the water L.C. She disappears for an instant then reappears clinging to Rock C. . . Thrusts her down. She disappears. . . Shot heard U.E.L.H. Danny falls into Water behind C. Rock. . . Myles sings without. . . Swings across by Rope to R.H., fastens it up, then fishes up Double of Eily—lets her fall. Strips, then dives after her. Eily appears for an instant in front. Then double for Myles appears at back and Dives over Drum. Myles and Eily then appear in front of Center Rock. Tableau. Curtain.[38]

Dialogue in many climactic scenes of the melodrama of this period was of secondary importance, and, as in the silent film, pictorial action, pantomine and business, dominated. Actors were unwittingly being trained for the silent film. There was no task here of creative interpretation or of dialogue. It was only necessary to carry out the action routine as outlined by author and stage manager. Drama depended essentially upon the sensational action, the spectacular scenic conceptions, and the cleverness of the overall episodic pattern.

Boucicault was a master in all three departments. He exploited visual appeal. His original production of *The Colleen Bawn*, an adaptation from the novel *The Collegians* by Gerald Griffin, at Laura Keene's Theatre in New York, grew out of a set of steel engravings of scenes around Killarney.

My dear Laura:

I send you seven steel engravings of scenes around Killarney. Get your scene painter to work on them at once. I also send a book of Irish melodies, with those marked I desire Baker to score for the orchestra. I shall read act one of my new Irish play on Friday; we rehearse that while I am writing the second, which will be ready on Monday, and we rehearse the second while I am doing the third. We can get the play out within a fortnight.

Yours, etc.

D.B.[39]

The play was written around the pictures, for the scenery had been fully commissioned while he was still writing the second act. This pictorial aspect of the production was enthusiastically received in its première in the sixties. The play was mounted "with all the care that always distinguishes the stage management at this theatre; the scenery, which is all new, and painted expressly for the play by Messrs. John Thorne and Minard Lewis is beautifully appropriate. We would particularize 'The Lakes of Killarney by Moonlight' by Thorne, 'The Gap of Dunhoe' by Lewis and 'Water Cave' by Thorne."[40]

But with this play, as with the others, the conventions upon which its staging depended gradually wore thin, and, by 1887, revivals found complaints against traditional scenic counterfeits. It was presented at the Hollis Street Theatre, Boston, a typical well-equipped metropolitan theatre, in November, 1887. Criticism displayed new standards, calling attention to the fact that "the scenery was not of the first order. A conspicuous and delicious absurdity was the display of a pretty house—worth, say $2000.00 or more—for *Myles' Hut*." [41] This abuse of the conventions in 1887 was further compromised when, on January 25, 1896, the revival by Mrs. Boucicault (Agnes Robertson) and John Douglass at the Princess' Theatre in London employed real water in "Douglass's famous tank." The intention, of course, was to increase the realism of the spectacular drowning sequence in an effort to compensate for the growing disfavor of the traditional staging. The *Saturday Review* of London claimed that it destroyed precisely the realistic effect it had set out to achieve.

> I have lived to see *The Colleen Bawn* with real water in it . . . the real water lacks the translucent cleanliness of the original article, and destroys the illusion of Eily's drowning and Myles-na-Coppaleen's header to a quite amazing degree; but the spectacle of the two performers, taking a call before the curtain sopping wet, and bowing with a miserable enjoyment of the applause, is one which I shall remember with a chuckle whilst life remains. [42]

This is fundamentally a proclamation against the mixture of the obviously real with the obviously unreal, which attracts attention to itself and in the end kills the illusion of the whole stage picture. A real water tank appears as nothing more than a tank, although it may claim to represent a lake. If consistency within the conventions had been maintained, there may, at least, have been a basis for their continuation. Such compromises were merely stopgaps. They marked both the breakdown of the nineteenth-century staging conventions and the readiness of audiences to shift to more spectacular and more realistic pictorial mediums.

This production in 1896 on the one hand offered real water tanks and on the other asked audiences to tolerate conventional scene changes. Austin Fryers has stated the case of the melodrama audience of the nineties: "When, therefore, in one act we have as many as six changes of scene, it requires more than the usual amount of make-believe to ignore the flitting figures of gas-men and scene-shifters, and the various contumacies of the scenery, so as to concentrate one's attention on the acting and the play." [43] Audiences would no longer put up with such distractions to pictorial continuity as were required by the outworn conventions.

When on January 20, of the same year, the play was repeated at the well-equipped Bowdoin Square Theatre in Boston, the water-cave scene was managed in the traditional way with the result that "its mechanism, its ropes, its waters, and its boats must be conspicuously unconvincing."[44] Another critic declared: "If one were to characterize this presentation of the play in a single word he would say 'crude.' "[45] And so it seems that neither water tanks nor the conventional trappings would satisfy the realistic demands of audiences in the nineties.

A medium was needed which could satisfy the pictorial leanings of the period with both realistic and spectacular effects at the same time. The motion picture had already been demonstrated, and its capacities in these two modes, the realistic and the romantic, were soon to be utilized in the filming of melodrama.

All of the Boucicault melodramas indicate that material superbly suited to the screen was being attempted upon the stage. The Henry Willard promptscript of *The Octoroon; or, Life in Louisiana*,[46] as produced at the Howard Athenaeum in Boston in 1863, describes a steamer ablaze in the middle of the river surrounded by burning bales of cotton. A two-dimensional profile cut-out represented the steamer and "red fire," arbitrarily used, simulated the conflagration. This spectacular effect was heightened by the appearance of McCloskey "seen swimming down stream, in the river landing L. behind some reeds." The steamboat is then blown up. The large profile steamer, afire at the wharf, is cut loose and drawn off the stage. A smaller steamer cut-out is subsequently introduced upstage in the middle of the stream, this "Small Steamboat to work on and be blown up." The blast was easily counterfeited with an exploding squib and appropriate sound and light effects. As the boat disappeared amidst flying pieces of stage carpentry and bits of wreckage, the crash machine was manipulated. Cinematic material presented in this fashion upon the stage relied upon the usual absurd scenic frauds.

This scene begins a pictorial continuity and cross-cutting sequence which builds suspense to the final curtain and closes the play on two climaxes in rapid succession. The explosion of the steamer forms the first episode in this sequence as McCloskey comes out of the river and makes an exit, with Wahnotee, the Indian, following in pursuit. The next scene, Act V, scene 1, cuts over to a parallel line of action. Zoe obtains the poison from Dido, intimating that she is planning to use it. The action flashes back to the first line to see McCloskey being trailed relentlessly by Wahnotee through The Cane-Brake Bayou. The next scene cuts across to still a third parallel line of action to show Pete and Scudder hurrying to tell Zoe that she is no longer a slave and thus prevent her from taking the poison. This Scudder-Pete line of action crosses the McCloskey-Wahnotee line in Another Part of the Swamp. It has become a double chase sequence. McCloskey, running into Pete and Scudder, pleads for help. They give him a knife, and he goes screaming off as Wahnotee closes in one him. Now the scene cuts back to the Zoe-and-the-poison line of action at The Parlor at Terrebonne. Pete and Scudder arrive, but too late; Zoe dies from the self-administered poison. This culminates two of the parallel lines. The McCloskey-Wahnotee chase sequence reaches its climax immediately after the death of Zoe and is shown as a tableau, pre-set behind the flats of The Parlor at Terrebonne. "Stage becomes dark, the scene opens and discovers the scene of the landing. Paul's grave R. the River at back. McCloskey is stretched across the grave, with his neck traversed with blood. Indian Wahnotee standing over him. Red fire. Slow curtain." The sensational fifth act has been developed with parallel lines of action forming two chase sequences which build into and are resolved by two pictorial climaxes, the self-poisoning of Zoe and the knifing of McCloskey by Wahnotee, the whole business being mounted in a kaleidoscopic fashion suggestive of a motion-picture montage.

Significance is to be seen not simply in the use of this cinematic technique, and in the presence of a rudimentary montage sequence, but in the very manner of their treatment. Events in parallel lines of action are seldom if ever merely suggested. Each incident contributing to suspense is pictured on the stage. Scene changes were made not with the use of the curtain but with the fading out and in of lights, or in full view, in the merging manner of the screen's "lap dissolve," thus providing an agreeable development of its episodic pattern. It would seem that, in the handling of such material, a motion-picture technique had been evolved many years before the arrival of cinema. Its further growth upon the stage was limited by the conventional staging methods which showed evidence of breakdown in the decade from 1885 to 1895.

In *Forbidden Fruit*,[47] first produced in New York at Wallack's Theatre on October 3, 1876, and in London at the Adelphi on July 3, 1880, Boucicault employed an old device which, in this case, enabled him to give his technique of cross-cutting between parallel lines of action a more realistic scenic treatment. The first act shows the chambers of lawyer Dove in the Temple represented by two compartments, the outer office on stage right connected by a door in the separating partition to the inner office, stage left. Similarly, in the third act at the Cremorne Hotel, two adjoining rooms as well as the intervening corridor are put upon the stage. Boucicault, recognizing the growing taste for realism, yet not wishing to sacrifice the scenic speed necessary to the play nor its pictorial variety, used box settings of a dual or even triple nature. Discredited and clumsy conventional scene changes were thus eliminated, and cross-cutting between parallel lines of action could be managed without scene waits.

The device of the dual box set was an old one. Early in the century the same romantic tendencies had been given this type of realistic treatment. As Allardyce Nicoll has pointed out, two cells with a separating partition were used in the 1808 Drury Lane production of "Monk" Lewis' *Venoni*.[48] Two rooms were also placed simultaneously upon the stage in Colman's *Actor of All Work* (Haymarket, 1817).[49] And in *Jonathan Bradford* by Fitzball, produced at the Surrey Theatre in 1833, "the interiors of four rooms were placed upon the stage at one time."[50] In 1846 at the Lyceum, Edward Sterling's *Above and Below* was staged on two floors, simultaneously shown.[51] It is likely that the early-century use of this device resulted in some pictorial cross-cutting between parallel lines of action, yet because it failed to meet the spectacular requirements of the romantic mode of the nineteenth century, it found no widespread usage until the conventional methods of handling changes and spectacular scenes fell into disrepute during the seventies, eighties, and nineties.

One of the most spectacular of Boucicault's melodramas was *After Dark; or, Neither Maid, Wife nor Widow*. Its original production was in London in 1867 and in the following year at Niblo's Garden in New York. Thereafter revivals took place throughout the century. Its pictorial sensations included a harbor scene with surface traffic moving behind an attempted murder by drowning. The hero dives head-on from the bridge into an open trap to make the rescue. The DeWitt version[52] describes the conventional pictorial manner of the sea-cloth, the backdrop river skyline, wings and borders to simulate the bridge and its stanchions, and the open trap for the final heroic header. Late-century revivals which introduced a real water tank produced incongruous results similar to those previously noted.

But the chief spectacle of the play was the scenic innovation of the railroad scene. Needless to say, the conception itself as well as the manner by which it was exploited in the script was cinematic. Chumley has been secured to the rails outside a stone cellar in which Old Tom has been incarcerated. Suspense arises from the obvious chase sequence: will Tom rescue Chumley before the train arrives? The editorial pattern of the stage pictures is rudimentary. Chumley is lashed to the tracks. Then the scene is flashed to Tom on the forestage frantically striving to break through painted cellar flats. "Cellar in 1st grooves; dark circular hole center in Flat, showing through it the platform on which train of cars cross R. to L.; only the wheels of them are visible from front."[53] Chumley is on the other side. After a single speech, Tom breaks through the wall and the scene is run off, "dissolving" into a fresh angle of the same episode. The underground railroad is shown from the other side of the wall which Old Tom has just penetrated. As the lights come up, Tom squirms through a hole in the wall to rescue Chumley on the rails.

All the flats are stone walls. . . A, a circular hole (like that of the previous scene) surrounded by stones which will fall out and make room for a man to pass through; B,B, tunnels with lines of rails, curving into that on stage, painting on flat represents them running off into distance . . . [cars] used are to be sufficiently heavy to keep the rail; car in profile with lights within and profile passengers' faces at windows; red fire under locomotive at fire-pan; red light at front; red lantern at last car; no works required; see the wheels run very freely; the moment Tom and Chumley are clear, run the train across; decline the rails to L. till at wing, then give it an uprise abruptly to check it in a few yards.[54]

The entire sequence as well as the effect itself depended upon two-dimensional conventions. Within these conventions a spectacular motion-picture sequence had been attempted. Like the cinema, the dramatic unit was the episode, which depended less on dialogue than upon descriptive action. The obvious counterfeits of painted passengers, red fire, rails and tunnels painted in perspective to merge with the practical ones on stage, and so on, may have satisfied early audiences but were viewed with open mockery in the days of the early film. For instance, at the Grand Theatre, Fulham, London, on April 23, 1900, "the crowning joy is the *Underground Railway on the Lines*. We tremble to think what would have happened to that train if the body of Gordon Chumley had remained to block its way."[55] Real water tanks may have been possible in this theatre of spectacular pictures, but real railroad trains were somewhat beyond reach.

Competition in the presentation of these faked spectacular scenes was bitter. Augustin Daly claimed the railroad-train effect had been stolen[56] from his *Under the Gaslight* produced at the New York Theatre, August 12, 1867. In an original prompt copy of Daly's play belonging to G. W. Wilson,[57] the scene is described in detail.

Railroad station at Shrewsbury Bend. Up R. the station shed. R.H. platform around it, and doors at side, window at front. At L.1.E. clump of shrubs and tree. The Railroad track runs from L.4.E. to R.4.E. View of Shrewsbury River in perspective. Night. Moonlight. The switch with a red lantern and Signalman's coat hanging on it L.C. The signal lamp and post beside it.

Laura, the heroine, insists upon being locked in the signalman's hut for safety, while Snorkey prepares to flag the train in order to relay information which would prevent murder. Byke, the villain, enters, overpowers Snorkey, and binds him to the rails as the approaching locomotive rumbles and blasts its whistle. Laura, unseen, has been watching from the hut. Byke exits. The rumbling of the train on the rails increases and the whistle is sounded repeatedly. Laura, locked in the hut, is smashing at the door with an ax. The locomotive headlight flashes around the bend. She breaks out of the hut, reaches Snorkey as the headlight beam shoots down the rails, and as she drags him off he gasps: "And these are the women who ain't to have a vote." Then, with a blast, the train of cars roars past "from L. to R.H."

The cinematic editorial form has not been so cleverly developed here as in Boucicault's version. Climax nevertheless does occur at the intersection of parallel lines of action which have been pictorially developed. The stage antecedent of such early screen material as *The Train Wreckers*[58] is obvious, yet even into the early days of the film, conventional methods were retained upon the stage. In an 1896 production it was noted that "the engine and cars are of wood and canvas."[59] Changes, of course, would have been difficult. It is not the intention here to dispute whether Daly or Boucicault was the first to use the two-dimensional railroad train upon the stage. There are, indeed, records to be found of the production of a play entitled *London by Night* by Charles Selby at the Strand Theatre in London on January 11, 1844, which employed the same device.[60] It is significant merely as an illustration of the conventional presentation upon the stage of spectacular scenic effects which belonged properly to the screen.

Daly's *Under the Gaslight* also employed the river scene. According to the G. W. Wilson prompt copy, the usual staging deceptions were utilized.

Foot of Pier 30, North River. Sea Cloth down and working. A pier projecting into the river. A large cavity in front. Bow of vessel at back, and other steamer, vessels, and piers in perspective on either side. The flat gives view of Jersey City and the river shipping by starlight. . . Byke enters sculling a boat, R. 2d. E. and fastens his boat to the pier, L.H.

A fight takes place on the dock and in the boat, and when the harbor police "patrol boat appears at R. with lights, Judas throws

Laura over back of pier . . . Ray leaps into water after Laura."
Dialogue, again, is subordinate to the visual appeal as the climax
is developed out of a spectacular action routine.

In Boucicault's *Formosa; or, The Railroad to Ruin,* first performed at Drury Lane, August 5, 1869, and a favorite of nineteenth-
century audiences, an actual boat race was staged in the fifth scene
of the fourth act.

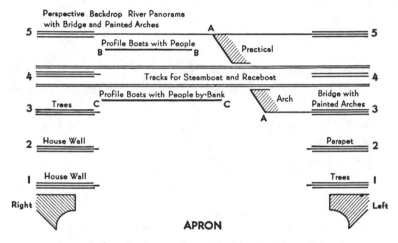

*Ground plan showing staging method for Boat Race Scene of
Boucicault's* Formosa *(from the DeWitt version, HTC)*

Trees R. and L. Sky sinks and borders in upper entrances. House
wall R. 1st and 2d E. AA—bridge openings, river with two large arches
shown, the rest of the arches continued in painting on flat; BB a profile line of boats with people looking L. CC, line of third grooves, profile of people in boats looking left supposed to be by bank of river.
The stage 1st and 2d E. is supposed to be on the bank, above the river
level. From under archway L. 3d. E. across to off R. 3d. E. double track
for steam boats and two race boats supposed to be forty-five feet long,
with profile eight rowers—to work—which are worked across. . . On
the bridge L. 2d. E. behind parapet, group of profile figures, men and
women, miniature, to work, jump up and down, as if to see the end
of the race; these face R. A flag, of the winner's colors, ready on the
bridge, on a staff, to be held up.[61]

The climax of the play, a boat race, contains few lines of dialogue
but a carefully developed plan of stage action. One wonders where,

in this staged motion picture, real actors could have mixed with the two-dimensional profile rowers and cheering spectators which were all operated mechanically in the fashion of puppets on the ends of strings. Material belonging properly to the screen was again staged with the flat scenic conventions. These conventions, and with them the entire theatre of action-melodrama, were on the point of collapse at the time of the film's arrival. A. B. Walkley reviewed a production of this play at Drury Lane, May 26, 1891, saying nothing much more than that he slept through two acts.[62]

Pauvrette; or, Under the Snow, another of Boucicault's spectacular pieces, first performed at Niblo's Garden, New York, October 4, 1858, received somewhat better notices, at least with early audiences, for its sensational avalanche of snow. "In the construction and 'getting up' of this piece Mr. Boucicault has once more displayed those great and peculiar talents in which he stands unsurpassed, and which generally secure popular success to his work. *Effective situations* and *telling mise-en-scene* are Mr. B's strong points."[63] Boucicault's devotion to the "effective situation" was synonymous with that episodic style of writing characteristic of the silent film. His "telling mise-en-scene" was devoted, in this case, to the artificial creation upon the stage of spectacular natural phenomena.

> The summit of the Alps, Rocks and precipices occupy the stage. A rude hut on one side in front. A bridge formed by a felled tree across the chasm at the back. The stone-clad peaks stretch away in the distance. Night. . . Storm, wind. She [Pauvrette] throws her scarf around her, and hastily ascends the rock—utters a long wailing cry—listens. . . Descends to her hut. Maurice cries for help. Takes her alpenstock and a coil of rope, and re-ascends the rock. The wind increases—the snow begins to fall. She crosses the bridge and disappears off left. Bernard appears below on the rocks, L. He climbs up the path. . . Pauvrette appears on the bridge, leading Maurice. . . They cross the bridge. . . They descend and enter the hut. . . Large blocks of hardened snow and masses of rock fall, rolling into the abyss. Pauvrette falls on her knees.

Then, when they have entered the hut,

> The avalanche begins to fall—the bridge is broken and hurled into the abyss—the paths have been filled with snow—and now an immense

sheet rushing down from the R. entirely buries the whole scene to the height of twelve or fifteen feet swallowing up the cabin and leaving above a clear level sea of snow—the storm passes away—silence and peace return—the figure of the Virgin (in window) is unharmed—the light before it still burns.[64]

What may not Dion Boucicault have accomplished had he lived some ten or fifteen years longer into the days of the motion picture, where, on location, his camera could have recorded such scenes with a realism impossible to the conventional stage? His setting was always his most important actor. Drama was dependent upon the spectacular pictures contrived and set into motion upon the stage. Without these there would scarcely have been excuse or reason for the play; indeed, there would rarely have been a play at all.

Such cinematic qualities so thoroughly exemplified by the work of Boucicault, are typical of all nineteenth-century melodrama. *Peep o' Day* by Edmund Falconer was first produced at the Lyceum in London on Lord Mayor's Day, 1861; Broadway Theatre, New York, January, 1868; Wood's Museum, Chicago, January 31, 1867; Howard Athenaeum, Boston, December 31, 1867. Thereafter, throughout the century, it provided a popular piece for both provincial and metropolitan revival. Attempting material with certain obvious motion-picture characteristics, its stage production, as in the case of the Boucicault melodramas, was dependent upon the conventional techniques. Its famous third-act scene is described in a review of a later London production.

Sensationalism was never carried to a higher pitch than in this dread *picture,* and what wonder was it that the spectators once more felt a thrill of horror as they *watched* Black Mullins digging the grave; *watched* poor Kathleen, his intended victim, endeavoring to elude the snare so artfully laid for her destruction; *watched* the manly Harry Kavanagh risking life and limb in his perilous leap in order to rescue her; and *watched* the faithful Barney O'Toole dancing with glee upon the lofty rock as he sees the villain brought to grief.[65]

The appeal of this climactic scene was entirely visual, depending upon setting and pantomimic action and, for the most part, dispensing with dialogue. The scene takes places in an old quarry surrounded by precipitous cliffs with only one entrance. The Broadway Theatre production was staged in the following manner, described in the promptbook of John Moore:[66]

Dark. Music. *The old quarry of Foil Dhino*, or *Dark Valley*. Moonlight seen above the precipitous peak, which casts a shadow L.H. Path from upper flies L.H., descent of three steps to ledge, which terminates in an abrupt precipice L.2E. Bridge (rough plank with guiding-rope) across from projecting ledge L. to projecting ledge R., which thus form a chasm. Winding path—steep descent from R. ledge, down to stage, terminating about R.2E. Large blocks of stone scattered about on stage, pretty well up. A mountain ash tree growing L.H. close to wing, its boughs reach top of precipice L.H. The quarry, having long been disused, shows a great deal of verdure. The stage set with grass and ferns. Mullins discovered digging a grave L.C. well down in front. A mound of upturned sod or clay on stage by grave. Large size block of stone a little above and L. of grave.

Stage manager John Moore has penciled into the margin: "Mullins discovered in Grave Pit digging. Continue music until he lays spade down. Mind stones in box for pick-axe to strike against." Within the two-dimensional scheme much of the setting had to be practical. In the first grooves were forest or rocky hillside wings. The projecting precipices forming the gulch were profile cut-outs, but required solid platforms behind them to support the weight of at least two persons. Into the rock of the right-hand precipice a winding path was cut for descent to stage level. The lefthand precipice was reached as if by a path down from the flies. The bridge across the chasm was practical, and so was the ash tree growing from its foot. The scene would be closed by a landscape painted on flats or backdrop.

Spectacular action within this practical but conventionalized pictorial setting was thoroughly worked out in the promptscript. Mullins comes out of the grave:

As he ascends steps R.H. Kathleen comes down L. to edge of precipice just as he reaches and crosses bridge to L. She is concealed from him by a shadow cast by peak; as she reaches edge of precipice L. branch of tree bars her passage—she starts, looks down and discovers with horror, the declivity. She turns and perceives Mullins crossing bridge, is alarmed and crouches down and watches him off L. She then, after a short pause, crosses bridge and descends steps R. to stage.

When Mullins returns and goes after her below, the visual details of the action and business are carefully explained in Moore's hand-script, but no mention is made at all of the interpretation of character or dialogue. "She dodges under his arm and hides L. hand." Mullins cannot find her. Afraid she may escape before he can kill her, he dashes up the cliff and "rips up planks of bridge with Pick Axe. Wood Crash as Bridge falls." [67] Escape or rescue thus blocked, a vicious struggle ensues, all carefully planned as if for a silent film.

> Kathleen screaming violently all through the struggle. Kathleen dodge a little—Kathleen rush a-x and gains foot of ascent. He catches her, his left hand seizing her back hair, his R. hand on her shoulder, he seeming to pull her only by the hair. Drags her back to L. corner, she struggling with back towards him, her head bent back. She gets away makes for R. hand corner. He follows, drags her to C. Punches her head violently. Break away, she to R., he to L. He seizes spade to knock her down. Harry down by this time, wrenches the spade from him and knocks him down. Lifts Kathleen from the ground. Tableau.

Harry's descent to the pit of the quarry without the benefit of a bridge provided a highly spectacular feat.

> At the moment she screams Harry and Barney appear on the ledge L.F. Harry runs along ledge to L.H. . . Sees the bridge down. . . Seizes the branch of the tree and swings himself off the ledge. It bends with him and lands him lightly down on the stage, just as Mullins has cast Kathleen on the mound of earth, and raised the spade.

Climax comes, in the usual fashion of this episodic style of playwriting, at the intersection of parallel lines of action. Characteristic of the period, it exemplifies spectacular action within a pictorial setting. To facilitate and to heighten the melodramatic values of this construction, the usual instantaneous shift in full view was employed either as a dissolve or with benefit of lights as a fade-out and fade-in. In an effort to overcome some of the artificiality of the conventional setting, great realism was attempted in the use of properties. In the New York production, the Fair Scene included "a great quantity of padded stones, fish, vegetables, dead cats, and other things to pelt with. . . Irish Bagpipes; Irish Harp;

Anything to improve Fair Scene; Live pig; see all the stuffed sticks in good order. . . Fir trees and green-branches to help [quarry] scene." It had been recognized that the traditional scenic method needed whatever support might be provided by realistic properties. The realism of live pigs or dead cats was undoubtedly sensational, but at the same time created a certain incongruity. On the other hand, a complete sacrifice of the conventions would have brought about the failure of the entire melodrama theatre. And so the whole business muddled along, stymied by such compromises, until the motion picture arrived.

Similarly with adaptations of Dickens. Whenever Dickens was transferred to the stage two basic qualities were invariably recognized: an episodic-pictorial construction, and an exploitation of spectacular scenes. George F. Rowe's version of Dickens' *Our Mutual Friend,* produced at the Olympic Theatre, New York, on June 4, 1866, was the usual clever piece of patchwork, for it was nothing more than "the tacking together of those scenes in the novel the best calculated to produce dramatic effects."[68] These "effects" fell into the typical category of scenes of violent action and spectacular setting. Act II, scene 5, included a murder, a drowning, and a rescue. Rowe's promptbook[69] directs Headstone to strike Eugene with an oar and throw him into the water. Lizzy returns, jumps into a boat, pulls him out, and drags him to shore. In Act III, scene 3, Riderhood in the Mill Weir Gatehouse quarrels with Headstone.

A struggle in which Headstone throws Riderhood and escapes out of the door. Riderhood rises and seeing Headstone on the lock gate, lets the wheel fly suddenly. The gates open slowly and the water rushes through. Riderhood draws a knife from his belt to follow. Headstone turns at the centre of the first gate and fires at Riderhood who falls but recovers. Headstone who has hesitated at leaping the chasm, seeing Riderhood following him, jumps. Riderhood leaps across after and seizes him, stabbing Headstone with his knife. They struggle madly but Riderhood cries, "I'll hold you living and I'll hold you dead." They fall locked together into the torrent.

This spectacular scene was managed with the traditional sea cloths behind the dam two or three feet above the stage. The locks opened toward the audience at the center and the escaping cascade was represented by the conventional waterfall machine, an endless belt of canvas working from a roller at dam level to a roller below the stage floor through a trap. Riderhood and Headstone fell through this same open trap to the accompaniment of suitable sound effects.

Racing melodramas were always popular on the nineteenth-century stage, as they have been since upon the screen. Occasionally they enabled the stage to meet the competition of the early film. Theodore Kremer's *A Race for Life* was not produced until 1904, nine years after the arrival of moving pictures, opening on November 21 at the New Star Theatre in New York. The story of the play concerned a race horse and a young couple in love. The horse won the race to secure the wealth, health, and happiness of the couple. It held the stage for several years in both provinces and larger centers. When it appeared at the Grand Opera House in Boston on January 8, 1906, one reviewer openly proclaimed: "It was the race that we spectators went to see, and no matter what stars of melodrama were on stage, the horse was the hero."[70] This exploitation of spectacular effects enabled stage melodrama to meet the encroachments of the film even after the methods of conventional staging had fallen into disrepute. Ironically enough, when the play next came to Boston, again at the Grand Opera House, on February 11, 1907, and despite the race's now being played in a "Real Rain Storm,"[71] moving pictures were offered on the same bill.

Presentations of melodrama were often accompanied by boasts of authentic stage pictures. When Augustus Harris' production of *Shamus O'Brien* by Jessop and Stanford came to the Star Theatre, New York, in December, 1897, it was hailed as "an admirable picture of the life of the Erin of a hundred years ago."[72] Earlier that year at the Broadway Theatre on January 4, 1897, its critics disclosed that it was "a most interesting combination of realism and romanticism."[73] The production of Watts Phillips' popular *Lost in London* at the Marylebone Theatre in 1887 was supported by authentic properties "in the shape of a real horse and cab—introduced in an effective snow scene."[74] In its production of 1899 at the Bowdoin Square Theatre in Boston, it was reported that "one of the strongest scenes was that of the coal pit in the first act, in which the weirdness of the diggers with the miners' lights . . . proved specially effective."[75] Stage pictures entranced these audiences of the 1890's. When it was revived later in the same year (September 18) at the Grand Dime Theatre, South Boston, the setting, "which shows the coal mine in Lancashire, where the miners, by the dim light of the lamps of their hats, dig thousands of feet below the ground for fuel," and the great snowstorm scene, "which shows a section of old London at night,"[76] were praised for their apparent authenticity.

This pictorial approach, striving to present authentic settings with conventional techniques, was common property of the melodrama stage. *The Romance of a Poor Young Man* from the French of Octave Feuillet, first produced at the Princess' Theatre in London in 1859 as *Ivy Hall*, held the stage throughout the century prior to being transferred to the screen as a feature film by the Biograph Company about 1914. On the stage a single sensational picture was, according to Dutton Cook, the only moving scene.

Real enthusiasm was excited upon only one occasion. This was, of course, the famous scene in the third act where Victor and Blanche are accidentally locked up together in the ruined Tower of Elfen. The lady charges her lover with a design upon her honour, and with having therefore prearranged her detention in the ruins. To vindicate himself, Victor, at the risk of breaking his neck, leaps down from the tower and obtains assistance. . . The suicidal-looking, headlong plunge in which Mr. Sothern indulges is perhaps more in keeping with his view of the excitable French gentleman he is personating, and moreover *"headers" are well-established means of moving an audience.*[77]

When it was produced in this country on May 16, 1887, at Daly's in New York, the scene again elicited praise as "Mr. Bellew jumped from the tower with great agility."[78] This melodrama apparently retained much of its popularity for the one spectacular scene, and any deletion would have undermined its success.

The quest for sensational stage pictures which could be handled with the conventional apparatus sometimes led to the use of the moving panorama. When Sifton Parry put on a piece called *The*

Odds at the Holborn, "the illusion of rapid locomotion [was] principally supported by a flying background and whirling wheels, while a man was being thrown out of a railway train in motion."[79] In the presentation of such moving scenic backgrounds, the stage was limited to the two-dimensional patterns of the period.

In larger and better-equipped theatres it was sometimes possible to combine pictorial-episodic staging requirements with a single spectacular scene of genuine three-dimensional construction. *Blue Jeans,* a melodrama by Joseph Arthur, was produced at the Globe Theatre in Boston in December, 1891. The growing dissatisfaction with the traditional techniques for the presentation of this "essentially kaleidoscopic"[80] dramatic form led to the introduction of a truly authentic stage picture. "It is conceded that the mill incident is the most sensational bit of intense realism ever vouchsafed on the stage of this or any other country. So thrilling is this materialistic introduction that it is a common occurrence to see the audience rise en masse at its close and cheer like mad."[81]

Audiences were not dissatisfied with the pictorial approach to staging. They were merely displeased with the overuse of an outworn set of scenic conventions.

And such a saw-mill! None of your paste-board, imaginative affairs, but a real saw-dust producer, with wheels, pulleys, belts and ugly-looking buzz-saws. And they buzz, too! You don't see them just as the curtain goes down—as the average bit of stage realism is shown—but real boards are really sawed, and real saw-dust flies therefrom. . . its hero, having been stunned, is placed upon the board which is being sawed, and is slowly drawn to a seemingly inevitable death.[82]

Such scenic realism, employed for its obvious sensational values, could hardly have been offered to more than a small percentage of the audience beyond the range of the metropolitan houses. Limited in its circulation, it nevertheless reflects the tastes of audiences in the nineties for both realistic and sensational stage pictures. Unlike the realism of the Moscow Art Theatre or of the Théâtre Libre of Antoine, this type of pictorial setting was the chief actor in the play, attracting attention to itself and being employed for specific spectacular-action routines.

Alexandre Dumas' *The Count of Monte Cristo* was filmed in

1908, again in 1910, 1911, 1912, and in 1922, 1927, and 1934. It was first performed upon the stage in this country on December 25, 1848, at the Broadway Theatre in New York, and thereafter held the stage during the entire century, only to disappear after its appearance upon the screen. James O'Neill made a fortune touring it through the country for seventeen years and playing over 5817 performances. The most successful plays of this period advanced both episodic playwriting and spectacular scenery. In 1884, when he played at the Globe Theatre in Boston, one reporter wrote, "To condense a novel of such length and variety into a play seems an absurd undertaking: and so it would be. Yet a kind of sketch can be made, in which shall be shown, *as in a series of tableaux,* a few of the chief incidents of Edmond Dantes' career. . . this has been successfully done."[83] O'Neill's production ten years later in the same city at the Grand Opera House had not changed. "Of course, no one claims any merit in the piece as an example of dramatic construction. It is simply the piecing together of a number of scenes from Dumas' novel, with just enough coherence to relieve them of absolute farcicality."[84]

The staging of such pictorial continuity was always carefully prepared. For instance, the second act deals with Dantès' escape from the Château d'If. It must tell of the death of Faria in the prison, of Dantès' changing places with the corpse, of the guards carrying him out in the dead man's sack, tossing him, within the weighted sack, into the sea, and finally, of his escape and appearance upon the rock. In the J. B. Studley promptbook[85] of the 1873 Charles Fechter production, subsequently reused at the Mount Morris Theatre in New York in 1884, the continuity was handled in the following way. The first scene of this act is a tripartite scene showing the two cells of Faria and Dantès at the Château d'If with the rampart above them.

The two cells of Edmund and Faria separated by a wall. A space excavated in its thickness for their escape, opening by a hole in each cell. Above the cells a Rampart, where the Sentinel Guard paces. Edmund is discovered in the opening in the wall, Faria kneeling near the hole leading to it. Sentinel paces to and fro on the Rampart. Clock strikes Eleven.

Action could be played in three areas simultaneously, with the dramatic emphasis shifting from one to the other. By this technique a narrative continuity was developed by cutting from a scene in one stage area across to a scene in another area where parallel action has been transpiring. At the end of this first sequence Faria died, and just as Dantès prepared to enter Faria's cell, there was "Thunder and lightning. Storm. . . The cells sink slowly. . . The sea and the rocks seen beneath a stormy sky." In this way the sequence of stage pictures was blended by means of a dissolve change. Now, into this stormy sea scene came the third scene, "Platform of the Chateau d'If. Steps cut out in the rock leading to a sort of Jetty from the second floor; a Door of the secret Dungeons on the first floor." The episode of the jailers' taking Dantès out of Faria's cell in the dead man's sack has not been shown. The continuity cuts down to show the jailers as they come out of the prison carrying the sack.

They swing and let the sack into the sea, come down the steps. . . They recross the stage and Exeunt into the Prison. Moon breaks out lighting up a projecting rock. Edmund rises from the sea and seizes on it—he is dripping—a knife in his hand—some shreds of the sack adhering to it.
Edmund: (on rock) The World is Mine!!

The entire act depended upon the flow of one pictorial setting into another, a series of rapidly changing, dissolving views. Dialogue may have been used, but the story grew out of descriptive action and stage pictures. In the fashion of the nineteenth-century melodrama, this appears to have been a staging with traditional techniques of what later became a motion-picture shooting-script.

This pictorial quality was fundamental to the popularity of the nineteenth-century melodrama. Audiences were moved and critics proclaimed that "there have been few more *striking stage pictures* seen in modern times than when Dantes, rising from the waves, brandishes aloft the weapon which has stood him in such good stead and shouts in triumph."[86] Spectacular settings were exploited to enhance the episodic, cinematic construction. The play opened on the Catalans Village with the Harbor of Marseille in the background. Originally this had been handled with conventional methods.

Scene 1st. Port of Marseilles. Set Waters and Foreground: Set Scene, trap open behind foreground with steps; all the entrances are made from the trap: set house on platform, L. 2d. E; rock masking balcony to house. . . Ship works on from R.H. . . . The Ship is seen entering Port, she furls sails and anchors—all hurry off down the cliff towards the port.[87]

By 1900 this conventionalized spectacle was no longer satisfactory, and the Leibler and Company production, with O'Neill still in the leading role, offered much more realistic settings. Moving pictures had been demonstrated five years before this company came to the Boston Theatre on September 17, 1900. Pictorial values dominated and, "although Mr. O'Neill's name appeared in large type on the playbill, it was really the scenery that was the star of last evening's performance."[88] There were only nine scenes in this version, but all employed spectacular settings.

In the scene representing the port of Marseilles, for example, we are given a most delightful water view, with a foreground crowded with the picturesque populace standing in groups, or moving about, all intent upon the arrival of the Pharon, which presently is seen in the offing. The ship moves gracefully through the water, making a complete turn as it sweeps into the harbor, where it drops anchor. In a few moments young Dantes, the mate in charge, is rowed ashore by a boat's crew and the action of the play begins in earnest.[89]

The romantic mid-century novel of Dumas *père* found a highly realistic and sensational staging at the turn of the century. "The second act opened with another front set, and then came the prison of the Chateau d'If, a massive-looking affair, which finally split itself into sections in the most surprising fashion showing the open sea, the escape of Dantes and the stirring tableau 'The World is Mine.' " Expense was not spared in the reproductional treatment of Dumas' spectacular, romantic conceptions. The lavishness of certain scenes suggested what was soon to happen in Hollywood. "The simulated conservatory and ballroom is not only beautiful to look upon, with its grand proportions, its harmonious blending of color and its elegantly attired moving multitudes, but it is almost *overpowering in its stability and massiveness.*" While this speaks of a solid, three-dimensional picture, this very quality set up barriers to its circulation and the size of it potential audience. "It is only in the large cities that a stage can be found big enough to accommodate the great interior, and hence the astonishment which the scene itself produces is increased at thought of the seemingly reckless prodigality of the producers."

Thus, while the Leibler production may have been acclaimed for its "series of 'illustrations' that accompany the text," these pictures were not available to the largest portion of the nationwide audience whose shifting allegiance was soon to popularize the motion picture. The insufficiency of provincial stages was no deterrent to the exhibition of films. Paradoxically, the more successful the stage might become in its creation of spectacular and three-dimensional stage pictures, the more certain became its failure to reach audiences throughout the country.

In October, 1896, *The Great Train Robbery,* by Scott Marble, was produced on the stage of the Bowery Theatre in New York. This may or may not have been E. S. Porter's inspiration or the source for his early photoplay. Marble's melodrama circulated on the stage in the years when Porter was demonstrating a syntax for the silent film. There is no question that the play possessed cinematic attributes and, indeed, certain scenes suggest their screen counterpart. Reviews of this original stage production, indicative of the values which saw the fusion of stage and screen, cannot fail to impress those who may have seen Porter's photoplay of the same name.

The most deserving participant in *The Great Train Robbery* doesn't get his name into the People's playbill. He is the scene painter, and he must have been busied for a long time by this scenic outfit, for it is complete and handsome. . . Act third shows the place of the express train hold-up. At stage right is the station, through whose open window the telegraph operator is seen at work. Just back of the station and parallel to the footlights runs a practicable side track but beyond in the painted perspective is what must be the main line. . . As soon as its double tracks come out from behind the station they curve to the left and are in sight for a half mile before they turn to the right behind rocky bluffs. At one side of them are towering cliffs, on the other a river, and the perspective is excellent. Posts displaying signal lights are seen at each side of the roadbed, the nearest ones being illuminated. The light in the signals grows dim as the distance increases, a spot of bright paint replaces it in the next ones, and the most distant posts in the rows seem dark. In the fourth act the picture is of a cañon in the mountains. Again, there is a practicable structure at stage right—a hut made of logs, and at the back, extending far away, are the steep walls of the cañon, the creek winding along away down between them. . . these quiet and pretty scenes are soon dimmed by the smoke from guns and revolvers, but not before their beauty has had a chance to impress.[90]

The physical aspects of this realistic, pictorial setting were exploited for sensational action. "In the third act a realistic 'hold-up' was shown, a train being stopped at a lonely mountain station and the express car blown open by dynamite. . . In the last act, in the famous Red River Cañon in Texas, a fierce fight takes place, and there is shooting galore."[91] When, in the following year, the play revisited Boston, "Seven Indian chiefs are introduced this time in all the glory of their war paint and other warpath toggery, and there is also a real live grizzly bear who contributes no small part to the sum total of entertainment."[92]

In the days which saw the fusion of stage and screen, drama was fancied in visual terms. The more elaborate the spectacle, with its trains, its hold-ups, explosions, gun-fights, Indian chiefs, and real live bears, the more successful the production. In this way the stage of the nineteenth-century melodrama unwittingly roared its swan song, for this type of theatre played directly into the hands of the film-makers. It was a glorious but futile parting gesture. When in March 1904, a year after E. S. Porter's film of the same title was released, the original production of *The Great Train Robbery* came to the stage of the Grand Opera House in Boston, reviews made no mention whatever of the usual spectacular effects.

The Clansman, adapted by Thomas Dixon from his own novel, was produced on the stage in the early years of the twentieth century. It was transferred by D. W. Griffith into the film as *The Birth of a Nation.* Why should this play, "as crude a melodrama as has ever slipped its anchor and drifted westward from Third Avenue,"[93] have served as the source for this epic motion picture? An answer to this will be developed in a subsequent discussion of Griffith's cinematic treatment. When the author of the play defined drama in 1905 as "a process of reasoning in which living pictures are used instead of words,"[94] he makes clear statement of the case of nineteenth-century melodrama and of the values which, in this particular instance, must have attracted D. W. Griffith.

The melodramas discussed in this chapter are typical of the period preceding and surrounding the early film. The method of their production characterizes the methods recorded in the promptbooks of the Harvard Theatre Collection. We have noted, first of all, that, in the matter of dramatic construction, the nineteenth-century melodrama employed an episodic technique. Time and space limitations were ignored and large numbers of scenes were pictured upon the stage for the development of the narrative. This resulted in either a progression of pictorial episodes defining a single line of action, or, more frequently, brought about cross-cutting between two or more parallel lines of action or flashing back to earlier actions. Such an editorial pattern was of a cinematic order and was similar in its aims and conception to that demonstrated by Porter and elaborated by Griffith as basic motion-picture syntax. In its execution it resulted in such filmic devices as the dissolve, the fade-out and fade-in, or the change in vantage point within a given scene.

In addition to its episodic construction, nineteenth-century melodrama exploited the pictorial tastes of the times. Visions, tableaux, and all manner of spectacular scenes were woven into the episodic fabric of the play. The entire melodrama stage hinged upon the pictorial value of settings and their physical aspects.

Unfortunately, this motion-picture construction and these spectacular conceptions depended to a large extent upon conventional staging. From the material presented in Chapter One concerning (1) productional methods in general use prior to and in the years during which the motion picture made its debut, (2) the physical equipment of theatres, in both town and country, of the period, and (3) specific productional techniques described in the Harvard promptbooks, it is clear that at the time of the arrival of the film, the extensive provincial audience was generally offered nothing better than conventional staging. The more solid, three-dimensional, and realistic a production, the more limited its circulation. Even in metropolitan theatres, where scenic realism may have been possible, it was not the usual thing. Irving, Belasco, and Mac-Kaye were outstanding for the unusual realism of their spectacular settings. But the melodrama, strongest single root of the cinema, was more a provincial than a metropolitan form, and hence retained its conventionality even after realistic reforms had been felt in the cities.

Throughout this period melodrama relied upon a large variety of settings and upon speed in their change. Since both of these qualities depended upon the conventional methods of existing staging facilities, melodrama and pictorial realism were incompatible and actually impossible upon the stage. This condition presented a temporary impasse, for the romantic tendencies of the times demanded melodrama, while the growing realistic bias became impatient with the conventional scenic counterfeits which made the staging of melodrama possible. In an effort to combat the waning popularity and the breakdown of these traditional techniques, individual realistic properties were introduced. Water tanks, buzz saws, carriages, dead cats, live pigs, horses, dogs, chickens were all employed, but while conventionalism governed the over-all production, such realistic items usually destroyed the illusion of a stock stage picture.

In the face of the breakdown of the traditional methods, these compromises were rarely successful, and by 1909 Walter Prichard Eaton reported, "Popular [stage] melodramas, since moving pictures became the rage, have decreased fifty percent in number."[95] With the breakdown of the conventions came the gradual withdrawal of stage melodrama. The film, boundless in its capacity for both spectacular and realistic pictures, naturally fell heir to the cinematic objectives which had been the principal appeal of this form upon the stage. The arrival of the motion picture in 1895 was so timely as to appear preordained. Audiences had been carefully prepared for the new medium both by century-long support of conventional stage melodrama and by the late-century rebirth of theatrical realism. Lewis Jacobs, in his excellent treatment of the history and development of the film in America, seems to have overlooked this underlying influence of the stage upon the rise of the film. Without detracting from the obvious virtues of his work, there are manifold grounds for disagreement with his statement that "Porter distinguished the movies from other theatrical forms."[96] Porter merely translated into the idiom of the motion-picture camera the mid-century aims and methods of the melodrama branch of this graphic theatre of realism and romance.

THREE

PICTURE PLAYS:
THE SPECTACLE STAGE

 The melodrama, chiefly significant for its cinematic constructional pattern, also utilized the spectacular stage picture. Certain plays, to be discussed now primarily as spectacle stagings, possessed melodramatic qualities as well. Between the spectacle and the melodrama there is considerable overlapping. However, while the melodrama usually depended upon stock productional techniques and thus showed itself in disagreement with certain tastes of the period, spectacle plays attempted a more realistic, three-dimensional *mise en scène,* and in this way revealed the growing taste for spectacular realism which the melodrama alone could not altogether satisfy.

The zenith of mid-century spectacular staging had been reached with the work of Charles Kean, who, "almost more of an archaeologist than an actor,"[1] required historical documentation for even the botany in his scenes.[2] Such archaeological exactitude, however, found considerable romantic glorification in its scenic treatment. Soon new realistic urges were reflected in the Robertsonian reforms of the 1860's and 1870's, in the work of Augustin Daly in this country, in that of Antoine and the Saxe-Meiningen on the continent, the Independent Theatre in London, finally reaching the ultimate in pure naturalism with the work of the Moscow Art Theatre. The growth of this "slice-of-life" naturalistic theatre exercised an influence upon the popular theatre and upon that stream of romanticized pictorial productions flowing through the work of Charles Kean. Romanticism and realism were simultaneous tastes of the entire cycle of theatrical expression

emanating from Garrick: the more romantic a dramatic conception, the more realistic tended to become its production. With
such a combination of these two qualities, realistic spectacular effects, suggesting an aesthetic movement toward the ideal of the
motion pictures, resulted. The box-office success of this alliance
seems to have indicated a deep-rooted taste for this pictorial type
of theatrical entertainment many years before the arrival of the
motion-picture camera.

The fusion of stage and screen is to be found in the years which
saw the preliminary exploitation of the realistic and spectacular
scenic style in the theatre, the natural assumption of this mode by
the motion picture, the decline of its theatrical popularity, and
thus its eventual withdrawal from the boards.

W. W. Burridge reported in 1900 that "the modern theatre going public demands that the best acting be supplemented by beautiful pictures," and added further that "the artist of the stage picture must have the capacity to reproduce topographically a copy
of a certain place, with the truthful representation of certain objects."[3] The prime requirement imposed by audiences upon the
scenic artist was realism of the quality suggested by George Gros-
smith when, in describing a farmyard painted by Joseph Harker,
he exclaimed, "I can almost smell the hay."[4]

We need go no further back than the seventies. Tom Taylor's
adaptation of *The Vicar of Wakefield,* produced at the London
Aquarium in 1878, opened with

the vicarage, where the rustics assemble, with vocal and instrumental
music, to congratulate the Primroses upon their silver wedding. Everything tells of comfort and ease. Ripe apples weigh down the over-
laden boughs, and are, in an exquisite scene, shaken by Sophia into
the lap of her admirer, Burchell. The young urchins climb furtively
up the ladder and pluck the tempting fruit. A cask of beer is broached
in the adjoining yard.[5]

The novel presented superb material for the three-dimensional
pictorial mode of staging.

Similarly with the dramatic poem. The many theatrical adaptations of Tennyson's *Enoch Arden* in this period provide a pattern
which traces the growth of realism in pictorial staging during the

last part of the century. A point was eventually reached beyond which improvement became impossible. Hence, with the arrival of cinema and a two-reel film version by D. W. Griffith, *Enoch Arden* disappeared from the stage. The play was first produced at Booth's Theatre in New York on June 21, 1869, and after being rewritten by Arthur Mathison, was presented again on September 25, 1869. The manuscript promptbook of Felix A. Vincent[6] indicates a pictorial, episodic construction with cross-cutting between simultaneous lines of action. This staging retained the conventional manner of the melodrama. For instance, the third act opens on a Room in Annie's Cottage, where Philip is looking after Annie in Enoch's absence. The scene dissolves to an Autumn Wood, where "Philip Enters R.3.E. and proposes to Annie. She asks him to wait another year and the scene changes during dance" to a Forest Glade with "Lively music at change." Here a nut-gathering sequence is staged in autumn foliage to show the passage of time until, finally, another change returns to A Large Room in Annie's Cottage where Annie and Philip are again together as in scene 1. Philip exits and Annie turns inquiringly to the Bible, wondering whether to marry Philip now or to wait longer for Enoch. All four scenes were not strictly essential to the drama. The story, its characters and situations, could all have been developed within the room in Annie's cottage. The other scenes merely provided pictorial illustration. At this point in the direct sequence of episodes there is a cut across to a parallel line of action, that concerning Enoch. This is presented with the conventional device of the vision. Annie opens the Bible asking, "Enoch, where art thou," and blindly choosing a passage to guide her, reads in response, "Under a palm tree." Felix Vincent here marked on his script: "Flats to draw and vision scene at back. Tropical. . . Music tremolo until end of Act. . . Light Fire. Vision—Enoch sitting under a palm tree. Red or white fire R.U.E. Picture, Slow Curtain." The fourth act illustrates further episodes in the Enoch line of action. The fifth act cuts back to the Annie-Philip line and, at its end, the two parallel lines intersect, thus creating climax and, eventually, resolution.

The cinematic pattern of this adaptation, involving direct pictorial continuity, cut-back visions, and tableaux, was staged in its original production in the traditional manner with wings, borders, backdrops, or flats. Stock lighting effects were used to spectacularize the pictures, and music, cinema-wise, heightened emotional sequences, entrances, and bridged scenic transitions. Vincent's directions for the use of music are numerous, including such notations as "Slow peculiar music till curtain," "Lively music till Annie and children off, then change to slow music till Philip is on," or "Tremolo pp. Outside R. at back." This entire production, music, lights, and scenery, was of such conventional quality that its 1872 presentation in Boston received no further acclaim than that "the stage was appropriately set." [7]

But by 1889 great changes had been made. The Newton Beers production of that year boasted special scenery by Mr. Hoyt and Mr. Albert. It provided the kind of pictorial staging that could have inspired Griffith's two-reel screen adaptation in 1911. The original Mathison version, which had only five acts, was episodically enlarged into "seven acts and thirty episodes," [8] thus increasing the pictorial opportunities. The *Chicago News,* describing its presentation on July 8, 1889, at Hooley's Theatre in Chicago, interestingly records that a scenic artist, Henry E. Hoyt, was "enthusiastically called before the curtain by the audience." [9] If the original adaptation was cinematically constructed, the Newton Beers version seems to have made much of this value in the staging. Here were thirty pictorial episodes and a complete denial of the manner of the well-made play. Two scenic artists were used to create an elaborate spectacle which swamped the original melodramatic values in the "pomp and panoply of scenic investiture." [10]

Special scenery rehearsals were conducted for the Chicago opening. An account of such a rehearsal, appearing in the *Chicago Herald,* July 7, 1889, suggests, in the original if not in the following condensed version, an early motion-picture scenario.

Act One: Scene One—Rugged coast scene in Cornwall.
          Two—Procession entering the chapel.
          Three—A beautiful bridal bower.
Act Two: Scene One—Interior of fisherman's cottage, with a distant view of the Sea . . . the ship *Good Fortune,* China bound, with Enoch on board, sails down the bay in full view of the audience as it passes Annie's cottage. This mechanical marine effect closes the act.

Act Three: Introduces the tableau of the wreck of the ship *Good Fortune* in the tropical seas.

Act Four: A faithful reproduction of a Cornish fair scene of olden times, with the sports and pastimes of the peasantry of the period. . . They gather in front of a colossal head of the titular divinity of the locality, the great Magog, fitted with ingenius mechanism, warranted to startle the spectators.

Act Five: The ghostly walls of England, a line of gruesome, shadowy cliffs, rising abruptly from the sea. . . Afterward comes the return of Annie to her cottage, where she invokes heaven to give her some token of Enoch's fate. . . the wondrous vision of the Isle of Palms is disclosed; the humble cottage disappears, and a transformation unfolds itself to the audience. Opening with the tropical night scene follows scene, light gradually growing, until a glorious burst of sunlight reveals Enoch under a palm tree, upon which beams the blazing light of day.

Act Six: Another view of Enoch's island home. A full-rigged ship appears in the offing; she tacks about, furls her sails, drops anchor, squares her yards and lowers her jollyboat upon the moving waters; the boat is manned by a working crew, and is seen approaching the island gradually increasing in size as it nears the shore, which it reaches—a full-sized ship.

Act Seven: The return of Enoch to his native village. . . reaching his old home, only to find it deserted and bearing a bill of sale, he is greeted by crowds of merry children, who mock the stranger's uncouth dress and appearance. This scene revolves and shows an illuminated night view of the house and grounds of Philip Ray. There are clouds and transparent effects introduced in this scene. The last scene is placed in the vestry of the ancient Chapel in which Enoch was married.

Thirty changes have been introduced, exploiting "a vast field in the way of stage pictures, startling effects and brilliant climaxes." [11] The construction of such pictures was by no means fully naturalistic, but considerable progress in the discard of stock methods was achieved. For example, the revolving stage in the seventh act was evidently brought into use for the handling of solid, three-dimensional settings. The entire approach to this staging appears to have been far beyond that of the conventions, for when the play visited Fort Wayne, Indiana, on July 3, 1889, "owing to the size of the stage, it was impossible to produce it entire." [12] Thus, while metropolitan audiences may have enjoyed elaborate scenic realism in keeping with the tastes of the times, provincial theatregoers were still crossed by the limitations of their conventional facilities. Metropolitan productions moved toward the cinematic ideal, providing both material and inspiration for the work of such film producers as D. W. Griffith, while the theatre of the provinces lagged far behind, fettered by inadequate and outmoded equipment.

Throughout this period Shakespeare provided a frame for the hanging of elaborate pictorial productions. The Coghlan production of *The Merchant of Venice* at the Prince of Wales's Theatre in 1875 presented the play as a vast and realistic pageant. "Superb views of Venice are presented. The gay, idle, insouciante, and withal mysterious life of the Queen of the Adriatic, is depicted with as much truth and color as in the pages of Consuelo."[13] Whether this is to be construed as an archaeologically correct production, with stage pictures which were entirely three dimensional, is not the only consideration here. What also matters is that audiences were hungry for this pictorial feast, and that the other values of Shakespeare seem now to have been subordinated to spectacle.

Cavaliers and rufflers, "witty as youthful poets in their wine," play in the street jests that may lead to "cracked crowns," or whisper beneath half-opened lattices, vows that may bring a dagger slit in the doublet. Music of endless serenades rings through streets ignorant of all noise or traffic. The idlers upon the quays and banks raise themselves to hurl execrations at the passing Jews, and the busy masque of medieval Venice defiles with marvelous fidelity before our eyes.[14]

The realism of stage pictures, whether architectural or in the two dimensions of painting and flat scenery, seems to have attained considerable perfection in this and in many other similar productions of the period. Sir John Martin Harvey, at the opening of the Theatre Exhibition in Manchester early in the century, cited J. Comyns Carr's description of the work of such popular scene painters as Hawes Craven or Joseph Harker. Their trees were so realistic that the foliage "seems actually to move in the breeze . . . water seems to murmur as it glides between the verdant meadows . . . birds are vocal in the leafy lanes, and the whole melting scene, illumined by the setting rays of the sun, dies down into the grey hush of twilight before our very eyes."[15]

The taste for spectacle during these years gave rise to the panoramas. Joseph Harker, writing of his visits to America late in the century, tells of painting a series of panoramas for Pain, the manufacturer of pyrotechnics: "Panoramas at that time were all the rage in America, and some very fine spectacular shows were presented, among them *The Great Fire of London, The Destruction of Pompeii, The Burning of Pekin, The Burning of Moscow,* and *The Fall of Sevastopol,* with representations of other great disasters."[16] Oftentimes included within the scenic scheme of a spectacle play, these panoramas, which are indicative of the pictorial tastes of the time, form an interesting bridge between stage and screen, for, as shall be seen, they found a direct continuation and improvement in the earliest film expression, that of the reproductional, topical episodes which filled the period from 1895 to 1902.

Every effort was made to give these two-dimensional scenic displays a realistic appearance. Some of them, Harker reports, were as large as four-hundred feet in width and over sixty feet in height. "Various real objects such as houses and trees were set up in front of the canvas background, and the whole lighted . . . to heighten the general effect."[17] Fireworks were utilized to build the scenic display to a spectacular climax. While the effect created by a panorama was certainly inferior, save in terms of color, to the simple topical episode on the screen, yet its production was a much more expensive and complicated task, and at the same time its audience was limited.

During the Franco-Prussian War, "in order to cope with the demand for realistic portrayals of battlefield scenes,"[18] all qualified scenic artists worked under great pressure. News events and scenic spectacles were popular. Frankenstein's *Panorama of Niagara* reached a length of one-thousand feet.[19] Archaeological reconstructions were not entirely two-dimensional. Harker's panorama of Pompeii, with its spectacular view of the eruption of Vesuvius, was "enhanced by an awe-inspiring effect of molten lava flowing down on the doomed city."[20] Despite this sensational realism the show had trouble in Boston, for the "Temple Columns," which were "made of wood and grained to look like marble, refused to sink in the lake, into which, following the fire, they were made to fall."[21] Apparently someone had forgotten the customary practice of weighting them with lead.

And of course, in race-track melodramas, where scenery was shown in motion, the panorama was invaluable. Or, as in the case of Wagner's *Parsifal*, at the Bayreuth Festspielhaus, the journey to the Grail was depicted proceeding before a moving panorama. When J. Comyns Carr and Joseph Harker were engaged for its staging at Covent Garden, they at first preferred not to use the full-length panoramic treatment of the journey to the Grail. They substituted "in its place a series of visions of parts of the journey." Although these visions were tied together with musical effects, eventually the panorama was employed: "nothing less, it was firmly believed, would satisfy the public or the critics."[22] But whether moving panorama or dissolving visions, either technique exemplifies a motion-picture approach to theatrical staging.

Spectacular realism became the magic formula for box-office success. *The County Fair* by Charles Barnerd opened at Proctor's Theatre in New York in March 1889, ran for four years, and, weathering the competition of the films, was still playing in some provincial centers as late as 1914. The original production, wrote the *New York Dramatic Mirror* on March 16, 1889,

might be more aptly termed a landscape poem, for it is the idealism of rural realism. It is a Georgic of New England. The beauty of the scene in the third act probably has never been excelled. The spacious stage is completely filled with a real barn, with live stock and horses, while through the open doors the hillside pastures and fallow fields are seen bathed in rosy sunset.

The big scene at the fair is a real horse race. "Four horses with mounted jockeys appear in a bunch on the track. The horses are kept in motion on the treadmill principle and the scenery moves so as to simulate the running of the horses."[23] Treadmills and a moving panorama provided a spectacular race, with horses plunging and snorting against the painted landscape. At the London production at the Brixton, April 12, 1897, the "scene of the horse-race, with its real horses galloping upon moving ground, proved, as before, wonderfully real, and was much applauded, as was also the farmyard scene with its profusion of real farm produce."[24]

The British staging of the horse-race scene employed a revolving stage.[25] When it was done in Boston in 1891, naturalistic pictorial touches were worked out for the farmyard scene. Detail was carried to the point where "the Jersey cow chews her cud, and the noble horse caresses his devoted jockey."[26] Realism continued into areas of sound and even of smell. "The play is much concerned with the superficial details in the way of local color, such as reproducing the farmyard odor—the sweet breath of the cow, the smell of the hay, artistically tempered into a suggestion quite delightful—the rustle of the corn husking and of the figures of the Virginia Reel."[27] In its quest for realistic stage pictures this production became "photographic in truthfulness."[28] The stage, having gradually moved towards the reproductional ideal of the camera during a period of a hundred and fifty years, the ultimate in scenic truth seems to have been achieved at about the same time that motion-picture machinery made its appearance. Audiences supported and encouraged such elaborate and romanticized scenic productions to the point that managers eventually attempted material of such cinematic nature that its presentation upon the stage was not always as satisfying as *The County Fair.*

Such a play was *Quo Vadis?* As a motion picture it was to become one of the most successful of the early spectacles and one of the wedges by which the feature film forced its entrance. Its scope was much too vast for an agreeable stage expression. Yet, under the spur of the increasing popularity of the early moving pictures with their topical episodes, the stage seemed driven to more realistic and spectacular productions, and a *Quo Vadis?* rage sprang up in England and America in the season of 1899-1900. Laid in Roman times, this popular novel by Henryk Sienkiewicz offered stage producers a rare chance. Simultaneous showings, in the fashion of the film, were held in many metropolitan centers. A version by Stanislaus Stange was presented in Chicago on December 12, 1899; another by Chase had been playing the tank towns under the management of A. Benedict since the twenty-first of November; two productions opened simultaneously in New York on April 9, 1900, one from the Stange adaptation at the New York Theatre and the second by Jeanette Gilder at the Herald Square; Wilson Barrett presented it at Edinburgh on May 29, 1900, in London at the Prince of Wales's on June 18, and again at the Elephant and Castle on March 4, 1901; a company appeared at the Castle Square Theatre in Boston on April 16, 1900; and other productions could be seen in San Francisco, Pittsburgh, Denver, and so on. Openings were heralded with great fanfare and high hopes, but it was not altogether successful.

Failure came because of the gigantic scope of the spectacle being attempted. For instance, one of the climaxes of the play is a scene in the Roman arena where gladiators and wild bulls fight each other for life. The *New York Sun* review of April 15, 1900, found both New York showings inadequate, complaining, "It is a good rule for playwrights never to tantalize an audience by having interesting things go on just out of sight." In both of the rival productions the arena episode, with its cinematic implications, was presented without putting it on actual exhibition.

The stage at the Herald Square is set heavily and massively with the seats of Nero and his official adherents overlooking the amphitheatre. The view is from the rear, with steps leading up, but no portion of the arena exposed. The tyrant takes his place, and gloats over the torture of the Christians, whose death songs are heard, and whose martyrdom is attended by cries of approbation from the populace.[29]

That the stage should have attempted this novel is remarkable evidence that it was playing directly into the hands of the screen, for the only way in which the theatre could handle such moving-picture material was simply by not staging it at all. It had become necessary to tell the audience what it was impossible to show them. As the hypothetical battle between man and beast was about to begin offstage, one actor informed another (and, incidentally, the audience) that "the man is to have no weapon, and on the horns of the beast the maiden, Lygia, is to be fastened." While Nero and his company exclaimed with delight, "The giant is gripping the bull's horns and striving to break its neck," the audience, unable to witness the scene, was naturally displeased. In the other version at the New York Theatre, "Nero and the courtiers retire to their seats,

— 77 —

but Vinicius and Petronius remain on the wall to describe the fight in the arena." The most interesting and the most spectacular episode, the one which should have epitomized the objective of such a production, could not be produced.

Wilson Barrett's Edinburgh and London production attempted a compromise by showing this scene in a final tableau. The entire third act is an elaborate chase sequence developed with seven scenes, beginning at

The Exterior of Nero's Palace, a striking pictorial achievement by Mr. Perkins. . . Lygia during the commotion caused by the entry of the Christian leaders has escaped from the feast. . . In the next scene, A Street in Rome, from the practised brush of Mr. F. W. Ryan, the fugitives enter, pursued by Nero's soldiers, but, favored by the strength and prowess of Ursus, they escape. Reaching The City of the Dead, the Christians and the soldiers come into conflict. . . Lygia and her friends are made captive. . . Her doom is decreed and in the Prison of the Arena, a characteristic effort by Mr. Stafford Hall, we find her calmly awaiting the end, which is to be facing the wild beasts in the amphitheatre. . . Then in the Corridor of the Circus, by Mr. H. P. Wall, Petronius describes sights he sees in the arena beyond, where Lygia, bound to the horns of the bull, is being hurried to her death. He then tells the breathless listeners how Ursus, entering the ring, has thrown himself upon the infuriated animal and rescued Lygia from a fate that seemed inevitable. At this junction the intervening scenery is withdrawn, and we see Lygia lying senseless on the ground, with Ursus beside her struggling with the expiring bull, a tableau that evoked loud applause from all parts of the theatre.[30]

This final tableau, a gesture in the direction of satisfying obvious audience demands for the spectacular gladiator scene, could hardly have rivaled a cinematic treatment of it. The play, of course, utilizing all the techniques of melodrama, sought to heighten these with spectacle. "Quo Vadis? is a livid melodrama breathing strongly the Boucicaultian method. . . It bears the general appearance of being episodical rather than convincingly connective. The play depends largely upon the carpenter and the scene-painter; upon the effective and drastic application of the best principles of stage management."[31]

To the values of melodrama discussed in the preceding chapter, Quo Vadis? had added the spectacular "panoramic largeness of outline."[32] The conception behind this production was entirely cinematic. Its presentation upon the stage, although highly realistic, left much to be desired. It was soon taken over by the screen and, as one of the earliest feature-length films, had tremendous popularity in this country and abroad. Thus the stage, ardently devoted to the development of an audience for motion pictures, soon found itself eclipsed by the screen. *Quo Vadis?* passed from stage to screen but did not return.

Ben Hur, which became in 1925 one of the greatest film spectacles, found its stage expression on November 29, 1899, at the Broadway Theatre. Like many nineteenth-century stage successes, this, too, was taken from the novel. Adapted by William Young from the prose story of Lew Wallace, it was produced by Klaw and Erlanger. In the first act alone fourteen scenes[33] were billed, each with its own scene painter. Emphasis from first to last was placed upon the pictures, and the scene painter usurped the author's prominence on the program. In the original version there are six such acts and an additional seventeen tableaux. This endless stream of scenes resulted in a dramatic pattern akin to the editorial fabric of the cinema. For instance, Act I provided the following sequence of stage pictures: A Lonely Desert, Joppa Gate, Dasmascus Gate, Herod's Palace, Imperial Gardens, House-Top, Street in Jerusalem, House-Top, Imperial Gardens, Roman Galley, Grove of Daphne, Lake by Moonlight, House of Simonides, and Salon in the Palace on the Island. It can be understood why critic Henry B. Shelley should write: "There is no other drama which depends so little upon individual effort of character presentation. Most emphatically . . . it is *Ben Hur,* the *visualized presentation* of a book as familiar as household words the people are eager to see."[34] With this large number of scenes, each an elaborate and detailed stage picture, some lasting but a few moments, oftentimes employing little dialogue but merely illustrating the novel, the stage seems to have come very close to the standard of the early motion picture.

This photographic ideal was carried into the treatment of the many stage settings. The climactic chariot race[35] was run on a treadmill by real horses dragging real chariots. A wheel of Messala's chariot was geared to work loose and fall off after a given number of revolutions. Ben Hur's treadmill was drawn into the lead a second before the lights went out. Uneven wheels were calculated to give the chariots a bumping, rough-riding effect. Behind the galloping horses and bouncing chariots passed the panorama with its painted arena and spectators. Its purpose was to heighten the realism of the race, which was ostensibly being run in a circle.

The panorama of spectators is in three separate pieces, the back and two sides. These are on rolls which are moved by electricity and they must move at exactly the same speed so as to give the effect of an unbroken panorama. In the front of the stage is a low wall which flows swiftly backward to heighten the illusion of the running horses.[36]

Yet in spite of all this, audiences which had known but four years of the motion picture had already recognized the limitations of the stage and the possibilities of the screen. The following report by Hillary Bell appeared in the *New York Herald*, December 3, 1899:

In the play we see merely several horses galloping on a moving platform. They make no headway, and the moving scenery behind them does not delude the spectators into the belief that they are racing. . . *The only way to secure the exact sense of action for this incident in a theatre is to represent it by Mr. Edison's invention.* The management could hire Madison Square arena for a veritable chariot race and vitascope or vitagraph it. The pictures on a screen, after the fashion of the Jeffries-Sharkey fight at the New York Theatre, would be closer to realism and more faithful in illustration of the finest passage in General Wallace's romance than these horses galloping nowhere at the Broadway. [My italics.]

This seems to have been as much a complaint against the contrived working of the horses as against the incongruity of mixing painted pictures with flesh-and-blood pictures. Two-dimensional photographs in motion would have been preferable. By 1902 the much-vaunted chariot race appeared completely counterfeit, and it was suggested that "if it needs must be given on the stage, [it] would be greatly improved by the stilling of the rapid whirling and completely disillusionizing scenic background."[37] From the first, Clement Scott had complained, "There was movement, but no action. It was impulse, but no race. I wanted an arena, a round track, not a flat one. I wanted the idea of the clatter and the dust and turmoil."[38]

The stage might attempt to compete with the screen in such spectacular effects, but these spectacular efforts obviously left much to be desired. The great picture of the galley had somewhat better success.

> The hold of the ship takes up the entire width of the stage. The oarsmen are placed in tiers, one above the other, around the sides, each tugging wearily at his huge blade. There is a sort of official stroke, who beats time for the slaves by regular taps on a drum. . . When the triremes come into close quarters the slaves are manacled to stanchions at their oarlocks, and if the vessel sinks the galley slaves go down with her.[39]

This scene fades out as the raft scene, "a marvelous picture of the tumultuous sea,"[40] fades in. The sinking of the trireme was managed in a simple mechanical way by dropping the vessel through the stage floor after the wreck. When the lights are brought up, Ben Hur and his captain Arrius are seen tossing on the raft.

In the last act a three-dimensional mountain is put upon the stage. The Mount of Olives occupies "the entire stage, stretching into the flies almost to the walls of the theatre, and is built of a number of frames rising irregularly toward one side. Upon these frames platforms are laid and covered with painted cloth. Scenic trees are set up on the mountain slopes and a well-painted canvas encircles the whole."[41] When the screen version of this spectacular production is considered, these detailed and three-dimensional staging efforts appear merely as rudimentary attempts to achieve pictorial realism. Nevertheless, *Ben Hur* does represent a certain climax in the cycle of theatrical practice emanating from Garrick.

Passing consideration has been given to the use of music in nineteenth-century methods of staging. The haphazard musical practices of melodrama often gave way to a more careful aesthetic discipline in the spectacle plays. For *Ben Hur,* music was especially composed by E. S. Kelly, and the *Boston Transcript* remarked: "It is so seldom that you hear incidental music that really adds anything to a play; this does. Some strokes are simply capital; for one,

that wolfish snarl of the brass, and the Egyptian enchantress re-
tires foiled in the last act.[42] Throughout the performance music
accentuated the episodes and was as carefully prepared and integrated as in the later screen version.

When the curtain rises on the opening tableau, showing the wise
men in the desert, beside their kneeling camels, awaiting the appearance
of the star in the East, the first suggestions of the star theme are heard,
developing into orchestral fullness as the light increases in intensity. As
this instrument of the drama closes, the tread of the camel is simulated
by the orchestra, suggesting the journey of the wise men over the arid
waste of sand to the City of David, where the child is to be born whom
they seek.[43]

Pictorial drama, whether stage or screen, required musical support,
and while this may have been a far cry from S. M. Eisenstein's
modern theory of sound montage, the origins of current practices
may be discerned.

Throughout the nineteenth and early twentieth centuries, the
novel provided the stage as steady a supply of material for spectacle
as for melodrama. That the stage should have continually borrowed such material from the novel, where the original conception
suffered no discipline from the physical limitations of the stagehouse, implies the obvious cinematic bias of the period. When
Kipling's *The Light that Failed,* adapted by George Fleming, was
produced at the Hollis Street Theatre in Boston on October 19,
1903, a review appearing in the *Boston Herald* was headlined
"Series of Scenes rather than Play."[44] It was further noted that, "as
is almost inevitable in the adaptation of a popular novel for the
stage . . . the play is episodic."[45] Others complained that *"The Light
that Failed* is not a play at all in the regular sense of the word. It
is a series of scenes in the life of a remarkable artist, succeeding
one another naturally but with absolutely no intrigue, and no
technical dramatic development."[46] Either under the influence of
the success of the earliest cinema or of a great heritage of pictorial
stagings, Klaw and Erlanger tried to pass off this scenic illustration
of a novel as drama. Having pointed and prepared the way for the
motion picture, the stage now tried to compete with it. It came

off second best, for in this case its production at the Lyric Theatre in London on February 7, 1903, created "a desire that it had been left unadapted."[47]

A stage version by Virginia Calhoun of Helen Hunt Jackson's novel *Ramona* was offered at the Mason Opera House, Los Angeles, on February 28, 1905. The play, described as "a series of pictures, illustrative of Miss Helen Hunt Jackson's story,"[48] provided material for one of D. W. Griffith's earliest departures from the simple chase-melodrama technique. *Ramona* returned to the stage after it had been done for the screen. It was played at the Forty-Fourth Street Theatre in New York on April 5, 1916, as a "cinema-theatrical" entertainment. It was actually "a novelty in moving-picture shows" rather than a stage play, for "each act and the prologue begins with an actual scene with people who sing and dance, and each blends into moving pictures telling the tale of Helen Hunt Jackson's story of the Mission Indians of Santa Barbara many years ago."[49] The stage, recognizing the superiority of the film in pictorial narration, was now satisfied merely to provide introductory material.

A scriptural tragedy, *Judith of Bethulia*, in four acts and seven scenes by Thomas Bailey Aldrich, was produced on December 4, 1904, at Daly's Theatre, New York. Showings appeared throughout the country. In this instance, as in many other productions of the early century, the stage seemed determined to drag its audience back out of the nickelodeon with ever bigger and better picture plays. In San Francisco, Ashton Stevens called it "a series of picturesque essays";[50] in Boston, at the other end of the country, a couple of years after E. S. Porter's *Life of an American Fireman*, and just a year after his *Uncle Tom's Cabin* and *The Great Train Robbery* had been shown, each of its seven scenes was described as "a most vivid picture."[51] There is no need to go over the many cinematic attributes of its construction, with its dissolving scene changes, its reliance upon music for transitions, mood, character values, and emotional heightening, or its cut-backs, its pictorial continuity, and so on. It would be enough here to recognize another attempt by the stage to compete with the photographic realism of the screen and to discover the extent of its success or failure.

The appeal of its production at the Grand Opera House, San Francisco, on January 6, 1906, was entirely pictorial.

If sumptuous scene and magnificence and beauty of costume could carry a play, *Judith of Bethulia*. . . would be a brilliant success. For its pictures alone the play as here produced is excellently worth seeing. Particularly effective is the courtyard of the tower with its wonderfully solid walls and a bit of blue hilltop beyond. The tent of Holofernes is another splendid picture. . . Lavishly *satisfying to the eye* is the whole play, in fact.[52]

While the three-dimensional stage pictures were pleasing, the implied complaint here against the play itself was more openly expressed in other reviews. When the same Nance O'Neill production played in Boston it was remarked that "the play as a whole [was] uninteresting, not to say dull";[53] and in San Francisco, Ashton Stevens, quick to catch the capacities of the screen, proclaimed, "The whole thing might be read at a ladies' club to an accompaniment of moving pictures. It is vivid only in a moving-picture way; even the tent scene."[54]

The Nance O'Neill promptbook, "just as it was last used," may be found in the Harvard Theatre Collection.[55] Here the staging of this spectacle is described. The limitations of the stage are plainly apparent. When, at the Eastern Gate of Bethulia, the dramatic action hinges upon the malignant movements of the mob, this surging mass of humanity is designated by a number of supernumeraries held back by two spearmen, stage right and left, and supported by offstage voices. This has always been the most successful method for managing crowd scenes upon the stage. Its suggestive force is always measurable. At the same time, when this is compared with Griffith's treatment of the same surging multitudes a few years later, the cramping of such spectacular, cinematic conceptions onto the stage becomes appalling. This promptbook and the opinions of the foregoing reviewers have stated the case clearly. They indicate that, despite its natural limitations, the stage had played thoroughly into the hands of the screen and that, despite decreasing popularity, it was continuing to do so.

Thomas Dixon compressed two of his novels, *The Clansman*

and *The Leopard's Spot,* into a single play, which was produced as *The Clansman* at the Liberty Theatre in New York on January 8, 1906. It was a bad play; indeed, the *New York Dramatic Mirror* announced, "It is difficult to do justice to so bad a play as *The Clansman.*"[56] This was the play which became, under the direction of D. W. Griffith, an early American screen epic, exerting considerable influence toward the introduction and establishment of the feature film, and upon subsequent cinematic methods of the silent era. The two qualities of the stage version which had attracted Griffith were those of melodrama and spectacle. Speaking of the play, two reviewers remarked:

> Whatever one may think of the nature of the drama . . . one must admit that the night meeting of the Klan was an impressive stage episode.[57]
> Doubtless there are features in *The Clansman*—spectacular and other—which may appeal rather forcibly to the lovers of crude melodrama.[58]

What had been, on the stage, crude and sensational melodrama, became on the screen a "thrilling historic spectacle,"[59] the great epic of *The Birth of a Nation.*

Another novel, G. B. McCutcheon's *Brewster's Millions,* was adapted by Winchell Smith and Byron Onglay. Its production at the New Amsterdam Theatre on December 31, 1906, with special effects by Frederick Thompson, attempted to put upon the stage the spectacular scene of a solid, three-dimensional yacht laboring in a great storm. A reviewer notes, oddly enough, that this scene was "hardly a part of the play, and . . . struck many in the first night audience as having been dragged in by the heels, as it were."[60] The play might very likely have gotten by under its own power; nevertheless, an expensive and complicated scenic arrangement was developed for the staging of this unnecessary effect.

> The back of the stage is draped with a "cyclorama drop" of sheeting, and behind the yacht are a series of "wave drops" suspended from the rigging loft and swinging clear from the floor, hung so that the first is slightly above the yacht's rail, the second a few inches higher and so on. Stereoptican lamps, with cleverly devised slides, concealed in the cabins of the yacht, but with their standards on the firm stage itself and

not upon the moving deck, throw cloud effects upon the cyclorama drop and water effects upon the wave drops. Clockwork devices move the slides in the wave lamps so that the proper undulatory, back and forward, up and down wave motion is cunningly simulated. In order to add verisimilitude to the waves the drops are kept in constant alternating motion by stage hands, who pull them back and forward with cords. . . Several dynamos pour blasts of air through tubing across the stage, creating drafts which make the clothing of the players and the pennons on the yacht flutter wildly. By the orifice of one of them is a machine that throws out salt, whirled across the deck by the wind to represent spray. Four or five small electrical devices make realistic flashes of lightning.

Against the cyclorama drop is a runway on which stand the town and shores of the bay, silhouetted out of tin. The little houses are neatly equipped with electric light switches, so that each or all of them can be illuminated. Then there is a pigmy lighthouse whose dot of light is made to alternate automatically. When the yacht puts out to sea these objects are moved by hand along their groove across the stage to the left, the effect being an impression that the ship is really in motion and the shore line is slipping by. . . An illustration of the lengths to which Mr. Thompson will go to add one touch to his picture is contained in the steam whistle that sounds a terrific toot when it gets under way and again as a signal of distress. He insisted upon having a real whistle of formidable size placed on the yacht itself. Not being able to connect it with the boilers of the building. . . he installed a battery of seven or eight tanks of compressed air in order to get his pressure.[61]

In spite of these elaborate and carefully planned devices, the scene was not convincing. While the "yacht labors in an excellent stage storm with roaring wind and tossing seas, the sails remain flat and gently swaying with the rocking of the boat—a fortunate thing, for if the vessel should come over on the port tack the foresail boom would carry away two feet of the funnel, the big whistle and a section of the main mast. Also, a yacht at anchor off a lee shore should not remain stationary in a choppy sea."[62] The same artificiality was apparent in the Boston showing at the Colonial Theatre on February 10, 1908. "The yacht rocks and sways in a quiet sea, while she is at anchor, and she rocks and sways when scudding before a terrific gale, with thunder and lightning, until her rudder breaks. . . And through it all the sails flap idly, and never a reef is taken."[63] These reviewers hardly realized how impossible it would have been to avoid the idly flapping sails which were "needed to hide the wires by which the wave drops are hung, and other parts of the internal machinery from the audience. If they were furled the entire effect would be ruined."[64] Unfortunately, the producers had not realized that it would also be ruined if the sails were not furled. No matter how far the stage might proceed in the spectacular direction, apparently it could not go quite far enough.

By 1909 much of the spectacle-drama audience had left the stage for the film. W. P. Eaton reported that in that year "eighty percent of present day theatrical audiences are canned drama audiences."[65] Managers tried to overcome this condition with ever more realistic and ever more spectacular productions. Even after the "canned drama" had established its superiority in this field, such pictorial offerings as *Treasure Island* appeared at the Punch and Judy Theatre, New York, December 1, 1915. Heywood Broun noted that "there are times when one feels the episodic rather than the dramatic nature of the entertainment."[66] The success of these episodes came through realistic stage pictures achieved at great cost with a complex crew and stage mechanism.

When the production was brought to the theatre the players were kept off the stage for several days, and the drilling of the stage crew was made the business of primary importance. This crew consists of forty-one men in addition to the head carpenter, electrician and property-man. Ten of these are stationed in the flies, twelve on the stage in the carpenter's department, eighteen electricians and eleven assist the property man.[67]

The play became "a graphic translation to the stage of Stevenson's thrilling story."[68] The most startling of its many pictures "showed the Hispaniola adrift and rocking like a channel craft while Hawkins and a pirate struggled in the rigging."[69] The spectacular episodes of this production seem to have attained a certain photographic ideal. Yet this achievement, which came only at great expense, fell far short of the accomplishment of the 1920 filming soon to be discussed.

Thus the pictorial approach governed both the melodrama and the spectacle plays of the period. But unlike the melodrama, with its large provincial audience and its need for speed, variety, and economy, the spectacle, more a metropolitan than a provincial form, welcomed the realistic reforms of the sixties, seventies, and eighties. To the stream of romantic picture-stagings flowing through Charles Kean had been added the realistic techniques of the Bancrofts, the Saxe-Meiningen, the Théâtre-Libre of Antoine, and the rest, Through the spectacle drama the demands for a realistic treatment of romantic material were temporarily satisfied.

This realistic movement in the field of the spectacle, plus the great popularity during the 1890's of the panorama, indicates the existence of an audience whose theatrical consciousness was on the photographic level. The motion picture, immediately upon its arrival, offered topical episodes of historical, scenic, athletic, or news interest, and thus acquired the entire audience of the panorama, which soon disappeared from the theatre. In the field of the realistic spectacle, the stage was not so easily disappropriated. The motion pictures naturally possessed qualifications in this field which offered the stage stiff competition from the start, and which were later exploited to form the basis for the third great advance in motion-picture method to be discussed in connection with the feature film. For a number of years after the arrival of the film, the stage, having made so much of the cultivation of this purely pictorial area, was reluctant to sacrifice it without a struggle. Hence we find stagings of a highly realistic and spectacular nature, belonging properly to the motion picture, being produced in the legitimate theatre even after the screen had established its success and popularity in this field.

In this rivalry between stage and screen, the stage continued to turn to the novel for material with spectacular pictorial qualities. The screen promptly borrowed these adaptations and, as shall be seen, was extremely successful in their filming. Indeed, upon the basis of such pictures, it was to establish a further superiority over the stage. Thus, since both the stage of the nineteenth century and the early film were equally beholden to the novel for material, the aesthetic similarity of the two forms is further demonstrated.

FOUR

THE PHOTOGRAPHIC IDEAL

 The main areas of the realistic-romantic theatre of the nineteenth century, the melodrama and the spectacle, are overlapping categories; melodramas were spectacularly developed and spectacles were melodramatically constructed. In evaluating the contribution of each toward the preparation of motion-picture values and techniques, it may be said that the former supplied its cinematic construction pattern while the latter offered a staging development approaching the photographic ideal. In the work of three leading producers of this period, Irving, Belasco, and MacKaye, these two motion-picture qualities were combined and in the combination reached a certain perfection.

I. HENRY IRVING

Henry Irving seems to have drawn inspiration from the success of Boucicault, let us say, with the melodrama and from that of Charles Kean with the spectacle drama, for his productions fall into two general groups, (1) the melodrama, and (2) Shakespearean and other historical spectacles. In either of these classes he thought of theatre in terms of the production and not of the play. He claimed "that the theatre is bigger than the playwright, that its destiny is a higher one than that of the mouthpiece for an author's theses, and finally that plays are made for the theatre and not the theatre for plays."[1] And so the leading manager of the late nineteenth century would have nothing to do with the drama of the theatrical revival in the 1890's. Irving's love for picture plays is described by Thomas Wood Stevens: "The Lyceum stage was splendidly pictorial and utterly romantic; the cold light of Ibsen glimmered in the north, but never penetrated the rich chiaroscuro where Irving moved."[2] Ibsen could no more have been successful under Irving's methods than under those of the early film. And Ibsen upon the screen of 1915 became a dismal flop. Irving seems to have had much in common with the early film, for he thrived upon melodrama and spectacle.

Irving and Melodrama

"Henry," writes Ellen Terry, "could always invest a melodrama with life, beauty, interest, mystery, by his methods of production."[3] He was not interested in the conventional mode of melodrama staging in general use through the provinces and in the so-called "10-20-30" metropolitan houses of the nineties. When Irving came into the management of the Lyceum after the death of Colonel Bateman in 1878, Boucicault complained about the detail and thoroughness of Irving's stage pictures, for "with such a theatre as the Lyceum in London . . . as many as 80 carpenters, 50 property men and thirty gasmen have been employed in one performance."[4] And so *The Bells,* adapted by Leopold Lewis from Erckmann-Chatrian's *Le Juif Polonais,* became

a striking example of superior study in stage setting and artistic atmosphere . . . The science of stagecraft and the art of management give rarely appropriate and realistic environment to enhance the mysticism and emphasize the vague terrors that chill the conscience and torture the victim of remorse. The blazing fire of the cheerful inn, the spiced wine that warms the visitors, the whistling winds and the drifting snows without make a charming picture.[5]

First produced at the Lyceum on November 25, 1871, it remained in Irving's active repertoire throughout his career.

The Bells exemplifies Irving's approach to the melodrama. In this case it was the fusion of the weird and fantastic, the romantic, with the real into stage pictures which "stand quite alone in our memory. The Polish Jew in his sleigh amid the falling snow, with the murderer creeping up behind, and the second vision of the trial, as Mathias sees it in his dream, with himself as the principal figure, a scene in which the management of light borders on the miraculous, are pictures quite worthy of a great painter's canvas."[6]

Irving was thoroughly aware of the spectacular leanings of his audience. To satisfy this taste, *The Dead Secret* was produced at the Lyceum in August, 1877. This play was nothing more than a good old-fashioned ghost story relying upon "the most primitive and venerable machinery of supernaturalism." Everything was shown, "luminous hands, bouquets fresh from Elysian fields," and even melodies were "condescendingly played by spiritual fingers upon material guitars."[7] The realistic presentation of the supernatural was one of Irving's special capacities. *Vanderdecken* by Wills and Fitzgerald, produced at the Lyceum, June 8, 1878, concerned the familiar Flying Dutchman legend. Joseph Knight unwittingly labeled Irving's work in this field when he declared: "If the play succeeds it must be on the strength of its weirdness and the admirable scenery applied to it."[8] In the prologue, where "by means of a magic-lantern a vision of the phantom ship is exhibited in the background,"[9] Irving made his first dramatic entrance into a beautiful stage picture.

The scene was of the landing-place on the edge of the fiord. Sea and sky were blue with the cold steely blue of the North. The sun was bright and across the water the rugged mountain-line stood out boldly. Deep under the shelving beach, which led down to the water, was a Norwegian fishing-boat whose small brown foresail swung in the wind. There was no appearance anywhere of a man or anything else alive. But suddenly there stood a mariner in old-time dress of picturesque cut and faded colour of brown and peacock blue with a touch of red. On his head was a sable cap.[10]

Spectacular entrances into spectacular pictures were part of Irving's graphic approach.

In the *Lyons Mail*, 1877, the sensational highway robbery was presented as realistically as the familiar stage coach holdup of the western film. "Whilst Dubosc surrounded by his gang was breaking open the iron strong-box conveyed in the mail cart the horses standing behind him began to get restive and plunged about wildly, making a situation of considerable danger."[11] The staging of cinematic effects usually spelled success for Irving. In *Lady of Lyons*, one of Irving's first independent productions staged at the Lyceum on April 17, 1879, a climax is reached with the departure of Claude Melnotte to join the army. A simple and sentimental farewell scene with Pauline would have satisfied neither Irving nor his audience.

As Irving stage-managed it the army, already on its way, was tramping along the road outside. Through window and open door the endless columns were seen, officers and men in due order and the flags in proper place. It seemed as if the line would stretch out till the crack of doom! . . . They would march into the wings with set pace, but the instant they passed out of sight of the audience they would break into a run; in perfect order they would rush in single file round the back of the scene and arrive at the other side just in time to fall into line and step again. And so the endless stream went on. . . No matter how often the curtain went up on the scene. . . it always rose on that martial array.[12]

The result, according to Ellen Terry, was that the "curtain used to go up and down as often as we liked and chose to keep the army marching."[13] Audience approval was directly proportional to the realism with which an effect properly belonging to the photographic medium had been simulated.

When on September 18, 1880, Irving staged the old romantic melodrama, *The Corsican Brothers,* the conventional methods were supplanted by new realistic techniques. The two-dimensional painted occupants of painted loges used in previous versions of the scene at the Opera House were eliminated. "The Opera House was draped with crimson silk, the boxes were practical and contained a whole audience, all being in perspective. The men and women in the boxes near to the footlights were real; those far back were children dressed like their elders."[14] To the simple romantic quality of the melodrama, Irving had added his own brand of realistic staging, even going to the trouble of grading the size of the occupants of the loges in order to heighten the illusion. As did the feature film to the single-reel photoplay, he had added realistic spectacle to conventional melodrama.

The editorial pattern for his series of episodes was the same as that of the earlier version. The difference was in the pictures themselves. With Irving it was not a simple painted forest, but

a forest as real as anything can be on the stage. Trees stood out separately over a large area so that those entering from side or back could be seen passing behind or amongst them. All over the stage was a deep blanket of snow, white and glistening in the winter sunrise. Snow that lay so thick that when the duellists, stripped and armed, stood face to face, *they each secured a firmer foothold by kicking it away.* Of many wonderful effects this snow was perhaps the strongest and most impressive of reality. . . It was *salt.* . . tons of it.[15]

This production seems to have come very close indeed to the photographic standard.

Henry Irving approached the staging of melodrama like a motion-picture camera in the hands of a competent artist. Using the cinematic pattern of the typical melodramatic form, he had, in these plays, moved directly toward the photographic ideal. His rise to the leading position on the London stage was predicated upon the pictorial realism of his productions. It is significant that his emergence coincided with that of the motion-picture camera. It would seem that both Irving and the cinema responded to the same social tension, and satisfied the same aestheic preference.

The peak of his success establishes a summit in the entire pattern of realistic-romantic theatre stemming from Garrick. Its attainment in 1895, at the precise time when the cinema made its appearance, marks the point from which reaction could normally have been expected. The presence of the motion-picture camera, however, provided a new medium which made it possible to prolong and heighten the development of this phase in the arts of the theatre.

Irving, Shakespeare, and the Historical Spectacles

Like critic Joseph Knight, Irving must have diagnosed that "to the majority of the audience the play is wholly spectacle, and Shakespeare's words might almost be regarded as a species of incidental music."[16] Irving could not deny his audience. He was by no means an isolated phenomenon, but simply the strongest single exponent of a trend that had been in progress for years. Shakespearean and other historical plays provided a prime opportunity for pictorial trapping.

Charles I by William Havard, produced at the Lyceum in October of 1872, was nothing more than "a series of pictures."[17] Its "episodic"[18] dramatic form was fully supported with stage pictures constructed "in solidity and architectural symmetry"[19] by Harker and Craven. The reality of these settings was enhanced by the costuming. "One of the most notable things of Irving's *Charles I.* was his extraordinary *reproduction* of Van Dyck's pictures. . . Each costume was an exact reproduction from one of the well-known paintings, and the reproduction of Charles's face was a marvel."[20] And, of course, Irving's direction achieved a number of "beautiful living pictures. . . by the players."[21] The one at its close, "with the royal family in the tented barge, gliding through the placid waters, [was] something to remember."[22] All this pictorial staging was amply strengthened, cinema-wise, by "illustrative music."[23]

Hamlet appeared at the Lyceum on October 31, 1874, and again on December 30, 1878. Its presentation in 1883 at the Chestnut Street Theatre in Philadelphia was "in the nature of an illustrated lecture."[24] Emphasis, again, was upon the pictorial aspects of the play. Every phase of the visual production, every pictorial detail, was calculated for its appropriate effect. An interesting example of Irving's thoroughness in these matters came in the poison-drinking scene.

In one of the final rehearsals, when grasped by Hamlet in a phrenzy of anxiety lest Horatio should drink: "Give me the cup; let go; by heaven, I'll have it!" the cup, flung down desperately rolled away for some distance and then following the shape of the stage rolled down to the footlights. There is a sort of fascination in the uncertain movement of an inanimate object and such an occurrence during the play would infallibly distract the attention of the audience. Irving at once ordered that the massive metal goblet used should have some bosses fixed below the rim so that it could not roll. At a previous rehearsal he had ordered that as the wine from the cup splashed the stage, coloured sawdust should be used—which it did to exactly the same artistic effect.[25]

Thus even the smallest visual details were carefully prepared.

This characteristic thoroughness, carried into all phases of such a production as *The Merchant of Venice,* first presented at the Lyceum on November 1, 1879, resulted in "scenes that, as real as circumstances permit of their being, flatter the eyes that have seen the city of the myriad canals."[26] Scenery was executed by four scenic artists, Craven, Telbin, Hann, and Cuthbert and provided a "succession of beautiful stage pictures, so artistic in conception, and so scrupulously complete in detail, that the impression could not be avoided that this very picturesque realism of the stage effects had a by no means contemptible share in enhancing the merits of the performance."[27] No effort was spared in this direction, the pictures were geographically correct, and the play proceeded within a graphic pattern of the life of the times.

Most of the street scenes were faithful representations of familiar localities in Venice. The stage management was about as perfect as can be imagined; every little detail that could lend truth and picturesqueness to the ensemble was made the most of. . . The young lazzaroni (or whatever such folk may be called in Venice) lazing about the quay in the first scene; the porters coming and going with packs of goods on their shoulders; the gay troops of maskers passing to and fro, whether on foot or in gondolas, in the night scene before Shylock's house; the crowd of curious spectators at the back of the court room in the trial scene, all afforded bits of local color.[28]

This, to be sure, was far from the original Shakespearean conception, and while it must have been an interesting production, it seems to have been more concerned with the life of the times than with the play itself. It reads like a motion-picture version. Much of the setting, furthermore, was in three dimensions, "particularly that which represents Shylock's house by the splendidly built-out and solid looking bridge with the gondolas passing to and fro."[29] This solid and practical realism was supported by music, enhancing the spectacle and heightening emotional sequences.

With the arrival of the film, Irving did not abandon his pictorial staging methods; neither did his approach immediately lose favor. In 1896, when he presented *The Merchant of Venice* in New York, it was reported that "the stage has never known such brilliant Venetian pictures."[30] When it was done at the Lyceum in 1898 with new scenery, it was again hailed for its "succession of striking pictures."[31] And as late as 1902, with its "palaces and prisons, the argosies, gondolas and watery ways, the wealth of marts and the frolic mirth of Venice," Irving, despite the presence and popularity of the early screen historical and geographical episodes, would not relinquish his well-known pattern. From first to last, Henry Irving's approach to the production of *The Merchant of Venice* was akin to the mounting of a motion picture on sixteenth-century Venice. Such techniques, cinematically conceived and three-dimensionally executed, carried pictorial staging into areas and levels earmarked for the screen.

Irving's persistence in relying upon external effects, pictorial settings, costumes, tableaux, visions, music, and so forth, had its influence upon his style of acting. Joseph Knight noted that in *Othello,* produced at the Lyceum on February 19, 1876, "such light as there is falls upon Othello from without, and is not generated within." If it were not for costume and makeup, "there are moments when we might fancy the character was Macbeth, or Julius Caesar with a brown face."[32] Does not this indicate that Irving's success as an actor depended upon his ability to represent rather than to create the character? His approach suggests the presentation of a recognizable type rather than an individual. External visual values coated his performance. He became "A Venetian Magnifico of the Middle Ages"[33] rather than Othello. And when the play was revived at the Lyceum in May of 1881, his love for such external values led him to elaborate the costume.

He now appears in much magnificence of a barbaric sort; jewels sparkle in his turban and depend from his ears, strings of pearls circle his husky throat, he is abundantly possessed of gold and silver ornaments, and his richly-brocaded robes fall about him in the most lustrous and ample folds. It may be, indeed that the actor has laid too much stress both upon the luxury and gorgeousness, as upon the Orientalism of his apparel.[34]

His acting strove to provide a picture of the man rather than the man himself. His popularity testifies to the simple photographic tastes of the times when visual proofs readily substituted for dramatic truths.

The productional care exercised in the offerings of Irving often focused upon archaeological exactitude. On such a basis he undertook, in 1880, to mold Tennyson's *The Cup* into an effective stage piece. Here he boldly hung upon the closet work of Tennyson sufficient archaeological trapping to make it worth the price of admission.

James Knowles reconstructed a Temple of Artemis on the ground plan of the great Temple of Diana. The late Alexander Murray. . . made researches amongst the older Etruscan designs. Capable artists made drawings from vases, which were reproduced on the great amphorae used in the Temple service. The existing base and drum of a column from Ephesus was remodelled for use . . . William Telbin painted some scenes worthy of Turner; and Hawes Craven and Cuthbert made such an interior scene of the Great Temple as was surely never seen on any stage.[35]

This correct scenic accouterment encompassed a scale sufficient to include great crowd scenes. "Something like a hundred beautiful young women were chosen for Vestals; and as the number of persons already employed in *The Corsican Brothers* was very great, the stage force available for scenic display was immense."[36] Mammoth spectacular scenes were marshaled. "Gorgeously armoured Roman officers" forced an entry into the Temple to create a "peculiarly strong"[37] effect. Such treatment insured the success of material not inherently dramatic. A picture play had been devised from closet poetics.

These productions, elaborate as they may have been, were only preliminary to what has been considered the first great Shakespearean production made by Irving under his own management, that of *Romeo and Juliet,* at the Lyceum, May 8, 1882. In the short preface to his published acting version, he proclaimed that he had availed himself in its production "of every resource at my command to illustrate"[38] the warm Italian life of the story. He surrounded himself with three of the ablest scene painters of the day, Hawes Craven, William Telbin, and Walter Hann. A special musical score was composed by Sir Julius Benedict. Results were extraordinary. The London *Era* exclaimed:

Many times as this tragedy has been performed, it is in no wise an exaggeration to say that never until its production under Irving's direction had there been fully realised the possibilities in the play for scenic effects, nor had a most beautiful realism in those scenic effects haloed the personages of the drama with an actuality that made them living Montagues and Capulets. Well we remember how the force and charm of these pictures lifted the whole work above cavil.[39]

Irving sought to create a photographic reproduction of the time, the place, and the very events of the play. His success in achieving such spectacular and realistic stage pictures is comparable to that of D. W. Griffith in such films as *The Birth of a Nation*. His substitutes for the military scenes of battle and gunfire were equally effective in their own right and were limited only by the physical capacities of the stage. The play opens in

the market-place of Verona with side streets and at back a narrow stone bridge over a walled-in stream. The "Several persons" [of the rubric], mostly apprentices of the Capulet faction, entered, at first slowly, but coming quicker and quicker till quite a mass had gathered on the hither side of the bridge. The strangers were being easily worsted. Then over the bridge came a rush of the Montagues armed like their foes with sticks or swords according to their degree. They used to pour in on the scene down the slope of the bridge like a released torrent, and for a few minutes such a scene of fighting was enacted as I have never elsewhere seen on the stage. The result of the mighty fight was that during the whole time of the run of the play there was never a day when there was not at least one of the young men in the hospital.[40]

Irving's pictures eclipsed earlier efforts. This particular production, with its pictorial achievements and its elaborate use of such devices as the instantaneous scene-shift, the dissolve, fade-out, fade-in, and so on, suggests the staging of a motion picture. Its cinematic values are manifest in the closing series of sets.

When the dialogue in Friar Laurence's cell ended, a darkness fell and grew upon the whole house, until the stage faded from sight. A slender thread of mournful melody from stringed instruments sustained the continuity. . . Presently the obscurity became less oppressive, and then an ashen haze seemed to hang across the proscenium, through which there was first perceived dimly and in distorted form, and afterwards more plainly. . . the barred entrance to the tomb of the Capulets. Anon. . . other and lesser tombs took shape. . . Then, as the illumination of the picture assumed the distinctive characteristics of moonlight, the beams were intercepted and broken by the thick foliage of yews and willows which took their place in a churchyard. . . The ghostly gleam quickened and vibrated all over, and the picture was finished. It had been painted before the very eye.

Before there was any movement in the picture the moonlight waned as though a cloud had passed before the silver orb, and the attention was wholly centered upon Juliet's tomb by a pale taper which flickered in the dark and inky entrance behind the iron gate. Then the action proceeded. Paris strewed his garlands at the gates; Romeo appeared and with desperate strength burst open the barriers to the tomb, and by his reluctant sword Paris fell, slain, within the portals of the sepulchre. Seizing his torch and dragging after him the lifeless form of his antagonist, Romeo disappeared, descending into the vault below. While the flare of his torch still reddened the damp walls of the entrance the picture faded from view. Silently it came; as silently it vanished. Once again the theatre was shrouded in darkness. . . Again the darkness became luminous, and the outlines of a deep cavern, hewn in solid rock, grew before the eye. It was the crypt in which rested the Capulet dead. High up in the background was seen an entrance from which a staircase, rudely fashioned in the rock, wound downward on the left to the cavern's floor, and through which the moonlight streamed and fell upon the form of Juliet lying upon a silken covered bier in the foreground.

Immediately the scene was developed Romeo appeared at the entrance leading from the churchyard above, bearing his flaming torch, and with the corpse of Paris in his arms, descended the rocky stairway to the bottom of the tomb. . . The action continued, and at length, when Juliet and Romeo were dead, and the Friar had fled the place, the murmurs of the approaching multitude grew into articulate cries, and then, as the entrance was darkened by the forms of those who jostled wildly in their haste for ingress, a curtain was drawn upon the picture. In a moment the drapery divided and the concluding tableau was revealed. The crypt was filled with a motley crowd, grouped on stair and floor, some bearing blazing torches which cast about a wild, red glare, and others in attitude of terror or of grief. . . From the churchyard came the voices of the friars chanting in measured cadence the prayers for the dead. . . The curtain slowly descended; the play was finished.[41]

The words of Shakespeare had lost their necessity. Everything had been done visually with pictorial settings, descriptive business, and mass tableaux. The realistic-romantic phase of theatrical expression had come a long way from the innovations of Loutherbourg and Capon. Indeed, it had come so far that, having climbed to the very doorstep of the motion picture, further progress seemed impossible without the motion-picture camera.

This same approach led Irving to one triumph after another.

He "finds Shakespeare a huge success, because he gives him the best accessories that the modern stage can afford," reported the *Boston Beacon* on the occasion of the Boston presentation of his *Twelfth Night*, November 5, 1884, at the Globe Theatre. The play itself became "a breathing, animated picture of the place, the people and the time."[42] Similarly in the case of *Coriolanus*. As usual, Irving wanted his stage pictures to be correct.

Alma-Tadema had made a specialty of artistic archaeology of Ancient Rome. . . He had so studied the life of old Rome that he had for his own purposes reconstructed it. . . He was familiar with the kinds of marble and stone used in Roman architecture, statuary, and domestic service. The kinds of glass and crystal; of armour and arms; of furniture; of lighting; sacerdotal and public and domestic service. He knew how a velarum should be made and of what, and how adorned. . . . He was learned of boats and chariots; of carts and carriages, and of the trappings of horses. Implements of agriculture and trade and manufacture and for domestic use were familiar to him. He was a master of the many ceremonial undertakings which had such a part in Roman life.[43]

And so Sir Lawrence Alma-Tadema was engaged to reproduce the scenery.

Irving was occasionally as clever as Boucicault with spectacular effects. *Faust,* for instance, at the Lyceum on December 19, 1885, afforded an unusual opportunity in the great duel scene.

The fight between Faust and Valentine—with Mephistopheles in his supposed invisible quality interfering—was the first time when electric flashes were used in a play. This effect was arranged by Colonel Gouraud, Edison's partner, who kindly interested himself in the matter. . . Two iron plates were screwed upon the stage at a given distance so that at the time of fighting each of the swordsmen would have his right boot on one of the plates, which represented an end of the interrupted current. A wire was passed up the clothing of each from the shoe to the outside of the indiarubber glove, in the palm of which was a piece of steel. Thus when each held his sword a flash came whenever the swords crossed.[44]

Flashing blades literally flashed. An effect from the files of gothic romance was realistically staged.

Other effects were not so easily gained, for "much of the scenery was what is called 'built out.' "[45] And, as always, the pictures simulated actual locales and details. Irving had to make "a trip to Nuremberg to see for himself what would be most picturesque as well as suitable."[46] All the stock-in-hand dissolving techniques of the pictorial theatre were used, particularly for the vision tableaux. In the last scene, "Margaret's prison fades away" and there appeared "the vision of Margaret's lying dead at the foot of the Cross with a long line of descending angels,"[47] all in the manner of the screen lap-dissolve.

The built-out scenery of *Faust,* the archaeological correctness of *Coriolanus,* and the epic spectacular quality of *Romeo and Juliet* were combined in the production of *Macbeth* at the Lyceum on December 30, 1888. Again Irving engaged a quartet of the best representational scenic artists of the day—Craven, Harker, Hann, and Hall—with the result that the "impressive grandeur of the setting [was] Miltonic."[48] Here there was none of the conventional "Palace Arches," "Oak Chambers," or "Forest Glades."

With Irving all was different. That "easy" progress of Macbeth's soldiers returning tired after victorious battle, seen against the low dropping sun across the vast heather studded with patches of light glinting on water; the endless procession of soldiers straggling, singly, and by twos and threes, filling the stage to the conclusion of an endless array, conveyed an idea of force and power which impressed the spectator.[49]

It was the spectacle which gave Irving's productions their power. Shakespeare's slightest suggestion blossomed into pictures of epic grandeur. And throughout the production "we are assured that the British Museum and all known authorities upon archaeology have been laid under contribution for correct patterns of the costumes, weapons, and furniture of the eleventh century."[50]

This correctness had a value for itself alone, and it was noted that "scenery reproducing exactly the features of medieval life. . . had not previously been seen."[51] Archaeology, plus the pictorial eye, plus the "setting aside all the traditions that have clung like barnacles to the play through many generations,"[52] led to an entirely new and fresh production. It was claimed that "never before in the history of the theatre has a play of Shakespeare been put upon the stage with such perfect pictorial art. . . *Mr. Irving sees the stage in his mind's eye as a painter sees the picture he proposes to put upon his canvas.*"[53] The pictorial trend of the realistic-romantic theatre of the nineteenth century found in Irving its most significant British exponent. In this case, any "comparison with other revivals—not excluding those of our own time, say from 1853, when Charles Kean's version at the Princess' Theatre was the talk of playgoing circles—would be not only out of place, but futile."[54] His pictures, even before the war-weary army trudges across the moon, caught the eerie and supernatural feeling of the play. "Out of the murky clouds that glower over a dread morass come the three weird sisters, miscalled witches. . . The sisters are not old men dressed up as women, dancing about a theatrical caldron, squeaking in shrill treble, and waving clothesprops in their hands, but three grey, gloomy women, dignified, mysterious, impressive with wailing women's voices."[55]

Irving sought to strip this supernatural business of its traditional hokum and to place it upon a recognizable yet spectacular level. This he achieved, first, by having the witches played "for the first time in the history of the stage by women,"[56] and, second, by surrounding them with appropriately ethereal stage pictures. They appear out of nothingness and disappear again into a void. They came in "out of the murky clouds" and then as "the clouds drift away, the King Duncan meets the Bleeding Sergeant."[57] Soon the army trudges on and then, as the witches fade into view, the soldiers disappear, leaving Macbeth and Banquo to hear the prophecy. In the last scene "in which the weird sisters appear, with its apparitions and its procession of grisly kings, all is so new, so fresh, so original and admirable. The cauldron is not stuck into the middle of the stage, but is thrust into a hollow of a rock, and Macbeth surveys the weird scene from an eminence. . . Once more the sisters have dissolved themselves into air and mist, once more the darkness of the night disappears."[58]

Returning to the witch sequence at the start of the play, the pictorial continuity cuts directly from the heath to Macbeth's castle, to show Duncan's arrival.

Macbeth's castle, shown first by moonlight as King Duncan and his train arrive in front of it, loomed forth from the grim shadows [of the preceding heath scene] like a mass of Gothic masonry. *Solid towers rose up from the stage,* and turrets frowned overhead amid the gathering clouds. The effect of them was enhanced tenfold by making the approach to the castle door lead up an invisible hill. It opened out into the middle of the stage close to a heavy archway leading into the castle. The royal train as they entered with flaring torches and drums beating, seemed to rise out of the earth.[59]

With Duncan's exit, the castle "opened up and disclosed the room where the new Lady Macbeth was about to appear with the fatal letter."[60] The scene shifts swiftly to its companion picture, the Courtyard. The setting is built out: "On the right a cloistered passage, a steep flight of stone steps leading to a gallery, and on the left a huge shaft, at the base of which winds the short ascent to the king's chamber. The wind whistles and howls, and the thunder rolls."[61]

These three-dimensional, architectural features were exploited for pictorial acting effects. For example:

Who that saw it can ever forget that picture of the horror-stricken Macbeth creeping round the worn stone Norman pillar up the narrow turret staircase to murder the sleeping Duncan. . .
A fine picture, this red-haired, heart-tortured woman, standing in that lonely hall whilst the murder shrieks are heard overhead.[62]

A marvelous effect is presently gained when the alarm has been given, and gradually the galleries, steps and courtyard are peopled by the excited, horror-stricken and vengeful throng, torches only lighting the scene.[63]

This entire "magnificent series of pictures"[64] represents a level in nineteenth-century pictorial realism beyond which progress without the motion picture would hardly seem possible. Indeed, "no more admirable stage picture could be conceived than that of Macbeth's dark and frowning castle. . . nor could the illusion of walls and battlements of wind and weather-beaten stone be carried further than it is."[65] In response to audience taste, the theatre of this period had been paving the way for the early film. With its photographic realism the motion picture was to find an audience ready and eager for the kind of theatre upon which Irving and his colleagues had based their success in the decades prior to its arrival.

With this picture drama came the usual coating of music. For *Macbeth,* Sir Arthur Sullivan composed an overture, the four entr'actes, the witches' choruses for the fourth act, and all incidental music. Musical illustration was as important as pictorial illustration. In the fourth act, with its great supernatural business, the witches' caldron, and the flying spirits, Sullivan took full advantage of the opportunity to provide

a musical accompaniment to the incantation scene that sobs and sighs like fitful gusts of wind; then comes a weird burst of melody in the 'mingle, mingle' song, and finally, when the scene changes from the witches cave to the shores of a Scotch loch under a wild, stormy sky, the crowd of Hecate's attendant spirits break forth into a magnificent Mendelssohnic chorus.[66]

Between the music and the pictures, the production seems to have buried the characters, the ideas, and, most of all, the words of Shakespeare.

Henry VIII offered Irving a great opportunity for archaeological pageantry. In the solid, three-dimensional quality of its settings it may not have equaled *Macbeth,* yet its processional pomp and panoply became a dramatic force in the development of the play, for "it was by the very luxury and extravagance of the nobles of the time that the power of the old feudalism was lowered."[67] The illustration of such a value, as Bram Stoker has explained, "naturally becomes a pivotal point of the play," for when the members of King Henry's court "were encouraged and incited to vie with each other in the splendour of their dress and equipment . . . their capacity for revolt was curbed by the quick wasting of their estates."[68] Hence Irving took great care in the presentation of the court not to minimize this graphic force and sought, of course, to restore the period.

Seymour Lucas, who undertook to superintend the production, carried on the usual archaeological research, even to the point of detailing assistants for months at "South Kensington Museum making coloured drawings of the many stuffs used at that time. . . Further months were occupied with the looms before the antique stuffs thus reproduced were ready for the costumier. Irving's own dress—his robe as Cardinal—was, after months of experiment, exactly reproduced from a genuine robe of the period kindly lent to him by Rudolph Lehmann, the painter."[69] Accessories were equally lavish. When one of the company was dissatisfied with his costume diamond collar, he "borrowed a real one from one of the Dukes, whose Collar of the Garter was of a magnificence rare even amongst such jewels."[70] On such a basis the play opened at the Lyceum on January 5, 1892, and enjoyed 203 performances. Yet in the midst of all this authentic *mise en scène* a single small oversight destroyed the illusion of an entire scene. A member of the audience registered written complaint: "The complete success of *Henry VIII.* was marred when the King kissed the china doll. The whole house tittered."[71] Such complete realism had been achieved in the rest of the production that this slight incongruity upset the illusion. The complainant offered the hire of his "real baby for the purpose of personating the offspring."[72] Anything short of absolute realism for this audience of the nineties failed to satisfy. Yet the physical limitations of the stage made compromises necessary.

Irving's production of *King Arthur* by J. Comyns Carr at the Lyceum on January 12, 1895, the year in which the motion picture appeared, again approached the photographic ideal. Scenery was designed by Edward Burne-Jones and executed by Hawes Craven and Joseph Harker. In the season following its London opening it was shown during September and October in Boston, and in New York in November. According to reports from Boston, it was "simply a beautiful poem in action, illustrated by a series of magnificent scenes."[73] Nothing in the play itself recommended success. The production "was lavished on a piece that, treating of legendary stuff, never evokes human interest, shows no strength of character development, and falls far short of arousing any keen interest."[74] The popular Irving formula was applied here, and in the typical manner of his other historical productions, "the constant succession of stage tableaux. . . [were] masterpieces in their composition."[75]

Great pictorial contrasts, appealing to all the senses, were employed. "Notably should be mentioned the Queen's Maying, which is redolent with the odors of spring, and from this to the clank of armor and the flash of a hundred swords in the following act is a contrast of mighty strength."[76] Electricity was used to enhance the realism of natural phenomena. Sunrise, sunset, and moonlight effects were created in an unusual way. "The drop scenes at the back, instead of being painted in opaque colors, according to the conventional way, are executed in aniline, or semi-transparent tints, through which coloured lights are made to shine from the back, giving a brilliancy of tone which makes a wonderful counterfeit of nature."[77] To the novelty of these spectacular effects was added a certain three-dimensional scenic quality. The Queen's Maying shows a whitethorn wood with part of a hillside visible upon stage and "winding up the hillside is a practicable path. On the left there is a wider alley between the trees which descends to the stage."[78] This solid hillside was utilized for pictorial groupings and action. Costumes "blended with mystic colors from the dreamland of Burne-Jones,"[79] accentuated the stage pictures, and even Ellen Terry's acting became "a series of pictures which will long be remembered."[80]

In this way a script which possessed little or no inherent dramatic value succeeded through the treatment supplied by Henry Irving and Edward Burne-Jones. Its presentation, a few months before the original motion-picture showings, achieved an outstanding pictorial realism for the American stage. "Never, on the American stage, even at Mr. Irving's own hands, was there a production with such prodigality of artistic coloring, wealth of mise-en-scene, reality and costliness of costume and suits of mail and armor, not to mention the thousand and one little details of construction."[81] Such was the formula upon which the success of Irving was based, and such were the aesthetic preferences which sponsored the most reproductional device yet known to the arts.

With the appearance of the film, Irving did not relinquish his pictorial approach. On the other hand, he strove all the more strenuously to achieve greater productional values. But something had gone wrong. He planned the presentation of *Richard II* and engaged Edwin A. Abbey, R.A., for the scenery. By 1898 over £1600 had been spent on scenery,[82] but plans were abandoned and the production was never offered. Whether backers suddenly realized that pictorial realism upon the stage had lost its hold, whether Irving himself was getting on in years and losing his grip, or whether the film had already made severe inroads into his audience, is, of course, impossible to determine. By 1903 his hitherto popular management at the Lyceum failed and, when J. Comyns Carr arranged for new financial backing for a production of *Dante,* translated by Laurence Irving from the original of Sardou and Moreau, "the 'backers' were unwilling that he [Irving] should be responsible for the management."[83] Adjustments were eventually made, and when the play finally opened on the thirtieth of April at Drury Lane, no expense had been spared. "The production was on a gigantic scale . . . the labour of preparation and rehearsal was endless, the expense enormous. The curtain went up on the night of production to an incurred expense of nearly thirteen thousand pounds."[84] According to present-day monetary standards this expenditure would represent approximately $150,000. Such an elaborate production should easily have satisfied the demands of his picture-conscious audience and held off whatever rivalry may already have appeared from the film. Yet the play ran for only eighty-two performances, a poor exhibition in comparison to *The Merchant of Venice, Romeo and Juliet,* or *Macbeth.* Thus, even prior to the competition offered by the great spectacular productions of the early feature film, the London audience of Henry Irving had dwindled into a fragment of its former size and he was soon driven to the provinces.

The theatrical conception of Henry Irving was entirely a productional conception. In exploiting this approach, his offerings fulfilled the taste for a cinematic kind of theatre. His success, marking a theatrical need for the motion picture, reached its peak simultaneously with the arrival of the film. His rise to popularity coincided with the final phase in the development of the motion picture, and, upon its appearance, fell into a decline. This would suggest that the success of his example, offering a certain stimulation to the promotion of the process, was subsequently undermined by its capacities and, as the motion picture brought the pictorial cycle of realism and romance into a higher level of perfection, was eventually deprived of its audience.

II. DAVID BELASCO

From Tom Robertson and Squire Bancroft at the little Prince of Wales's on Tottenham Court Road to the spectacular and scintillating cinematic showings in the mammoth auditorium of Radio City Music Hall is a period of artistic inertia, of imaginative laziness—a laziness not on the part of artists of the theatre, but rather on the part of their audiences. Audiences demanded proof, and, first of all, visual, scenic proof. They had not come into the theatre to participate imaginatively; this was an age of reason: they had come to be shown. But this was also an age of romance; they must be shown exaggerated and glorified as well as mundane and everyday pictures. Both of these needs the cinema filled, but before the cinema came David Belasco. His popularity continued into the years of the early film because his theatrical technique was highly cinematic.

While Henry Irving had been glutting his audiences with a graphic kind of theatre at the Lyceum in London, Belasco had been exploiting similar methods in this country. Under the influence of the new standards of realism established by the Bancrofts, Daly, Antoine, and the Saxe-Meiningen, Irving brought fresh pictorial values into the century-old forms of melodrama and spectacle. The work of Belasco achieved exactly the same thing, but with the development of still another dramatic area. Unlike Irving, Belasco showed a significant interest in the drama of intimate realism, of domestic problems and homely situations. In this he extended the reforms as well as the type of drama sponsored by the Bancrofts, Antoine, and Stanislavsky. Belasco rode the crest of that rising tide of theatrical reform whose final surge carried the theatre from the representational stagings of the Bancrofts to the photographic reproductions of the motion picture.

The development of this quality became the motivating force behind his entire theatrical endeavor. He himself asks: "When I set a scene representing a Child's Restaurant how can I expect to hold the *attention* of my audience unless I show them a scene that looks *real?*"[85] *The Governor's Lady,* the play to which he refers, gained its reality by the transfer of an entire café interior onto the stage of his theatre. This approach has been criticized because it depended completely upon settings, and because, as a result, Belasco's stage became the "paradise of the property-man." But this very quality "has made his chance for the world's moving picture anthology."[86] For Belasco forms a bridge between Tottenham Court Road and Hollywood, and thus occupies a salient position in the realistic-romantic development from Garrick to Griffith.

Belasco's work, beginning with his debut as stage manager in 1878, falls into three general classes: melodrama, historical spectacle, and domestic drama. The categories overlap, of course, but are convenient for discussion.

Belasco as a Producer of Spectacle

In December of 1878 Belasco adapted an old spectacle play by Watts Phillips entitled *Not Guilty* and staged it at the Baldwin Theatre in San Francisco on the day before Christmas for the holiday trade. This early theatrical effort, billed as a "Grand Production of the Magnificent Musical, Military Dramatic, and Spectacular Christmas Piece,"[87] identified his approach. He himself has admitted that it "was very spectacular, and with my customary leaning to warfare I introduced a Battle Scene, with several hundred people in an embarkation, as well as horses and cannon."[88] Contemporary opinion proclaimed it "about the most realistic ever produced on the stage."[89] With the aid of horses, cannon, and masses of supers, Belasco had, from the start, set up a formula.

Salmi Morse's *Passion Play,* which, in 1898, became the first long story film, was staged by Belasco at the Grand Opera House, San Francisco, on March 3, 1879. It was a spectacle, pure and simple, dealing with the life of Jesus Christ and consisting of "a long series of dialogues accompanied by pictures and tableaux."[90] But the dialogue, it seems, was of minor importance, since the story of the events leading up to the Crucifixion and the Resurrection was told by the sequence of stage pictures. For instance, in the episode entitled The Massacre of the Innocents, "many females appear, carrying babes, and a ferocious *Jew,* essaying to kill the infant *Jesus,* falls back astounded and overwhelmed by the aspect of the sacred infant."[91] The story and its drama was planned entirely from the visual point of view. The Betrayal of Jesus was played in a dual set: "On one side, a lighted room in which is reproduced a semblance of "The Last Supper" according to the admired picture by Leonardo da Vinci, and on the other a gloomy range of plains and hills dimly lighted by the stars."[92] This arrangement provided an interesting pair of stage pictures as well as the opportunity for cross-cutting between interior and exterior.

The story of the Passion, treated by artists of many centuries, offered prime material for spectacle production. And Belasco delighted in the many "opportunities which he discovered for pictorial display: he explored every accessible source for paintings to be copied and for suggestions as to costume, color, and 'atmosphere,' and, particularly, he made use of every expedient of 'realistic' effect."[93] Other pictures included The Agony of Jesus in the Garden of Gethsemane, The Arraignment of Jesus before Pilate, The Investiture of Jesus with the Crown of Thorns, and Golgotha, Under a Midnight Sky.

To heighten their effect, great numbers of extras were maneuvered through motion-tableaux. Belasco wrote, "We marshalled 400 men, women, children, and infants in our *ensembles*," and for choral effects, "We engaged 200 singers." In the scene of Joseph coming down the mountainside with Mary, "We had a flock of real sheep following in their wake."[94] This kind of Biblical spectacle later provided a wedge for the introduction of the feature film.

There was rarely any imaginative or suggestive kind of scenery, costume, or property. Even the supernatural was literally and photographically treated. "O'Neill [as Christ] came up from his dressing room and appeared on the stage with a halo."[95] The play itself William Winter described as "merely a goody-goody, tiresome composition, full of moral twaddle. . . written in nondescript lines of unequal length, halting, irregular, formless, weak, and diffuse."[96] The success of the production stands in evidence of the nineteenth-century taste for pictorial realism and of Belasco's successful illustration of the Biblical story. That Belasco, at the outset of his career, should have attempted such a production, later to become the first long story film, indicates that sixteen years before the demonstration of the Edison vitascope Belasco was staging material of a cinematic nature.

While still in San Francisco, Belasco collaborated with Peter Robertson in writing *The Curse of Cain,* produced by Belasco at the Baldwin Theatre on March 5, 1881. According to William Winter, this play had been produced simply "for the purpose of making lavish scenic display and startling theatrical effects."[97] Again, nothing was left to the imagination.

In the scene of the Gypsy Camp Belasco indulged to the full his liking for literalism,—providing for the public edification a braying donkey, neighing horses, cackling hens, crowing cocks, quacking ducks, and a rooting, grunting pig. In the Lighthouse Scene, as one account relates, having assembled his *dramatis personae* for the final curtain by the novel yet simple expedient of "washing them all up from the ocean," after a shipwreck, like flotsam, he introduced a frantic struggle between the villain and the hero, beginning on the wave-beaten rocks, conducted up a spiral stairway within the lighthouse and intermittently visible through the windows thereof, and terminating in the fall of the villain from the pinnacle of that edifice to a watery grave,—with which fitting demise, and the union of the lovers, the spectacle drew sweetly to a close.[98]

The obvious motion-picture values of such melodrama were presented with a photographic literalism.

Belasco rarely staged a play directly as written. He adapted Rider Haggard's *She* from the William Gillette version and presented it on the stage of Niblo's Garden in New York on November 29, 1887. Very little could be said for the play itself, but its production at the Hollis Theatre in Boston in November, 1888, drew the report that "as a series of striking scenes the piece has some claim to consideration."[99] The pictures were varied and unusual, and possessed a good deal of weird interest.

Whether it be on the deck of the African coaster, manned by divers dingy sailors where the Englishman triumphs over the aborigines by valor. . . or the sequent scene where, after the customary thunderbolt and rescue of the whites from drowning, the imposing head of an Ethiopian, colossally set in stone, is outlined against the stormy sky; whether it be the grim cave of the Amhaggar or the underground palace of She, where every most unpleasant reptile is used for ornamental purposes, and skeletons are as common as washstands in a furniture store; whether it be the dusky ravine and precipice. . . or finally, the blazing fountain of fire which turns She, after her bath therein, back to a woman 2000 years old—all is clever.[100]

No effort was spared to camouflage the play's lack of all but pictorial values. Belasco knew what his public wanted. Novelties of every sort heightened the pictures. Out of love for sheer spectacle the production nearly turned into a fireworks display. A report at the time of the original production stated:

> There must be a boom this week in lycopodium in the wholesale drug line, for *She* at Niblo's is ablaze with it. Flaming torches, fire-sprouting skeletons and gorgeous flash-boxes hold conflagrational revel on the stage at Niblo's. . . The stage looks like a smelting-works on a dark night, and the auditorium is perfumed with the exhalations of all the illuminating chemicals known to the stage mechanician.[101]

And in the customary manner of such sensational melodramas, "*She* is very liberally garnished with solos, choruses and incidental music, composed for the San Francisco production of the piece by W. W. Furst."[102]

The spectacle of *She* was managed with a considerable use of conventional devices. Later productions, such, for instance, as *Under Two Flags,* adapted by Paul Potter from the novel by Ouida, were developed with a great deal more care in the matter of realism. Apparently Belasco aimed here at the reproduction of a particular part of the world. His achievement, "a populous, tumultuous stage pageant,—a spectacle of Moorish scenery and military bustle,"[103] was presented at the Garden Theatre, New York, February 5, 1901, in apparent response to the stimulation offered by the photographic realism of the motion picture.

> Taste, thought, ingenuity, and sedulous care were expended on every feature of the pageant by Belasco, and the result was a magnificent spectacle—one of the richest and most impressive seen on our stage. Had it been brought here by Henry Irving or Herbert Beerbohm Tree, it would have been hailed as a transcendent exploit in stagecraft. Every scene was a picture, every picture was harmonious with the phase of the story to be illustrated, and in the transitions from the luxurious villa,

with its prospect of the tranquil ocean faintly rippling beneath the moon, to the desolate, rocky, weird and ominous mountain gorge, a climax of solemn grandeur seemed to take shape, color and charm, slowly rising out of a dream of romantic beauty. The drift of whirling mist over the darkening waves of sand on the bleak sea-coast would have seemed the most consummate of illusions had it not been excelled by the blinding terrors of a mountain tempest.[104]

Settings here seem to have come very close to the photographic ideal. The Byron photographs of this production[105] show that every effort had been made to increase its realism. For example, what the programs in the palmy days used to call a "rocky pass" became a solid, three-dimensional precipice. At the extreme height of the stage Bedouins could be seen hidden behind rocks and crags waiting in ambush for the girl Cigarette, unwittingly being misled by a traitorous Arabian guide. And yet, while the realism of this stage picture cannot be denied, its limitations in comparison to a possible screen treatment of the same "rocky pass" ambush sequence are equally obvious. Fundamental, of course, is the fact that such a sequence would gain much of its dramatic value through a pattern of cross-cutting between the waiting Bedouins and the blithe Cigarette. Hence it appears that while screen material was realistically presented upon the stage, this very fact made the development of the implied cinematic editorial pattern impossible.

As a result, Belasco sought to meet the photographic rivalry of the film with an increasing thoroughness in the preparation of each individual pictorial aspect. Cigarette has been sentenced to be shot. A simoom suddenly rises and, while the driving sand blinds the eyes of the Bedouins, she spurs her horse to escape up the hillside. The sandstorm effect was produced "by means of shadows thrown by a stereopticon upon a screen between stage and the audience."[106] These projections were combined with sound and light effects.

The wind sighs in the distance and rages as it comes near. . . The light of day fades to dimness. The sand that is blown in these storms of the African desert came lightly at first, but soon so heavily as to look like furiously driven hail. Rapid reflections on gauze curtains, in conjunction with the noises of the wind and the bending of trees, make a really awe-inspiring imitation of natural phenomenon.[107]

Here was a recognition that projected scenery could create as realistic an illusion as the actual presentation of natural phenomena at every performance. Opportunities of this kind were rarely lost. Even the "rosy touch on the snowy peak after the simoom has spent its fury is a wonderfully pretty effect."[108] Having taken "a story suitable for scenic illustration,"[109] and in a manner which audiences had "all come to expect from Mr. Belasco,"[110] "no pains or expense had been spared in carrying out that design!"[111] In this way a certain competition provided by the early-screen topical episodes, which reproduced photographically actual scenes of the same kind, had been met.

Madame Butterfly, a one-act tragedy of Japanese life adapted by Belasco from a story by John Luther Long, satisfied the love for stage pictures even before the play itself began by using a series of "picture drops" arranged at the proscenium in front of the actual setting.

A notably effective scenic innovation was the precedent use of "picture drops," delicately painted and very lovely pictures showing various aspects of Japan,—a rice field, a flower garden, a distant prospect of a snow-capped volcano in the light of the setting sun, and other views,—by way of creating a Japanese atmosphere before the scene of the drama was disclosed.[112]

Here Belasco presented static views in color of a type similar to the topical-film episodes on the Orient currently showing on the screen. His use of these pictures suggests the use of the panorama shot or certain montage devices for establishing locale, mood, and atmosphere in the cinema.

The original production at the Herald Square Theatre in New York on March 5, 1900, gained its popularity from its "pictures of Japanese life and domestic customs, its daring but successful admixture of European realism in dramatic art with some of the conventional Oriental stage customs, its brilliant display of color, its changing light effects."[113] It held the stage through 1907, at which time it was still reported that "the play is a gem of picturesque treatment."[114]

Lighting effects played an important part. Electrical lighting,

Belasco claimed, had "accomplished the feat of compressing an entire night into twelve minutes."[115] Electricity offered opportunities for new pictures without changing the physical setting. Through the control of color and intensity of light, temporal changes within the same set provided a series of pictures from sunset to sunrise. Belasco boasted that "the characters present on the stage are really secondary to the lighting effects."[116] This reflects a definite aesthetic preference of early-century audiences. Therefore, to increase the realism of his stage pictures, he eliminated footlights, which, situated below, cast unmotivated light and unnatural shadows and which, he averred, "are made unnecessary for any play, and are no longer a part of the illumination of my stage."[117] Belasco's great interest in lighting stems both from the potentialities of the new electrical-light supply and from his recognition that lighting effects were beyond the pale of the early motion picture, thus providing him with an area in which he might easily surpass the pictorial appeal of the film.

The production of his own *DuBarry* at the Criterion Theatre, New York, on December 25, 1901, marked a peak in the Belasco realistic spectacles. H. T. Parker described this play in the *Boston Transcript* as a production of "stage pictures of life at Paris and Versailles toward the end of the reign of Louis XV, with a scene or two from the Revolution as an epilogue."[118] On such a basis the play ran for 165 performances the first season and was revived at the beginning of the next on September 29, 1902, for the opening of the remodeled Belasco Theatre. "So beautiful" were the pictures "that the audience were distracted from the lines of the play and did not notice them closely."[119] Despite the distraction the play succeeded. Audiences had come to see and not to listen.

Belasco spared nothing and achieved a profuse realism. The lavish and accurate reproduction of costumes and properties of the period, apparent in the Byron photographs,[120] defies description. Nothing was artificial, everything was reproduced as if from a plaster cast of the original. Embroided costumes were not simulated with printed or stamped patterns, but showed the depth of genuine needlework with an amazing thoroughness of detail. Mirrors, draperies, statues, all sorts of boudoir accessories were accurately re-created. Everywhere the visual aspects were fully developed. For instance:

> In the fete in the *Park at Versailles,* the long façade of the palace, high on its terrace, stretches away into the misty night, aglow with lights, as though revivified. The jaded and frivolous court would have applauded the DuBarry's ingenuity when she bids the pedestal of a statue of the king to open and reveal a throne girt with little Loves. Dancers, acrobats, Pierrots, succeed each other on the scene. A throng of courtiers and their ladies, officers and aides, guardsmen and lackeys fill the background.[121]

Later, during this "optical offering that delighted the crowd," the stage was darkened and "illuminated balls were tossed about among the characters," quite in keeping with this type of drama which, it has become evident, was nothing more than "a series of circus scenes"[122] supported by elaborate graphic illustration. The famous boudoir of DuBarry displayed walls "covered with frescoes in the opulent, voluptuous manner of Boucher and Fragonard. Mirrors reflect her comeliness. Cupids everywhere, on pedestals, holding up sconces, drawing back the canopy of the great gilded bed, attest the business of her life."[123]

To such lush pictures of sensuous court life came the startling contrast of "the narrow streets of revolutionary Paris, with their high, plain, dingy houses on a raw winter morning with the jeering crowd of Jacobin riff-raff blocking the pavement and filling every window to mock DuBarry on her way to execution."[124] A regular cast of 55 was augmented by 135 men, women, and children lining this street, crowding windows and balconies to see DuBarry roll by in a tumbril drawn by a real horse. The architectural aspect of such a setting required solidity and practicability, with the result that the street of four-storied houses through which DuBarry rolled on her way to the guillotine had "to be literally built against the back wall of the theatre."[125] It was Belasco's "ingenuity as a mechanic and not his possibilities as a dramatic author, that the public cared for."[126] It was his skill in the creation of realistic and spectacular stage pictures that the public patronized.

Belasco understood well the source of his success and did everything possible to enlarge the physical capacities of his stage. To increase ease and speed in the handling of such large, practicable, and solid architectural settings, the Belasco Theatre was remodeled in 1902. For its reopening on September 29, with the revival of *DuBarry*, the entire stage was replanned as a mosaic of trap doors. In addition, the center of the floor became " 'an elevator,'—that is, in fact, a movable platform,—fifteen feet wide and thirty feet long. Upon this platform, when it had been lowered into the cellar cavity, were placed the paraphernalia required in the setting of the scenes. . . 'properties'. . . 'set pieces,'. . . which were then raised to the stage level for use."[127] In this way, solid and more elaborate stage pictures could be managed with greater ease.

While *DuBarry* reproduced the period of Louis XV, *The Darling of the Gods*, which opened on December 3, 1902, at the Belasco Theatre in New York, took place in Japan during the period of the "sword Edict." Less emphasis was placed upon the archaeological reconstruction of the period than upon romanticized pictures of the times. Five long acts held an audience "largely because of its interest in the wonderful pictures of another civilization than its own."[128] To satisfy this interest, Belasco created a spectacle of superb opulence. The original production cost, in 1902, $78,000, and it has been reported by William Winter that operating expenses left a profit of only $5,000 in two years.[129] This may reflect the decline of the popularity of the pictorial stage under the competition of the film.

Some study was devoted to "plates of Hokusai and other Masters,"[130] but the actual result did not stress historical accuracy. Rather, according to Winter, the play was "a unique fabric of fancy, wildly romantic, rich and strange with unusual characters. . . occasionally mystical with implications of Japanese customs and religious beliefs, opulent with an Oriental splendor of atmosphere and detail.[131] Scenes were carefully devised to "intoxicate the eye, drug the senses with their blending of hue and tone; even the nostrils were assailed by drowsy odors."[132] The production falls somewhere between circus and Henry Irving spectacle. Belasco's stage in this play was described as "a picture of many-colored costumes, tripping geishas, screen bearers, mousmes, jugglers, acrobats, incense bearers, richly and quaintly armored warriors."[133]

The great resort to pictorial sensation for its own sake brought here a degenerate form of the archaeological spectacle play of Irving. The combination suggests a certain similarity to the screen work of George Méliès. For example, the play opens with a picture called The Feast of a Thousand Welcomes, where "fireworks and lights and showers of paperlike confetti, following the acrobats and tumblers,"[134] and all manner of strange sights are introduced to impress the audience. The spectacle appeal of the production was achieved by all sorts of exotic excesses. In The Red Bamboo Grave, "the stage is literally strewn with suicides."[135] And finally, The Brink of the River of Souls shows a vast gorge in the mountain of Sheide. "The smoke-like water swirls and eddies and rushes downward toward the fire of Hades. Through the water shadowy forms of men and women pass, striving against the current to reach the harbor of paradise."[136] Romantic or supernatural sequences were seldom merely suggested but were usually realistically illustrated.

To these many pictorial values, architectural settings, costumes, lights, supernatural effects, fireworks, and tableaux were added the strains of a continuous musical accompaniment. "The incidental music was incessant. . . At times, when the band beneath was silent, tinkling Japanese instruments and shrill Japanese songs took up the burden."[137] Productional characteristics of the entire preceding century were excessively developed in this presentation. Belasco did not stand alone.

It would seem that the crescendo in the matter of magnificent stage production which began two weeks ago with *Mary of Magdala,* then modulated to *Julius Caesar,* surely culminated last night at the Belasco Theatre in the gorgeous, fragrant, fantastic Japanese drama by David Belasco and John Luther Long entitled *The Darling of the Gods.*[138]

Belasco forms one of the salients of the large movement toward the photographic ideal of this motion-picture kind of theatre.

From Japan he shifted his attention to the British Isles. *Sweet Kitty Bellairs,* adapted by Belasco from a story by Egerton Castle, opened on December 9, 1903, and ran till June 4, 1904. Pictures of a different age, place, and time were staged: "The old English city of Bath is shown in a beautiful picture, and therein is displayed a populous, animated scene, constructed to exhibit as a background the raiment, manners, morals and pursuits of Bath society, in the butterfly days that Smollett and Sheridan have made immortal."[139] From scenes of life in old England, his tragedy *Adria,* written in collaboration with John Luther Long, switched in the following season to a "wonderful picture of human life in the antique world."[140] Its presentation at the Belasco Theatre on January 11, 1905, sought to meet the challenge of the film by sheer scenic quantity, which brought nothing more than the defect of excess— "an excess of persons, objects, pictures."[141] Thence, from classical times he turned, on November 27, 1906, to "the sleepy, picturesque Spanish missions of Southern California,"[142] with *Rose of the Rancho,* based on *Juanita,* an earlier play by R. W. Tully. Both the subject and its pictorial treatment resembled in approach Griffith's *Ramona.* Although it was noted that the production was less significant as a play than as a scenic illustration, it nevertheless ran for six months. "The investiture of this play, indeed, blending old Spanish architecture with a semi-tropical wealth of natural beauty, was literally magnificent and considerably excelled the worth of the play itself."[143]

New realistic lighting effects were achieved and experimentation with color was attempted. Belasco wrote:

> To get the strong sunlight of my beloved California and the wonderful shades and tones of sunset, night and dawn as they come out there I had my electrician, Louis Hartman, carry our experiments to the point of making our own colors for our lamps, as we could find none on the market that would give me the desired result. . . I took *twenty-five electricians* with me to Boston, for the opening of *The Rose:* usually two or three are enough with any company.[144]

The care and attention Belasco gave to lighting was by no means accidental. Artificial lighting in the film had not yet become practical and was not in general use. Belasco met the competition of the new pictorial medium by moving into areas where he might still enjoy a limited monopoly. In *Rose of the Rancho* his choice of subject was unfortunate, for in the outdoor sequences, primarily because of the greater flexibility of the camera, D. W. Griffith's *Ramona* was soon to demonstrate the inferiority of the pictorial stage.

In the next season Belasco chose the early American period, presenting *The Warrens of Virginia,* by William De Mille, at the Belasco Theatre on December 3, 1907. Again, as William Winter reported, "The predominant element in it is picture, but it contains much incident."[145] In this play, Cecil B. De Mille, playing a small role, absorbed the Belasco approach for subsequent use in motion pictures. Combining melodrama with spectacle, the "stage dresses and pictures were, in every detail historically correct and characteristic of the period to which the play relates."[146] The arrival of the film did not discourage Belasco in his realistic-pictorial technique. Throughout the single-reel period of the early film he competed with the photographic medium on its own terms, even attempting plays which possessed no merit beyond that of his stage pictures. As late as January 8, 1913, *A Good Little Devil* offered a stage accouterment at the Republic Theatre "so beautiful, so full of the poetic feeling and allurement, conspicuously absent from the piece itself, that it gained and for some time held, and deserved to hold, popular favor."[147] Thus the basic pictorial approach in staging method continued with Belasco into the days of the silent feature film.

Belasco's effort in the field of the spectacle play coincided with the final phase in the development of the motion picture. Both came to satisfy a similar aesthetic preference, namely, the taste for pictorial realism. That Belasco presented on his stage many years before the cinema's arrival material which was later taken over as prime subject for the photographic medium throws light upon the forces, sociological and aesthetic, working behind the invention of the motion picture. The realism of his spectacle stagings reached a peak in the final decade of the century, at about the time of the original demonstrations of the vitascope. The immediate popularity of the new medium did not bring about Belasco's retirement from the spectacle stage. On the contrary, he sought to meet this new competition with ever more realistic and elaborate productions which encompassed a variety of historical periods and places and which, through successful experimentation with the new electrical-light source, developed areas forbidden to the early motion picture. In this fashion he retained much of his audience into the years of the silent film.

Belasco as a Producer of Melodrama

Whether in the production of spectacle or melodrama or in a combination of the two, Belasco's aim—to present a heightened form of pictorial drama—did not vary. He understood the growing dissatisfaction with the conventional methods of presenting melodrama and predicated his entire career upon an improvement of the techniques. With J. A. Herne he revamped a melodrama by Henry Leslie called *The Mariner's Compass*, and produced it first at the Baldwin Theatre in San Francisco on September 9, 1879, as *Chums*, and later at Hamlin's Theatre, Chicago, on November 17, 1879, as *Hearts of Oak*. William Winter claims that its realistic "trappings" were entirely Belasco's contribution.

Real water, real beans, real boiled potatoes, and various other ingredients of a real supper, together with a real cat and a real (and much discontented) baby, were among the real objects employed in the representation. . . Herne somewhat improved the play in the course of his protracted repetitions of it, after he parted from Belasco, but he always retained in it the "real" trappings which Belasco had introduced.[148]

This addition of the intimate details of daily life became a favorite Belasco technique for heightening the realism of his stage pictures.

The same style was still in use twenty years later when *The First Born* by Francis Powers was produced at the Manhattan Theatre, October 5, 1897. The popularity of the earliest topical films with their photographic reproduction of actual scenes from far and near provided a certain competition in the matter of realism in stage settings. The play took place in San Francisco's Chinatown. Every care was taken to reproduce "scenes and incidents in the life of the Chinese with which it deals."[149] The opening street scene in San Francisco "was very Chinese in appearance, with its open shop fronts, its working pipe repairer, its market folk, its porters with yokes and poles, its groups of school children, its

Babel of strange talk, and its general picturesqueness, animation and colour."[150] To heighten the illusion of the settings it was noted that "some of the minor groups and occasionally some of the principal characters speak in Chinese."[151] This visual and aural realism was augmented by an olfactory realism, described in a contemporary review: "The entertainment last night began with small whiffs of sickening, nauseating odor that was burned for atmospheric and not for seweristic reasons. The theatre was bathed in this hideous, tinkative odor of incense, and during the long overture, you sat there getting fainter and fainter."[152] Belasco apparently had found areas in which the screen could not pursue him. And, of course, "the orchestra contributes its share by inflicting upon the listeners noises that purport to be a fair sample of the Chinese notion of music."[153]

The play dealt with a sordid and sensational situation. A son's mysterious death must be avenged by his father. Murder is committed in full sight of the audience—a hatchet murder, omitting none of its simple and brutal details. Wang has been waiting in the shadows of the doorway. Quietly, he

sets down his pipe inside, rolls up his cuff from his wrist, seizes the short, shiny, little high binder's hatchet. . . Now comes Yek, trudging carelessly along. He has just passed the door when the avenger leaps upon him, chopping the hatchet half a dozen times into his neck and back. . . . Now he drags the body into the house, leaps back to the door, resumes his pipe and stands there in assumed serenity as the curtain falls.[154]

The entire production was mounted and played with a reproductional quality akin to that of the motion-picture camera.

Such sensational action was supported by equally spectacular stage pictures. Belasco's *American Born*, adapted from *British Born* by Merritt and Pettitt and produced on July 10, 1881, employed "a volcano in furious eruption,"[155] providing, in this way, the same kind of theatrical appeal that was to be found fifteen years later in the first screen topical episodes.

Prior to the arrival of the film, Belasco made certain attempts, in his presentation of melodrama, to increase the speed of scene changes. He saw the possibility for developing greater suspense and climax through more rapid pictorial cross-cutting between parallel lines of action. In this connection his production of Boucicault's *The Octoroon* at the Baldwin Theatre, San Francisco, June 12, 1881, is an interesting case. To develop maximum climax in the chase sequence between Wahnotee and McCloskey, he sought a staging technique which would facilitate rapid pictorial cross-cutting. To accomplish this, he wrote:

I used a panorama, painted on several hundred yards of canvas, and I introduced drops, changing scenes in the twinkling of an eye, showing, alternately and in quick succession, pursued and pursuer,—*Jacob McCloskey* and the *Indian,*—making their way through the canebrake and swamp, and ending with the life and death struggle and the killing of *McCloskey.*[156]

Belasco approached the pictorial development of the stage play much in the way that early film directors approached the chase sequence. In the need for a rapid succession of stage pictures Belasco had supplemented the conventional methods with the panorama. He had thus attempted, in a limited way, the kind of pictorial sequence which would suggest the motion picture.

Such productions as this, under the pressure of pictorial requirement, employed certain conventional methods in the eighties which would no longer be tolerated in the metropolitan areas of the nineties. Consequently, Belasco's melodrama, just prior to the appearance of the motion picture, attained a photographic realism. Embodying all the cinematic characteristics of the stock melodrama of the period, *The Girl I Left Behind Me,* by Belasco and Franklin Fyles, was offered at the opening of the Empire Theatre on January 25, 1893. Parallel lines of action were developed pictorially to provide climax at their intersection. Stage pictures here, however, were not conventional. The main line of action, frontier warfare between pioneers and Indians, takes place at

the stockade of logs surrounding the Post. There has been an all-night vigil, with fierce, intermittent fighting. The time is just before daybreak. The first faint gray of light is beginning to steal into the sky; there is a reflected glow of distant fires, and, far off, yet clear and indescribably horrible, are heard the "blip-blip" of the Indian war-drums and the shrill, hideous cries of the savage warriors.[157]

This battle is fought "from a period before sunset through sunset, twilight and into moonlight." The moon cannot be seen, but its rays are "shown piercing the darkness in the most natural way possible."[158] As dawn breaks, Kate Kennion, the heroine, to complicate the main line of action, begins a tributary line by asking her father to shoot her through the head should the Indians succeed in capturing the fort. Outside the Indians gain across the clearing. The fight mounts. "The patter of the bullets on the stockade"[159] is heard as pioneers fall wounded from the ramparts. Inside the old man is raising his pistol slowly to Kate's head. Outside the Indians are scaling the walls; inside the old man begins to repeat the Lord's Prayer. At this point suspense is heightened by the introduction of a third line of action, that of the United States Cavalry speeding to relieve the besieged garrison. Just as her father is about to pull the trigger, Kate imagines she hears hoofbeats. The old man does not hear them and accuses Kate of losing courage. She insists on waiting as the pounding grows louder. The Indians are on the point of breaking down the gate. Her father will wait no longer. She shrieks and grapples with him over the gun. Just as the Indians crash through and rush upon the couple, in dash troopers of the United States Cavalry "upon horseback."[160] Dialogue is of small consequence as the stage picture dominates: "The onrush of the dozen mounted cavalry men, covered with alkali dust, is something which will live in the memory. It is an exact copy of many such a scene."[161] Climax comes with the intersection of three parallel lines of action. The pictures, of course, were

put upon the stage in a very realistic way, even to the white "alkali dust" that gathers on the uniforms of the troopers. The fidelity to the real conditions of army life in the West is noticeable throughout every scene. . . The very chant of the attacking Indians was an example of this; the pages of Puck and Judge on the walls of the barrack room, the stockade near the gate.[162]

Belasco thus scrapped many of the conventional techniques. By using built-up scenery, adding a troop of mounted cavalry, and loading the production with many minor but significant realistic items, he had enhanced the cinematic characteristics of this popular form with realistic stage pictures.

Similarly, *The Heart of Maryland,* written by Belasco and produced by him at the Herald Square Theatre in New York on October 22, 1895, combined the two qualities of theatrical expression, the realistic and the romantic, which emanated from Garrick and culminated in the motion picture. Contemporary opinion conceded that it was "as perfect a combination of realism and romanticism as one can possibly conceive."[163] This production took place one month after the showing of the vitascope in the South. Unlike Boucicault, who had been content to focus his skill upon a single realistic scenic sensation while the remainder of his production floundered in conventionality, Belasco staged this melodrama with a thoroughgoing precision in the realism of all his stage pictures. When Boucicault brought out *The Octoroon* at the Winter Garden, "he bent all his energies upon the famous steamboat scene with its bales of cotton, its army of black slaves, and its tremendous explosion which brought the curtain down to a thunderstorm of applause. But the other scenes of *The Octoroon* were full of all sorts of aggravating anachronisms."[164] When Belasco picked up the thread of romanticism with the popular melodramatic form, he brought a new realism to the work of such men as Boucicault. "*The Heart of Maryland* is continuously careful and effective. Mr. Belasco has left nothing to chance. The play is brimful of scenes which depend, to a large extent, upon effective accessories; each of these scenes is perfect in its way."[165]

His first picture, showing the ancestral home of the Calvert family, "an old Colonial mansion, deep-bowered among ancient, blooming lilac bushes and bathed in the fading glow of late afternoon and sunset light, was one of truly memorable loveliness."[166] As the action progressed, the picture, through changes of lighting, took life. Sound effects were carefully planned and carefully cued: "When the clatter of horse hoofs has died away, there is silence on the stage. The trickle of the spring of real water is distinctly heard. The water comes from a rubber hose behind the canvas rocks."[167] When the army makes its entrance, the same realism is apparent.

Each man in the line is individual and different from his comrade, both in makeup and uniform. One has torn sleeves and a rough black beard, another has a whole uniform but a ragged hat and a scar over his right eye. A third is a sturdy old man with gray hair and clear cut features. A fourth has muddy boots. A fifth with bright red hair carries his arm in a sling. And so on with the rest.[168]

Like Boucicault, Belasco saw the value of a single great spectacular scene in the play and brought to it the same realism that characterized the rest of the production. In *The Heart of Maryland* it was the famous Belfry Scene. At the "exterior of an old church" Mrs. Leslie Carter, playing Maryland, stabs Thorpe, frees her lover, Alan, and induces him to escape. Thorpe regains consciousness and orders the bell to be rung that announces the escape of a prisoner. The stage grows dark, and as the lights are brought up again, the Belfry Tower, filling the height of the stage, looms into view. "With a supreme effort, Mrs. Carter rushes up the stairs of the tower and clutches the bell tongue. Then she swings backward and forward for fully two minutes, while audience and actor watch her with bated breath. The tower is forty feet high, but from the floor it looks to be sixty feet."[169] The bell, of course, will not ring and her lover is saved. It was this "white vision against the blackness of night"[170] that audiences came to see. Without sacrificing the basic spectacular requirements of this romantic form, Belasco added his own brand of realism, creating stage pictures which brought the entire cycle of nineteenth-century pictorial theatre to a level approaching cinema.

Later on, Belasco found himself competing with the new pictorial medium on its own terms, oftentimes with certain success. *The Girl of the Golden West,* presented at the Belasco Theatre, New York, November 14, 1905, takes places in 1849 around a mining camp on Cloudy Mountain, California. Such a locale could be presented in its entirety by the motion picture. Belasco attempted to paint this whole area on curtains, drops, and panoramas, and to introduce these in a cinematic fashion. The front curtain represented a panoramic landscape of the mountains in the distance.

It consists of a scene painted in "poster" manner, representing four trees well in the foreground, behind which is a stretch of neutral color dotted with . . . sage brush. Back of this stretch rise blackish green mountains over the central dip in which shines a setting sun, and above which are clouds of red, and yellow and gray. The sun is illuminated by placing a light behind it.[171]

When the play was about to begin, the house was darkened gradually, the sun faded out, and the "curtain" rose silently and unseen as the lights were brought up on a panoramic view moving vertically across the proscenium opening in the fashion of a motion-picture vertical panorama shot. The vertical sequence started where the front curtain stopped, at sundown, showing first the "heights of the mountains with the moon shining over them and the gleam of the light from the hut where the 'Girl' lives,"[172] and thence "booming" downward.

Moon, mountains, and hut rise slowly upward, and we see farther and farther into the valley until finally at the base of the mountain we have before us the red lights from the window of "The Polka," the drinking place where the "Girl" has her business. There is the sound of music and singing from the saloon, the "picture" fades and we are inside the saloon.[173]

The use of the vertical painted panorama here combined the "pan" shot with a "track" shot as the audience moved into the valley and toward the red lights of the windows of the Polka.

The settings themselves, with their innumerable properties, carried pictorial realism to a new level. The saloon, for instance, was

an elaborate setting and includes every bit of furniture, bric-a-brac, and decoration that possibly could be put into such a place. . . The second act shows the interior of the "Girl's" hut, and here stage setting is carried to the last limit. There is nothing there that might not be in such a place, but there is everything that possibly could. Mexican blankets, calico hangings, fur rugs, lace curtains, table spreads, everything hangable, layable or standable is put on the stage for that scene.[174]

This itemized style of setting was carried into the acting, where it resulted in an elaborate kind of pantomimic "touches" and highly pictorial business. For example, when Johnson, pursued by Sheriff Rance, comes to the "Girl's" hut looking for a hideout, she puts him in the loft. Rance arrives, searches the cabin, cannot find him, takes the Girl's word that he is not in the loft, and, about to depart, turns momentarily in the doorway "to speak to the *Girl*, holding a white handkerchief with which he has wiped the snow from his face; as he does so, a drop of blood falls from the helpless wounded man above him upon the handkerchief, then another,— and *Rance,* watching the little crimson stain grow, instantly comprehends."[175] In certain climactic moments the play hinged upon these pictorial "touches"; often they served as embellishments, comic or otherwise. On one occasion, ten minutes were devoted to watching "two Indians wipe whipped cream off a piece of paper in which Charlotte Russe had been wrapped, and lick the cream from their fingers."[176] These touches of detailed pantomime and of itemized property business are strongly characteristic of Belasco's method for heightening the realism of the stage picture.

And, as usual with the melodrama, at least one of these pictures must attain spectacular proportions. In this play it was a blizzard scene equaling, if not exceeding, the reproductional thrill of the cinema. William Winter has described it in detail.

Nothing of the kind which I have ever seen in the theatre has fully equalled in verisimilitude the blizzard on Cloudy Mountain as depicted by Belasco in the Second Act of this fine melodrama,—such a bitter and cruel storm of wind-driven snow and ice as he had often suffered under in the strolling days of his nomadic youth. When the scene, the interior of the *Girl's* log-cabin, was disclosed the spectators perceived, dimly, through windows at the back, a far vista of rugged, snow-clad mountains which gradually faded from vision as the fall of snow increased and the casements became obscured by sleet. Then, throughout the progress of the action, intensifying the sense of desolation, dread and terror, the audience heard the wild moaning and shrill whistle of the gale, and at moments, as the tempest rose to a climax of fury, could see the fine-powdered snow driven in tiny sprays and eddies through every crevice of the walls and the very fabric of the cabin quiver and rock beneath the impact of terrific blasts of wind,—long,—shrieking down the mountain sides before they struck,—while in every fitful pause was audible the sharp click-click-click of freezing snow driving on wall and window. . . the operation of the necessary mechanical contrivances required a force of thirty-two trained artisans,—a sort of mechanical orchestra, directed by a centrally placed conductor who was visible from the special station of every worker. . . the perfectly harmonious *effect* of this remarkable imitation of a storm necessitated that at every performance exactly the same thing should be done on the stage at, to the second, exactly the prearranged instant.[177]

Having once accepted the standards of the motion picture, Belasco's attempts to meet its competition carried him further and further into the development of productional aspects until, indeed, he discarded the robe of the dramatist for that of the stage mechanic. And it was such mechanical magic that enabled him to survive the cinema while his colleagues either failed or fled to the provinces. Even as late as 1915 his production of *Vanderdecken,* an old nineteenth-century favorite, succeeded on the same basis. The romanticized pictorial approach remained Belasco's forte into the years of the feature film, reviving old material with new reproductional stagings even as did the cinema.

Belasco and the Drama of Intimate Realism

The quality which may be defined as that of intimate realism colored the entire body of Belasco's production. Certain plays, however, were written particularly for this style of presentation and boasted it as their chief merit. As early as 1884 his *May Blossom,* produced at Madison Square Garden, succeeded largely through its development of the "Robertson-Antoine" realism of homely and intimate details. It was typically sentimental, and it was "this great heart interest. . . added to its pictures of homely life, well filled in as regards details, which has given to it an already long lease of life."[178] Representative of Belasco's appeal here is the scene in the woods where the children bury a pet bird: "Eight little children take part in the burial of a bird, and their pretty prattle and songs and picturesque grouping make a charming and touching scene."[179] These sentimental and romanticized pictures, intimately developed and replete with significant details, were exactly the same kind of thing that D. W. Griffith used in his first release, *Adventures of Dolly,* in 1908.

When Belasco collaborated with Henry De Mille in writing *The Wife* for production at the Lyceum Theatre, New York, November 1, 1887, they strove to embody in the script the realism of the pictorial "touches" style of acting and characterization. The

players were given the opportunity "to display all those idiosyn-
cracies and qualities which have given them rank and popularity."[180] With its over-supply of pictorial-pantomimic acting, this
production was conceded to be "the best example of a modern
society play interpreted according to the naturalistic methods of
the modern school which is now before the public."[181] This homey,
"daily-routine-of-life" kind of acting was facilitated and heightened by solid interiors, real properties, and reproductional lighting
effects. In the first act, for instance, Jack and Kittie "sat on the
bough of an apple tree, from which they plucked real apples, which
they proceeded to devour,"[182] meanwhile evolving a private little
scene. The same intimate approach is initiated by realistic lighting
effects when the wife reveals to her husband love for another man.
"The room is lighted only by the reflection from the fireplace. The
spectator's vision seems to actually penetrate the privacy of domestic life."[183] A touching scene of family life takes place as if behind the "fourth-wall," gaining much of its dramatic effect through
the emotional quality of its naturalistic lighting. The productional
values here are the same as those described by Vachel Lindsay in
speaking of the early film: "The Intimate Motion Picture is the
world's new medium for studying. . . the half relaxed or gently
restrained moods of human creatures. It gives also our idiosyn-
cracies. It is gossip *in extremis.*"[184]

In continuing the Robertsonian reforms, Belasco realized a
quality which later became the special possession of the intimate
motion picture. Productionally speaking, his success in competing
with this class of films was due largely to the fact that artificial
lighting was inadequate for indoor photography until about 1905-
1906, and that not for still another five or even ten years did it
achieve a flexibility, practicability, and realism comparable to that
of Belasco's. Lighting, then, provided Belasco with a sort of limited
monopoly in this drama of intimate realism.

Zaza, adapted by Belasco from the French original of Pierre
Berton and Charles Simon, and staged at the Garrick Theatre,
New York, January 9, 1899, carried this intimate realism into the
casting and elaboration of minor, background roles. According to
Winter, it was "not so much a play as. . . a series of loosely jointed,

sequent episodes."[185] To capitalize upon the episodic construction of the play, a dual box set made pictorial cross-cutting, from Zaza's brilliantly lighted dressing room to that of the supers and chorines, instantaneous. Here a half-dozen men not connected with the show had access to the actresses. Here rakes and rounders, old and young, mingled with manners as free and easy as those of the women.

The men range from a doddering old rake to a boyish loafer, and the women from a besotted matron to a shy young debutante. The beverages are as strong as brandy and as weak as beer. All these characters are enacted as carefully as though they were to figure throughout the play instead of being merely incidental. They are distinct individuals, they behave naturally.[186]

This thoroughness in the minute details of casting, in the use of properties, and in over-all character interpretation of even minor roles gave Belasco's productions an aura of real life comparable to the photographic ideal.

Belasco often selected his company and his leading players with this single quality in mind. David Warfield's style of acting lent itself particularly well to Belasco's approach. A number of plays, "manufactured" by Belasco and his collaborators, featured Warfield. *The Auctioneer,* by Klein, Arthur, and Belasco, produced at the Hyperion Theatre, New Haven, September 9, 1901, exploited the intimate and minor details of surface reality. According to the *New York Times,* there was "not the least suggestion that the makers of this play—it would not be fair to say authors—have gone to any great trouble to get beneath the surface of things in the conglomerate and intensely human phases of life that have their being east of Broadway."[187] Warfield excelled in this itemized pantomime of surface realities. Large sections of the play were made up of stage "business." For instance, "the second act, which occupies the better part of an hour, probably has less than 400 lines of dialogue." To support this naturalistic style of acting, the old auctioneer's shop was loaded with all sorts of secondhand whatnots, clothing, jewelry, sporting wear, cookery, footwear, haberdashery, household linens, tools, as if it "might have been transported from Hester Street itself." Warfield, turned loose in the midst of this bric-a-brac, automatically achieved the kind of theatre Belasco was after. "Simon's dealings with customers in the first act gave peculiar pleasure. To see him deluge a pile of clothing with water from a watering-pot, then smoke the pile with a tinker's stove, and mark the lot 'Damaged by Fire' . . . surely nothing of this was of much worth yet it afforded an immense amount of amusement."[188]

Similarly, the scene outside a fashionable dry-goods store "was shown as if the corner of Twenty-third Street and Sixth Avenue had been moved bodily to the Bijou's little stage."[189] Even in this early day the photographic quality of this setting was being compared to that of the motion picture.

This Twenty-Third Street scene, with its moving panorama of people, and the exterior of a large dry goods establishment in the foreground is a revelation in the art of stage simulation of street life as it really exists in busy Gotham. One would imagine they were gazing at a motion picture reproduction of the original instead of at men and women and painted canvas scenery.[190]

Whether or not he intended it, Belasco now found himself in competition with the film. Sacrificing pictorial variety, he had achieved a photographic realism upon the stage. Lighting effects, as yet impossible to the screen, were used to create "twilight in an old second-hand shop, just as eloquently beautiful as though it were falling in a rose garden."[191] This kind of reproductional beauty, plus the naturalistic style of acting of which Warfield was a master, provided Belasco with areas of pictorial staging still free from the competition of the cinema.

Belasco was careful to avoid effects which could be surpassed by the screen. *The Music Master,* another "assembly-line" play by Klein, Morris, and Belasco, again starring Warfield, and opening in Atlantic City on September 12, 1904, called for a vision sequence, stock-in-trade effect of the nineteenth-century melodrama. Von Barwig dreams of his past in Leipzig. Discarding the usual two-dimensional wing-and-border settings and vampire traps, the stage mechanics arranged a series of scenes solidly built and mounted on movable platforms or wagons. It was required that a double take Warfield's place on the forestage scene while Warfield played

31. *The Count of Monte Cristo,* Duel Scene (with James O'Neill).

32. *The Count of Monte Cristo,* Port at Marseille.

33. *Treasure Island*, Gangplank of the *Hispaniola* (1917).

34. *Treasure Island*, Battle at the Stockade (1917).

35. *When Knighthood Was in Flower,* Act I (1901), with Julia Marlowe.

36. *Sag Harbor* (1900), with James A. Herne and W. T. Hodge.

37. *Brewster's Millions*, Sailboat Scene (1906).

38. *In Old Kentucky*, Plantation Scene.

39. *The Bridge,* Fight Scene (1909).

40. *Under Two Flags,* produced by Belasco (1901).

41.   Henry Irving as Shylock (1879).

42.   Henry Irving as Macbeth (1888).

43. *Romeo and Juliet,* Crypt Scene designed for Irving's production (1890).

44. *The Dead Heart,* scene designed for Irving's production (1889).

45. *King John,* scene designed by Hawes Craven for Irving's production.

46. *DuBarry*, produced by Belasco (1901), with **Mrs. Leslie Carter.**

47a. *DuBarry,* properties used in Belasco production (1901).

47b. *The Warrens of Virginia,* produced by Belasco (1907).
Left to right: Cecil B. De Mille, Emma Dunn, Frank Keenan, C. D.
Waldron, Raymond Bond.

48. *The Return of Peter Grimm,* produced by Belasco (1911), with David Warfield.

49. *The Auctioneer,* produced by Belasco (1901), with David Warfield.

50. *Aladdin.*

51. *Arabian Nights.*

52. New Comic Pantomime.

53. *Cinderella.*

54. *Forty Thieves.*

55. *Forty Thieves,* advertising streamer.

56. *The Sleeping Beauty.*

through the "flash-back" vision sequence. But, at the last moment, Belasco must have recognized that this had become a clumsy device compared to the kind of dream sequence already seen upon the screen in *The American Fireman*, for "to the surprise of everyone [he] ordered the scenes cut out."[192]

A Grand Army Man, written in conference according to formula by Pauline Phelps, Marion Short, and Belasco, and starring David Warfield, was a similar case. It opened at the Hyperion Theatre in New Haven on September 23, 1907, and moved to New York as "the most realistic American play that has been presented in New York City within the memory of the writer."[193] There were only four scenes. Having given pictorial variety over to the film, Belasco achieved within each of his stage pictures a reproductional quality akin to that of the camera. "The whole performance, down to the last detail of the setting, seems at first glance minutely photographic."[194] For instance, in the rural court scene, described by Franklin Fyles as "one of Belasco's finest studies in realism,"[195] every item of setting and property was painstakingly reproductional. "It was poor and shabby, with worn benches, bare 'gas fixtures,' strips of dilapidated railing, pulpit-like bench, and a dozen other material details."[196] When in the following year Belasco opened Eugene Walter's *The Easiest Way* at Parsons Theatre, Hartford, on December 31, 1908, the same photographic care was apparent.

Nothing was forgotten: the rooms shown were reproductions of fact,—from the rickety wardrobe, with doors that will not close and disordered sheets of music and other truck piled on top of it, in the boarding-house chamber, to the picturesque, discreetly arranged disorder of the opulent apartments, the signs of a drunken orgy, and the artfully disclosed and disordered bed. All that stage management could do to create and deepen the impression of reality was done.[197]

These reproductional interiors, with their realistic lighting, enabled Belasco, even as late as 1908, to develop an area beyond the competitive reach of the motion picture.

As the capacity of the screen in this direction increased, Belasco was driven to extremes. *The Governor's Lady* (1912) became, in Belasco's words, "a play in three acts and an epilogue in Child's."[198]

It was reported that a section of a Child's Restaurant was actually transported to the stage of the Republic Theatre. A peak seems to have been reached in this staging of the drama of intimate realism beyond which progress apparently was impossible. The pattern was continued by Belasco with success into the years of World War I and the feature film, and has, of course, since been exploited by the motion picture, even to the present day.

With the uncanny instinct of a showman, Belasco, soon after the arrival of the motion picture, had apparently sensed an irrefutable rivalry and had recognized that his work, while moving in the same plane as the film, must not run directly against its competition. Thus, while he never abandoned his reproductional techniques, he strove, through the drama of intimate realism, to outrival the screen by an exploitation of certain specific areas. These were essentially two, namely, (1) acting in the restrained, naturalistic, pictorial "touches" style, loaded with graphic business,[199] and (2) settings of interiors, reproductionally lighted, architecturally constructed, and filled with a multitude of realistic, authentic, and recognizable details. In these two areas Belasco suffered little interference from the early motion picture.

The end result of the realistic reforms which had occurred during the sixties, seventies, eighties, and nineties could hardly have been anticipated by the reformers. That an entirely new medium should have appeared, better satisfying the same audience preference they had striven earnestly to meet, could hardly have entered the minds of Daly, Bancroft, Antoine, or the Duke of Saxe-Meiningen. Yet before the century was spent, these aesthetic tastes had crystallized. Their cumulative demands had grown so large and so urgent that it now seems that the cinema alone could fully have satisfied them. This scale and urgency is reflected in the work of Belasco and his colleagues.

To the spectacle, to the melodrama, and to the drama of intimate realism, Belasco brought his own gift of the photographic ideal. To the cinematic conception embodied in these theatrical fields, he imparted a cinematic productional quality, thus satisfying the taste for theatrical motion pictures years before the motion-picture camera. With the arrival of the film Belasco did not relinquish his audience, but, by newer efforts in the same old pictorial directions, he sought, and, in many instances, succeeded in meeting the competition of the film. Thus, under the influence of the motion picture, Belasco continued the century-old graphic style of theatrical production beyond the point at which reaction might otherwise have occurred.

III. STEELE MACKAYE

Each of the great triumvirate in the nineteenth-century pictorial theatre of realism and romance represents a particular stage in the culminating phase of this cycle. The contribution of Steele MacKaye was cut short by death just a year before the vitascope was exhibited. The popularity of Irving reached its peak simultaneously with the arrival of the film, and subsequently lessened as he was rapidly relegated to the provinces. Belasco came closest to the photographic ideal—not prior to the cinema, but after its popularity had been established. Chronologically speaking, MacKaye came first, Irving second, and Belasco last. But Steele MacKaye's contribution to the realistic development of romantic staging was, in his short career, of a larger scale than that of his colleagues.

His basic approach to theatre will be found, first of all, in his plays and dramatic productions. His attempts to enlarge the physical capacities of the stage in the cinematic direction will be found in his mechanical inventions. And lastly, his spectacle stagings, utilizing this inventive ability, illustrate the vast expense and effort consumed to satisfy an aesthetic preference so easily filled by the cinema.

MacKaye as Author and Theatrical Producer

MacKaye was not a revolutionist. From the start his contributions, while creative, dared no transgression against the pictorial mode of theatre then in vogue. In 1875 he adapted *Rose Michel* from the French of Ernest Blum for A. M. Palmer. It was produced on November 23 of that year at the Union Square Theatre with scenery by R. Marston. Nym Crinkle (Andrew C. Wheeler) wrote that MacKaye told his "story from first to last. . . by action."[200] This adaptation had something in common with the silent film, for another reviewer, writing that "pantomime and picture are unquestionably the prime essentials of good drama," proclaimed that to test the excellence of this play "it is only necessary to take the language out."[201] This provides an excellent definition of pre-cinema theatrical standards. Dialogue was unimportant, as "each incident lived in the memory as a vivid picture."[202] The photographic analogy present in this production was not lost. "So cunningly have the playwright and the manager set this fable in vital tints, so deftly have they fashioned its living parts, that every phase of it is a photograph in itself, either of character or of situation."[203] This pictorial kind of playwriting was supported by equally realistic stage views which "are rather built than painted,"[204] and "which leave nothing whatever to be added for the imaginative eyes."[205]

MacKaye's own plays, in keeping with nineteenth-century theatrical traditions, were melodramatic, dependent upon external effects, and replete with the cinematic conceptions of this dramatic form. Oftentimes, as in the film, such plays would find successive productions under fresh titles while the spectacular effects which sponsored the original venture remained the same. *Through the Dark*, first produced at the Fifth Avenue Theatre, New York, on March 10, 1879, was revived as *A Noble Rogue* at the Chicago Opera House, July 3, 1888, and as *Money Mad* at the Standard Theatre, New York, April 7, 1890. The plot, of course, was "very much on the dime-novel order,"[206] but audiences came to see the pictures which were both sensational and realistic. A great model of the Clark Street drawbridge was mechanically reproduced on the stage for the Chicago opening. Dramatic conflict arose from the physical aspects of this setting. At the moment that the villain of the piece, Hack Murray, pursuing the hero's father, overtakes him by sleigh at the foot of the bridge, "the bridge swings open for a vessel to pass and prevents the son from going to his father's assistance and the latter is overpowered and thrown into the river."[207] When the show moved to New York as *Money Mad*, Nym Crinkle wrote glowingly:

Nothing in all the important sensations of English melodrama can compare, in structural audacity and pictorial effectiveness, with this bridge scene, as MacKaye now presents it. The very idea of swinging a causeway fifty feet long across the whole stage for the passage of a lake propeller at least sixty feet long, will cause a success of wonderment.[208]

In Boston, "a smoking, snorting tugboat"[209] followed the steamer. At the Grand Opera House, San Francisco, to heighten suspense and climax during the attempted murder, the steamer became 112 feet long and a tank of real water was used for the drowning. The steamer, as in the other productions, was rolled up in the fashion of a panorama, and the bridge was swung out over the audience. As the steamer passed slowly through the night across the proscenium opening, "a realistic illusion of soft cabin lights, ship's gongs and marine whistles sounding . . . electrified the audience, above whose heads . . . the cries of the hero . . . rang out through the auditorium, as he shouted frantically to the play-characters on the stage."[210]

Dialogue itself had no significance. The plot hinged entirely upon the situation and the reproductional, mechanical aspects of the setting. Indeed, the photographic realism of the entire scene nearly broke the aesthetic distance, for the cries of Wilton Lackaye to the bridgekeeper, who refused to close the draw, and the curses, grunts, and pleadings of the figures fighting in the dark became "almost too real to be pleasant."[211] While the motion picture, blessed with a greater aesthetic distance, might carry this sort of sensational realism to a higher level, the stage had apparently reached its limit with this particular production.

Steele MacKaye's many melodrama productions all possess the cinematic qualities characteristic of the period. That he was at the head of the procession racing toward the photographic ideal can scarcely stand dispute. *Anarchy; or, Paul Kauvar,* written by MacKaye for production in Buffalo on May 30, 1887, and in New York at the Standard Theatre on December 24, 1887, was called "a superb realisation upon the stage of one of the grandest eras in human history,"[212] and, according to Nym Crinkle, surpassed the efforts of even Henry Irving: *"Paul Kauvar* is a play of action, action, action. . . You are asked only to look and vibrate.—So with

Mr. Henry Irving's productions. . . But this is the point: *Mr. Steele MacKaye has outreached with pictorial art all our importers.*[213] The play, obviously, did "not belong to the order of dramatic composition that depends mainly upon dialogue for success," but like the motion picture, "its vital elements are action, incident and situation."[214] These concepts of playwriting were supported by realistic and spectacular stage pictures which could "speak to the heart as no words of poet, historian or dramatist could speak."[215] Nym Crinkle, holding that as a stage artificer MacKaye had no equal, described the vision effect at the end of the first act where the hero dreams of his beloved, Diane, at the guillotine as "electrical":

> I have never seen a theatric picture whose subject was so terrible, whose action—as the heroine mounts the scaffold in her grey dress and falls into the horrible arms of the executioner—was so quick a combination of life and illusion. Had it been done by Mr. Henry Irving, this dream scene would have been recognized as an unparagoned triumph of realism. But nothing that Mr. Irving has attempted in this country at all approaches it in artistic ensemble, in pictorial effect, or in mechanical execution.[216]

None of the gruesome details were spared and it is no wonder that Diane fainted into the arms of the executioner who, while she mounts the steps leading to the platform of death, "takes from the bloody knife the dripping head of the last victim."[217] Speaking of this tableaux, the contemporary press proclaimed, in terms which indicate its clear relationship to the film, that the production's "most skillful invention is a silent picture."[218] This spectacular scene is close kin to one of the earliest topical-episode films, the *Beheading of Mary Stuart,* made in 1895. Motion tableaux, silent pictures, were used throughout *Paul Kauvar* to picturize its significant and climatic moments. Two more, The Conquest of Evil and Liberty, were added several weeks after its New York opening to counterbalance Anarchy. It has, indeed, been noted that Steele MacKaye, with this production, "presented . . . a vital sequence of 'living pictures' in motion, more than a generation before the advent of the modern vitagraph."[219]

These tableaux derived much of their vitality and realism from the groupings, vocal patterns, and movements of the mob. Percy MacKaye, Steele MacKaye's son, has made the following claim:

> *Paul Kauvar* was the first American play (perhaps the first modern play) technically builded upon mass effects in production, visual and aural; that is, the large ensemble situations, the half-distinguishable dialogue of the mob (which appears in no printed or manuscript text), the tempo and flux of its rhythmic sound-surges were structurally . . . intrinsic parts of the plot and motivation, not introduced for mere whirling clamour and spectacle, but to clarify and impersonate dramatic significances of the play's national folk-theme.[220]

Thus, in the fashion described by early screen critic Vachel Lindsay as the "Motion Picture of Crowd Splendor," MacKaye had developed a dynamic, personalized mob which, as a unit, became the most significant single dramatis personae in these scenes. The pattern of aural-visual relationships presents an interesting analogy to modern methods in the sound film. The connection here between Steele MacKaye and D. W. Griffith will become more obvious in subsequent examinations of the early motion picture, for, like the great mobs of *Judith of Bethulia* or *Intolerance,* the mob of *Paul Kauvar* became "a hideous rabble of maniacal men and women, inflamed with passion and liquor and led by Carrac—a notorious and bloodthirsty monster. *Human realism cannot go much further than it has gone in this mob.*"[221] John Carboy of the *New York Despatch* wrote: "The demoniac madness; the wild fury, the bloodthirsty desperation and the brutality of a Parisian revolutionary mob, have never before had so truthful and impressive a showing upon the stage in this country."[222] Even David Belasco conceded that this amazing mob scene "was the first genuine, thrilling mob we ever had."[223]

And, as with the earliest of motion pictures, the incidental music "was suited to the action, as Paul Kauvar's entrance was heralded by a certain figure, and the onslaught of the mob was accompanied by the anarchic theme."[224] MacKaye's success, then, with this play, as, indeed, throughout his career, came from the exploitation of external productional values: scenery, mass movements, spectacular action, tableaux, visions, all on a reproductional level and thoroughly integrated by music. His approach to theatre was entirely in terms of motion pictures and, ironically enough, the performance of *Paul Kauvar* in London at the Crown Theatre, Peckham, April 9, 1900, was followed by "an exhibition of Edisonograph war pictures."[225]

There is hardly need to elaborate further upon MacKaye's techniques in the staging of melodrama. His intentions, achievements, and contributions are clear. His conception of theatre was largely visual, and his concern with language small. He exploited the optical qualities of theatrical presentation through reproductional scenery, thrilling action-tableaux, spectacular sequences, and gripping visions. His stagings often achieved a three-dimensional, architectural quality sometimes surpassing those of Henry Irving but always moving toward the photographic ideal.

MacKaye's achievement as writer and producer of melodrama forms the least significant part of his contribution to the American theatre. His cinematic leanings and accomplishments were even greater in the other two branches of his theatrical activity.

MacKaye as Theatrical Inventor

In the theatre of melodrama Steele MacKaye conformed to the pattern set by his colleagues and predecessors. Like Belasco and Irving, he continued and enlarged upon the basic traditions of the nineteenth-century theatre of realism and romance. But between the lines of the preceding section is to be found an occasional suggestion of dissatisfaction with existing staging facilities. Steele MacKaye, more so than his colleagues, was an inventor of staging devices. This genius was focused upon carrying the legitimate stage into the orbit of the motion picture and marked his greatest contribution to the theatre of the nineteenth century.

In 1879, the Madison Square Theatre was remodeled under MacKaye's direction. It was opened on February 4, 1880, with his own play *Hazel Kirke*. All changes were governed, according to MacKaye, by the desire "to focus attention, time and money on the creative art of the stage picture itself."[226] He recognized the value of musical accompaniment to support the external nature of his staging technique and at the same time felt the need for eliminating the distraction of an orchestra playing directly in front of the stage picture. A platform was built above and behind the proscenium opening and here the musicians sat, invisible to the audience, playing their musical illustrations for the stage picture below. In addition to this, an elevator stage[227] was installed. This was designed, according to MacKaye, to enable him "to sort and distribute our scenery upon three floors, instead of huddling it upon one; to control the waits between acts, avoiding tedious delays; and to produce scenic effects impossible upon any other stage."[228] Sensing the new dislike of metropolitan audiences for the conventional staging methods and not yet willing to sacrifice speed and variety in his scenic pictures, he was able, through the use of the elevator stage, to fulfill the pictorial requirements of this romantic theatre with solid, built-out, and practicable settings. This was one of MacKaye's early solutions of the breakdown of the conventions.

When, five years later, on April 6, 1885, the New Lyceum Theatre was opened, the distraction of the orchestra playing its descriptive music in front of the stage picture was eliminated in a spectacular fashion. Its platform, properly counterweighted, was flown above and behind the upper edge of the proscenium opening just before the beginning of the play. It is also to be noted that, "for the first time,"[229] the stage of this theatre was completely equipped with electricity.

Further confirmation of his pictorial conception of theatre and of his belief that certain forms of drama might dispose of dialogue altogether was given in 1892, when MacKaye applied for a patent for a "Silent Unfolding Announcer Appliance for Theatres," stating that its purpose was "to provide means by which the performance or scene which is being exhibited may be automatically explained or interpreted by a silent unfolding announcer, without subjecting the audience to the annoyance incident to an oral explanation."[230] This and other devices were carried out and demonstrated in connection with his Spectatorium and his Scenitorium.

At the same time he filed application for patents for an "Illumiscope," "Colourator," and so forth, developing further techniques for heightening the scenic illusion. These were intended to provide means for the improvement of scenic illumination upon the stage and the increase of realism in scenic effects. To this end I have devised improved appliances for imitating the shades and tints of light which color the landscape, from the darkness of night, through dawn, sunrise, early morning, noon, afternoon, evening, sunset, twilight, moonlight into the darkness of midnight again; these appliances permitting the imitation of the tints of the hours to be produced completely, or in part, as desired, and facilitating the passage and blending of the various tints each into the other so as to illustrate the slow progress of the hours throughout the whole day. They also permit the imitation of clouds moving through the sky, and of cloud shadows moving over land and water.[231]

By means of this series of devices the color and lighting effects connected with the progress of time and other natural phenomena were projected and controlled by a fixed mechanical operation.

In the same year he claimed a patent for a "Sliding Stage." The purpose of this was similar to that of the elevator stage, but the technique called for horizontal rather than vertical movement. Specifically, he sought

to provide a sliding or movable stage and means for handling or moving and controlling the movements of stages or stage equipments and scenery with facility so as to adapt such devices to be easily moved forward or back, sidewise or in an oblique direction across or in front of a proscenium opening, and to readily change the direction of motion so as to produce the desired result in shifting set or other scenes or stage appliances or equipments.[232]

MacKaye's inventive strength was directed entirely toward increasing the physical facilities of the stage for pictorial illusion.

Next came the "Floating Stage," similar to the sliding stage but with greater flexibility in the choice of direction or kind of movement. Here MacKaye aimed

to provide an improved floating stage which is susceptible of a to and fro or rotary movement and may be propelled forward and back or in a curvilinear direction upon an artificial lake, tank or other body of water and sustained when desired in a fixed position in respect to other objects or other stages of the same kind arranged in a proximity thereto, so that scenery, paintings or other objects or persons placed on the stages may be exhibited to an audience through the usual proscenium opening of a theater or other structure adapted for the exhibition of spectacular, dramatic, or other performances.[233]

While the various types of movable stages were all calculated to provide a rapid and easy shifting of architecturally real scenery, his "Luxauleator" enhanced the spectacular appeal of such shifts by eliminating the ordinary curtain and providing in its place a curtain of light. This was devised to intercept "all sight of anything that may be placed or moved in the space at the rear of the proscenium opening or arch."[234] With centrally controlled electric lighting, this curtain of light could be manipulated for cinematic dissolve effects, or fade-outs and fade-ins, thus providing much more subtle and realistic transformation effects than were possible with the conventional wing-and-border system.

His "Cloud-Creator" or "Nebulator," a device for the projection of moving clouds, seems closely related to the motion picture. Here he provided "means for creating clouds or cloud shadows so as to produce the effect of clouds or cloud shadows moving upon or over a landscape or sky foundation or other scenic arrangement, for the improvement of realism in land and water scenic effects."[235] To these many machines for the reproduction of natural phenomena and the presentation and control of a number of architecturally real settings was added the "Proscenium-Adjuster." This was calculated to provide a greater flexibility in the pictorial arrangement of the stage. The change from a panoramic view to a close-up, from a gigantic cathedral set to an intimate fireside scene, could be handled instantaneously with any one of his mechanical stages plus this automatic adjustment of the size of the picture-frame opening. To accomplish this MacKaye devised "improved means for enlarging and contracting the proscenium opening at will, so that without a moment's delay and almost imperceptibly to the audience, except as to the result, and during the performance or exhibition, the opening may be enlarged or contracted in conformity with the requirements of the occasion."[236] In this way MacKaye could control the type of stage picture offered, in the fashion of the motion picture with its long or medium shot, its panoramic or tracking shot.

To these mechanical devices, all aimed at the enhancement of the pictorial aspects of production, must be added his sponsorship of a system of acting which arose out of and exploited a purely visual appeal. This system, in which he had gathered his first training from M. Delsarte in Paris and which has come to be known by this name, owed much of its favor in America to Steele MacKaye. At the New Lyceum Academy, the Delsarte method, depending upon the pictorial values of body positions and attitudes, became the foundation for his course in acting. Such a pictorial approach to acting was thoroughly in accord with the theatrical trends of the times and was fully exploited upon the stage by MacKaye himself. In his presentation of the role of Paul Kauvar it was noted that he

expresses everything by an ingenious system of physical symbols which conclude to be a demonstration of the theory invented by M. Delsarte, of whom Mr. MacKaye was at one time the apostle.

He acts by a kind of algebra so to speak. . .

It is only fair to say that he gets there just the same, and with an accuracy that fully bears out the simile. . .

His acting, in addition to these intelligible strokes, is further distinguished by a profusion of graceful but meaningless gesture and action, very much like a writing master's flourishes.[237]

Carried to its proper conclusion, such a system would have resulted, as would his over-all productional approach, in the complete elimination of dialogue. Drama then would have become a series of visual symbols, pictures envisioned by the scenic artist and created by the stage mechanic and by the body of the actor. Theatrical invention plus the rigid application of the system of Delsarte brought the theatre of the nineteenth century to the very threshold of the silent film.

MacKaye as a Producer of Spectacle

In 1886, MacKaye's pictorial proclivities brought him into an association with Buffalo Bill's Wild West Show. His reputation as stage artificer had reached William Cody, who engaged him to stage a series of mammoth pictures illustrating the struggle of the growth and expansion of America. This cycle, named by MacKaye

The Drama of Civilization, became the first of a new type of drama for America, a dramatic form which has since developed into one of the significant expressions of the motion picture, and which has been called by Percy MacKaye the "Masque of American Life." Many phases in the historical spectacle of the rise of America have since been reproduced. In *The Drama of Civilization,* the theme was the same as that exploited by the motion-picture epic of the 1920's, *The Covered Wagon.* MacKaye's scenario was completed in October and the production opened at the Madison Square Garden on November 27, 1886. Some idea of the magnitude of this romanticized reproduction of the growth of a nation and of the care and expense which were involved has been provided by Louis Cooke.

It was necessary to cut through solid walls, building temporary housings or lofts on the roof, to carry ropes and blocks, to handle the heavy set pieces and move the panoramas in order to produce some of the storm and atmospheric effects. Trenches had to be dug across 27th Street to connect with the steam plant in the old Stevens carshops. This steam was used to supply batteries of four six-foot exhaust fans, which operated one of the most effective cyclones that has ever been staged.

Preparatory to this, in the autumn before snowfall, men had been sent into the forest to gather up tons of fallen leaves and small shrubbery, sufficient to last through the winter. Two or three wagon loads were used at each performance, by throwing them in front of the great drafts, created by the fans which forced air through funnels that could be turned in any direction. . . The roar of the fans, and the rush of air turned upon the camps of miners and troopers, lifted the tents from their fastenings, causing the flags to snap in the gale. Then when the storm was at its fury height, the leaves would be turned loose, sweeping the arena with terrific force, lifting equestrians from their horses and creating other sad havoc. . . The light and cloud effects, the old Deadwood stage-coach striking a snag in the ravine and going to pieces, while the six mules escaped on a dead run, with only the forward wheels, dragging the driver by the reins—all this never failed to bring a tremendous final curtain call. . . The production included also one of the most realistic prairie fires ever presented, when we saw a stampede of real horses, cattle, buffalo, elk and deer, dashing madly across the plains.[238]

The panorama background for this spectacular epic, painted by Matt Morgan, was "a picture half a mile long and fifty feet high."[239]

The result, comparable in its conception to the James Cruze epic, *The Covered Wagon*, was not unlike a Thomas Ince western motion picture.

First Scene—"The Primeval Forest," with bear and antelope. Here the aboriginal Indians appeared, two tribes joining in a friendly dance, broken in upon by a hostile band, a fight ensuing, with antique weapons. . . *Second Scene*—a Prairie Encampment, with the old emigrant schooners and a realistic prairie fire. A Virginia Reel on horseback. . . *Third Scene*—a Cattle Ranch, where the cowboys' fun is interrupted by an Indian attack, which is beaten off at last by Buffalo Bill and a party of rescue. . . *Fourth Scene*—a Mining Camp in the Rocky Mountains. Here rides the "pony express" and the Deadwood Coach is robbed, though the road-agents are captured.[240]

And so on until, as climax, the camp was carried off by the cyclone. Tremendous and painstaking as the production of this spectacle must have been, it fades into obscurity when compared with the pictorial conceptions responsible for the development of the Spectatorium.

The aesthetic values embodied in the Spectatorium were purely visual. Here there was to be no pictorial illusion of reality but reality itself, the creation of pictures-in-the-round-in-motion, that is, three-dimensional motion pictures. As described by the American painter, Robert Reid, who was present at the Chicago Chamber of Commerce banquet in 1892 when MacKaye's ideas were presented, the Spectatorium was "in essence the birth of the modern art of the motion picture—only it was a picture-of-motion done in the round, to the life,—an *actual* 'movie,' not a photograph."[241] All the arts and all the sciences were evoked by MacKaye in a manifesto for "an entirely new species of building, invented and devised for a new order of entertainment entitled a spectatorio. . . to present the facts of history with graphic force.[242] All of the inventions discussed in the previous section were incorporated into the Spectatorium on a colossal scale.

There were to be twenty-five telescopic stages, all of which were to be furnished with *scenery of an entirely new species* devised by myself. The frame of the stage pictures was 150 by 70 feet, and the full range of the vision of the public, at the horizon of the picture, would have been over 400 feet. It would have required over six miles of railroad track for these stages to move upon, and their aggregated weight would have been over 1,200 tons. . . the machinery of the building. . . would have made each change within forty seconds. . . *An entirely new system of lighting* was to be used in connection with these stages, the aim being to arrive at as close a reproduction of the subtle light effects of nature as modern mechanism made possible. . .

There was also the cyclone machinery, the running of which would have required over 400 horse power, and the immense current-and-wave-makers, requiring an equal amount of force. . . This mechanism would have been capable of producing, in the most realistic manner, all sorts of land- and water-scape effects, and every kind of weather, as well as natural illuminating effects. . .

Among *the light realisms* were all the optical phenomena produced by the passage of time from night, through the early dawn, the rising of the sun, through all the hours of the day with their changing shadows, to the setting of the sun, followed by all the tints of the twilight, and the gradual appearance of the constellations, accurately depicted as they exist in the southern hemisphere—the stars softly stealing through the evening sky into the night, and thence through deepest darkness to the day again; also the falling stars and meteors, the milky way, the aurora borealis, the real lightning, and the real rainbow. . . Among *the weather effects,* were to be the clear day through all the subtle modulations of the approaching storm with real haze and fog and rain. In addition, the real wind effect of almost every degree of force, with the movement of real waves of water, presenting thus all the phases of the atmosphere produced by different degrees of temperature and humidity, combined with the many capricious aspects of the sea. . . *The purpose of this mechanism was to bring into the realm of art as perfect a reproduction of nature as possible.*[243]

The entire stage apparatus was to be powered by electricity and the performance controlled from beginning to end by one man from a centrally located overhead booth. The building was in the process of construction, intended to be the main feature of the Chicago World's Fair of 1893, when the financial "panic of '93" occurred. After hundreds of thousands of dollars had been invested and the building already in its final stages, for want of a few thousands more the entire project was scrapped and, soon after, the building torn down, not one public performance having been given.

Large-scale models, however, had been completed. *The World*

Finder, re-creating the trip of Columbus into the New World, intended for the inaugural performance of the Spectatorium, had been staged. An audience of newsmen at the preview of this projected production

saw the clear white lights of innumerable stars shining out of such a sky as only the Mediterranean reflects, and recognized familiar constellations. . . saw red beams of light streaming from the little church, in which Columbus knelt, while Padre Juan Perez said mass. . . lights in the windows behind which the crew of the *Santa Maria* were singing tipsy songs. . . saw the declining moon fade out. . . church and cottages disappear in the "darkest hour before dawn"; saw the stars gradually grow pale—outlines of church and cottages reappear dimly —a faint glow on the eastern horizon deepen imperceptibly, till [they] beheld what has been sung since Homer's day—the grey dawn stealing over land and sea—the despair of painters and the delight of poets.

This was the last touch. . . "That is dawn itself. . . The picture is as true as any I have witnessed, before sunrise, standing on the high bank of the Hudson and gazing seaward. *Mr. MacKaye, your art and your science together have solved the problem of absolute realism."*

As the glow of the rising sun deepened, a land breeze sprang up, filled the sails of the *Santa Maria,* covered the calm sea with ripples, rustling the leaves of trees on the shore. Not only did their shadows move with the swaying of the branches, but they shortened as the sun rose higher, just as shadows do in nature. The little fleet stands out to sea. Palos recedes. The beacon is passed. The *Santa Maria,* her brave captain and the quaking crew are tossed on the mysterious sea. . . It is rather too heavy a tax on one's imagination to determine the probable effects upon an audience of 10,000 when the completed spectacle is presented with all the accessories of finished actors and the music of great masters.[244]

The zenith of the pictorial theatre of the nineteenth century had been reached. The century-old quest for the photographic ideal was on the point of being realized upon the stage just two years prior to its demonstration upon the screen. F. R. Green, assistant to MacKaye in the construction of the miniature, has written:

When you think of the mechanical difficulties—the proscenium opening in a horizontal semi-circle—a curtain of light, invented by him, in order to change scenes—a tank of water, with panorama sky, meeting the horizon with perfect illusion—railroad tracks under water —cables to move the truck-cars (which held the scenery), operated by windlasses—and everything in relief, built up to cast real shadows from an electric sun—and consider that all was demonstrated to be practical: it is clear to see that there never was a theatre like his spectatorium, before or since, nor any approach to it.[245]

One wonders what Steele MacKaye might have accomplished had he lived to see the completion of the motion picture. Titles in flaming letters, in the fashion of the film, were used at each side of the proscenium as "the story of Columbus is told in letters of fire a foot long, a sentence at a time."[246] Everything had been directed toward the cinematic illusion. The curtain of light was used for dissolve effects and to accelerate scene changes. Scenery was prearranged upon twenty-five stages which could be controlled from the central booth. Lighting effects could be integrated from the same control.

Size and scale were, of course, tremendous. The ships of Columbus, for instance, were gauged to carry "50-foot masts."[247] Such magnitude had its effect upon acting which, of necessity, would become entirely pictorial. Actors "neither spoke, as in drama; nor sang, as in opera," but were "reduced, in that respect, to pantomimists."[248] A special school had to be set up for these actors, essentially "a pantomimic school, educating the student to understand and develop his natural resources of expression in physical action." And it was specifically stated that "elocution will not be taught."[249] Music, of course, was utilized to cement the episodic pattern of this epic-dramatic form and enhance its pictorial values. MacKaye had envisioned the same kind of thing as that of the early screen epics, *Intolerance, Ben Hur,* and so forth. Thus, while the $1,250,000 reputedly invested in the unfinished project was a loss, the aesthetic and historical value of the attempt must be recorded as the creation, before the arrival of motion-picture apparatus, of a motion picture in the life.

Despite the financial collapse of the Spectatorium, MacKaye managed to secure a backing of $50,000 in the following year to carry out the original plan on a smaller scale. An old theatre was reconstructed at 130 Michigan Avenue, Chicago, and "a fragmentary illustration of what the great Spectatorium might have been"[250] was launched. The Scenitorium, as it was called, seated only eight hundred and boasted a proscenium opening of only sixty by twenty feet. Nevertheless, it was reported that the pictures approached "so closely to perfect realism as to challenge nature herself."[251] The same scenario, *The World Finder,* was staged.

In the first scene (La Rabida) the stage, at first perfectly dark, blossomed with a sunny landscape of Spain. As the doors, in lieu of curtains, drew back, the rocky mount stood out with the glaring white walls and the red tile roof of the convent. In this scene, a beautiful incident was the celestial vision which illumined the darkest hour in Columbus' struggle. At this point, the sky was suddenly darkened; then from it burst a great congregation of angels, and Christ was seen, amid a number of the world's rejected, pointing to the earth floating in space, with the western hemisphere dimly outlined. . . The curtain of light blotted out the scene as effectually as any curtain ever devised. When the lights were again lowered, the witching outline of the city of Santa Fé came into view, its places lit up in the foreground, while behind twinkled the lights of the watchful moslem in the minarets of the mosques at Granada.[252]

The smaller-scale presentation of the scenes originally laid out for the Spectatorium was still in advance of contemporary pictorial staging. Electricity, too, was fully exploited for naturalistic lighting values, and it was conceded that "Mr. MacKaye is the first artistic scientist who has been able so to control electric lighting that he can give to stage views all the verisimilitude of night and day as perfectly and imperceptibly as if it were the very method of nature."[253] The two completed achievements of Steele MacKaye in spectacle staging mark a peak in the pictorial theatre of the realistic-romantic movement of the nineteenth century. Certainly nothing short of the great Griffith screen spectacle would have surpassed MacKaye's Spectatorium vision for *The World Finder.* That the dream of Steele MacKaye was to be consummated by the apparatus of the motion picture is not a coincidence. Both had come in response to a similar "social tension," aesthetic preference, call it whatever you will.

MacKaye reached the pinnacle of his expression just as the cinema was about to appear. Soon the motion picture picked up his work where it had been dropped by his early death and, exploiting the aims as well as certain specific techniques of MacKaye's method, carried the original premise of this pictorial theatre to its proper perfection. As A. F. Victor of the Society of Motion Picture Engineers wrote to Percy MacKaye in 1927,

> Many of the methods we employ nowadays in motion picture making were originated by your father for use in his Spectatorium. Whether his ideas were remembered and put to use later on, or whether they were rëdiscovered, it is difficult to state without a certain amount of investigation. . . It is especially interesting to note that the means employed by Steele MacKaye for the reproduction of atmospheric phenomena, and which were patented by him in 1893, are identical with those now in common practice. . . The cloud-producing scheme is an example of such priority of conception. . . *I find every indication that the thing which to-day has developed into the most powerful form of public entertainment was in his mind,* and that he recognized the appeal of that form of entertainment. . . Even titles and subtitles had been recognized by him as an essential to proper presentation, and these did not arrive in the picture industry until after many years of exploitation of the pictures themselves.[254]

Thus, in the brief span of his short career, Steele MacKaye, by virtue of his inventive genius, carried theatrical production from the artificiality of the two-dimensional pictorial conventions into the very realm of graphic authenticity and the staged silent motion picture.

FIVE

PICTORIAL FANTASY:
THE PANTOMIME-SPECTACLE

 That branch of nineteenth-century theatre called pantomime-spectacle provided another area for the development of pictorial staging. At the same time, despite the apparent paradox, pantomime-spectacle did not exploit pictorial realism but was a highly conventionalized and fantastic form. The cinematic potentialities of the pantomime-spectacle must have been as apparent to the creative eye of the early French film producer, George Méliès, as they appear now in retrospect. His immediate success upon the screen explains the disappearance from the stage of its most unrealistic dramatic form soon after the appearance of the most realistic medium ever provided the arts of theatre.

Differing from the realistic spectacle play, the pantomime was nevertheless pictorially conceived and presented. An early pantomime, *The Sleeping Beauty,* was first presented at the Park Theatre, New York, on January 18, 1828. During the week of May 26 of the same year, the third week of its run at the Walnut Street Theatre in Philadelphia, the principal scenery was exhibited alone, for a contemporary review by Charles Durang had already noted that it was "the only thing of merit in the drama."[1] These stage pictures which were the sum and substance of the play, while presented literalistically, were nevertheless fantastic. The second scene of the first act, for instance, was staged as follows, according to the Durang promptscript:[2]

Scene 2nd. The Interior of the Wood. . . Thunder and Lightning. Music.—Forte—Number 12. Lamps up when thick Gauze Cloud is

— *152* —

down. . . a thin gauze cloud slowly descends in front of scene—music —piano through which Aldebert speaks. "Protecting spirit of my Ethelinda's slumbers, assist and aid my purpose." As soon as the gauze cloud is within a few feet of the stage a thicker one descends. Thunder Ball. . . The scene being hid from the audience is removed, and the thick cloud passing off R. and L. discovered the Fairy Melzinna slowly in a car from L.H. surmounted by silvery clouds covering the whole width of the stage—thin gauze cloud ascends, Melzinna leaves the car, she advances, at her signal illuminated letters appear in the clouds.

With its artful use of various thicknesses of gauze cloud to simulate the dissolve and the fade-out, fade-in effect of the film, and with its traditional cloud machines deriving directly from the scenes and machines of the Italian Renaissance, a fantastic picture was spectacularly and graphically presented. The dramatic value of such stuff grew entirely out of these strange pictures sensationally manipulated.

This material, itself artificial, was presented during the greater part of the century with the counterfeit methods of traditional staging. A prompt manuscript of *Aladdin* belonging to Felix A. Vincent,[3] in use during the sixties, seventies, and eighties, indicated that the cinematic values of this fantastic dramatic form relied upon conventional usages. Complete with gong scene changes, vampire traps, cloud machines, and flying palaces, twenty scenes were set into five sets of grooves to create spectacular pictures of Oriental magnificence, which, according to the playbill for G. H. Gilbert's 1862 production (pasted into Vincent's promptscript for this production), "for Artistic Genius, Mechanical Skill, Superb Costumes, beautiful Music, Imposing Tableaux, Terrific Combats, Thrilling Effects, Comic Incidents and Splendid Marches, by far exceeds anything ever attempted at this Establishment." Many of the stock-in-trade pictorial practices of the melodrama were included in this great conglomeration of stage magic. And, as in the melodrama, the basic dramatic pattern was that of a narrative continuity developed with a single direct series of pictures or with cross-cutting between parallel series.

But unlike the melodrama, which sought, despite the artificial conventions of staging, a certain realism in its stage pictures, the pantomime-spectacle exploited the purely fantastic, spectacular effect. In this production of *Aladdin,* soon after the opening curtain, amidst "Thunder. . . Louder Thunder. . . See Vocal Score," the stage manager noted in the margin, "check bells for clouds to fall," and presto, *"The Magician's Study* disappears by working clouds descending. Discovering Orlock, seated in the clouds which envelope the scene." Then, when Orlock tells Abanazar where the wonderful lamp is to be found, "Music—Chorus repeated. Stage lights become dark—clouds and car work off up and discover *Barren Plain."* In this way, while the cloud scene covered the wings and borders of the Magician's Study, this was withdrawn in order to reveal the Barren Plain in the fourth grooves when the clouds and their car worked off up.

In the fifth scene, The Blasted Cedar, the stage magic is much more spectacular. "Kasrac takes some sticks to Abanazar; he makes a fire and throws into it—Loud Thunder and Gong—the charmed dust from the wand. Tree opens." To the accompaniment of thunder sheets, gongs, fire, and flash powder the tree bursts asunder to "discover a frightful chasm." Aladdin goes down as the stage manager signals "Gong to close tree." Then, with a "Whistle," the scene is changed in full view of the audience: "Lights up full. The *Magic Cavern,* a spiral staircase reaching to the top of the cavern R.U.E. The wonderful lamp burning in an avenue C. Over the avenue an emblematic figure of the Genii [*sic*] of the ring. Avenue of trees loaded with beautiful fruit—Aladdin discovered descending the stair. R.C." While the action has been proceeding continuously, the vantage point of the audience has been swung around, in the fashion of a shift in camera position and angle, to catch Aladdin as he makes his entry down into the cave. The "whistle" change added to the spectacular quality of the full-view shift from the Blasted Cedar in the first grooves to the Magic Cavern set up in the fourth.

Immediately upon Aladdin's entry more pictorial chicanery occurs. Plucking fruit, he fills his basket. He polishes a luscious piece on his sleeve and tastes it, as, without warning, "Music. . . Gong sounds. Statue of Genii disappears and chorus begins directly." In the meantime, action has been proceeding simultaneously on the ground level and editorial cut-back is employed. Abanazar, speaking from the ground level, is instructed, in a stage manager's note, to "throw Kasrac down the cavern. Gong and crash as the stone rolls over the entrance." The statue of the genie which had just disappeared comes magically to life. "Music. Kasrac, as if a sudden thought had struck him points to the ring on Aladdin's finger and rubs it. Gong. Star in flat opens discovering Genii of the ring. . . Red fire C." The pantomime is filled with this fantastic and spectacular trickery, all of which is utterly dependent upon the two-dimensional staging conventions of the period.

The artificial hocus-pocus of the magical scenic changes, of the appearances and disappearances, matched their naïve fairy-tale conception, and no attempt was made at subtlety. Gong changes, on the other hand, called attention to this productional sleight of hand. The second act is even more full of this supernatural contrivance than the first. At the Widow Mustapha's Bamboo Cottage, "Music. She takes up her apron and begins to rub the lamp. *Gong three times* and trap bell. The Genii of the Lamp appears close to her bearing a baton lighted. Widow M. faints and falls in a chair." Then, when Aladdin orders food, "Music. *Gong three times*. Genii waves his baton. Table comes down covered with delicious fruits, etc., in a silver service. Music. Bell for disappearance of Genii. Genii disappears." There is no need, of course, to wash dishes in this fairy-book world. The stage manager's gong is the open sesame to the unfailing devotion of the Genie's apprentices. When the table is cleared, the stage manager has but to signal: "Gong for table to work up. Music. Banquet disappears." In the next pictorial episode, At the Royal Baths, Azack orders the arrest of Aladdin and Kasrac, but Aladdin, perceiving his danger, rubs the lamp. "*Gong*. They rush through Vampire in R. and L. Flat. Music. The wall is seen to divide and Aladdin and Kasrac rush through the opening. Azack and Guards are about to follow when the wall closes and catches fast the sword of Azack. . . Whistle change of scene."

Tableaux, pageants, processions, and dances follow, with the most spectacular piece of stage magic coming in the third act. Abanazar has gained possession of the lamp and, going to Aladdin's palace, commands, "To Africa." Then, "Gong. Red Fire. Music.

Everybody on. The Palace rises and appears to fly through the air leaving a barren plain and distant hills. Enter Kasrac quite frantic." Aladdin is summoned and, as the stage manager signals for a whistle change, Aladdin, to the strains of "Brave Aladdin," rubs the magic ring. "Enter Genii of the ring—after chorus whistle—Aladdin and Kasrac are led off by Genii L. and are seen to traverse the air in a beautiful car with the Genii of the Ring. Whistle for change." Aladdin overtakes the palace, brings it back, and places it where it originally stood to provide the closing tableau. This final touch, the return of the profile palace with the characters of the play aboard, indicates the small stress put upon realism in the pantomime-spectacle and the great emphasis upon the graphic treatment of spectacular, fantastic effects. This stage magic, with its transformations, vampire traps, flash powder, disappearing genie, flying scenery and actors, all handled with a high degree of conventionality, was the direct forerunner of the work of George Méliès in the early film. In addition to its fantastic style, the pantomime-spectacle possessed most of the cinematic values attributed to the melodrama: the pictorial continuity with single or parallel lines of action; the insignificance of dialogue; the insistence upon spectacular physical action, pantomime, and tableaux; and the use of music throughout to heighten these many productional values.

The London season of 1879 brought the usual number of "pantomime stupidities, long-winded barbarities, founded on half a dozen nursery tales, long ago worn threadbare."[4] The subject matter itself was stale and worn out, but nevertheless this dramatic form retained its favor. In this season, while the majority of pantomimes "proved wearisome beyond endurance," the one at the Covent Garden was "saved by splendid spectacular effects."[5] The durability of this form, then, would seem to hinge upon the continual enlargement of productional values which, in turn, depended upon the enlargement of staging facilities. Apparently the pantomime-spectacle, because of the limitations of stage equipment more a metropolitan than a provincial form, had begun to cry out for a more fluid and spectacular pictorial medium than that of the stage.

The introduction of novel productional values served to sustain the popularity of the pantomime. When a new version of *Aladdin* by Alfred Thompson, now called *Arabian Nights*, was presented in the eighties, the closing episode was given quaint and capricious treatment. The fairy palace was actually built on stage in full view of the audience by legions of miniature workmen. "The arrival of the workmen's tiny wives with their doll babies in little perambulators is a very happy thought; and the capital pantomime into which the small performers have been drilled suggests the proceedings of adult artists seen through the wrong end of an opera-glass."[6] Anything was done for the sake of novelty, and an unusual picture, no matter how extraneous, had a marketable value. Production dominated and the play itself was not the thing to catch an audience. When Thompson's version came to Boston at the New Grand Opera House on January 9, 1888, the theatrical position of pantomime-spectacle was clear.

It is not necessary to criticize Mr. Thompson's work, for it is not the essential part of the play. It serves the intended purpose of joining in an intelligible manner the apparently endless series of transformation scenes, actes de ballets, songs, dances and specialty performances which follow one close upon another with bewildering variety throughout the whole evening.[7]

Prior to going to Boston, the production at the Standard Theatre, New York, on September 12, 1887, had employed a steam curtain, adding to the fantasy and heightening the spectacular qualities. A large audience attended this opening, "but their enthusiasm was only for the gorgeous scenery, novel effects, and ballets."[8]

The quest for pictorial sensations included all sorts of unexpected exaggerations. When William Muskerry's version of *Cinderella* was produced at Sanger's Equestrian Amphitheatre in 1886, a Grand Jubilee Apotheosis took the place of the customary transformation scene, "and as it introduced five monster elephants, including the 'Siamese Twins' and the Burmese sacred white elephant, a herd of camels and dromedaries, kangaroos, emus, ostriches, pelicans, parrots, and other 'wild fowl' selected from Mr. Sanger's zoological collection, it is more welcome than transformation ever was."[9] The success of pantomime was predicated upon the perennial elaboration of its pictorial effects. In the struggle for its survival, growing more intense as audience tastes became more clearly defined during the nineties, ever more fantastic and spectacular exhibitions were offered. Their success was measurable, as the popularity of the form boomed in the season of 1895-1896, with a large "exodus of our principal artists from the Halls this year to pantomime."[10] Nevertheless, novelties were merely stopgaps, and the introduction of cinema at this particular moment was soon to prove disastrous. A point was being reached beyond which fresh productional novelties upon the stage would become prohibitive.

The ultimate development possible to this form upon the stage may be seen in such a production as that of the *Grand Pantomime, Aladdin,* presented by Oscar Barrett at Drury Lane on December 26 of this peak pantomime year of 1896. Much progress had been made from the kind of production represented by the Vincent script. Five scenic artists, J. Harker, W. Telbin, R. Caney, H. Emden, and J. R. Barrett, were engaged. The opening scene, which, in the Vincent promptbook was done in a conventional Magician's Study, was here played in the Interior of the Great Pyramid, Egypt. Abanazar's first entrance touches off the hocus-pocus as "the Spirit of Life reanimates the Sphinxes and finally a mummy,"[11] which turns out to be Abanazar. When Aladdin later enters the Cave of the Lamp, a "revolving scene brings to view the interior of the Cave,"[12] thus replacing the traditional two-dimensional cave cut-outs with a more practicable solid setting. In the cave, Aladdin adventures "with malignant spirits, including a colossal centipede, which he cuts off with his magic sword into slices, which run off separately by themselves,"[13] much in the fashion of Méliès' magic in *A Trip to the Moon,* where, as each imp is killed by the adventuring scientists, three more spring up in its place. The closing scene shows Aladdin's Palace in Ivory and Pearl. "The effect of the highly ornate Chinese architecture, and of the long vista of steps and terraces, is brilliant in the extreme, and the splendour is heightened as group after group of performers make their way down slowly from the hidden depths to the front, arrayed in costly fabrics of well-harmonized tints."[14]

Elaboration beyond such a level as this became both costly and difficult. Witness, on the other hand, the economy of the Méliès' productions, the most expensive of which, *An Impossible Voyage* (1904), amounted to only $7500.[15] Not only was the film able to include a larger number of effects, but these effects were more fantastic. At the same time the motion-picture theatre, with a simple screen opposing a projection machine at the end of a hall, was able to replace the elaborate metropolitan stage machine and thereby vastly enlarge its potential audience. Production costs were decreased while box-office receipts were increased. The motion picture was, from the start, the more practical and economical medium for the pantomime-spectacle.

Like the other types of spectacle plays of the period, the pantomime depended to a large extent upon the use of music. In this production of *Aladdin* it became "all-important. . . Favorite music-hall melodies are deftly orchestrated, so as to follow without offense airs from *Faust, Romeo et Juliette,* and bits from Wagner's *Ring des Nibelungen. . .* the dramatic work of the authors is at all times assisted and emphasized by the composer."[16] For instance, as George Bernard Shaw has noted, "Aladdin's combat with the Slave of the Lamp is accompanied by the heroic strains of the famous Siegfried motifs; and the trombones blare out Alberich's curse on the King when mention is made of Abanazar's greed for gold."[17] The musical effects may have been naïve, but the procedure elaborated a practice which, of course, became a strong forte of the silent motion picture.

The pantomime productions of Oscar Barrett mark a peak in this type of staging. His *Cinderella,* produced on the Lyceum stage on Boxing Night of 1893, made spectacular use of the well-known fantastic situations. A wave of the fairy godmother's wand and

the ugly kitchen disappears, and in its place is a fairy boudoir where the sylph coquette summons looking-glass fairies, powder puffs, pin cushions, fanmakers, milliners, gloves, flourists, perfumers, and all the sprites attendant on a well-dressed lady's toilet. The stage is filled with these magic little damsels, and presently, by skill known only in fairyland, Cinderella appears beautifully dressed. . . slippers on her feet, whose jewel clasps are tiny electric lights. She drives away in her pumpkin chariot, twinkling with electric lamps, drawn by six dainty Shetland ponies, with lizards and rats and mice for footmen and coachmen.[18]

The Cinderella story was used as a skeleton for the hanging of spectacular effects. In expanding upon this technique, George Méliès soon dispensed with the traditional story and, substituting original stories of his own making, opened new fields for the introduction of cinematic magic. Barrett's *Cinderella* offered Méliès a precedent for the animation of inanimate objects by introducing a dance "in which the gigantic fire-irons take part."[19] Transformations of all kinds either form part of the story or are dragged in by the heels. For story purposes, the "cat is transformed by a fairy into a coloured footman,"[20] while the closing transformation, From Storm and Sunshine, seems to have been added for its own sake alone. As an illustration of Beethoven's Pastoral Symphony, it depicts "daylight, sunset, moonlight, the storm and avalanche, the rain, sunrise, the rainbow, the flight of the doves and the land of sunshine."[21] The unimportance of the dialogue or the book, and the complete reliance upon the visual aspects, was rarely camouflaged. When a version of *Cinderella* by H. G. French was presented at the Elephant and Castle in London on December 24, 1895, it was openly noted that the author had provided "plenty of opportunity for the introduction of those *incidental items on which, after all, the success of modern pantomime chiefly depends*."[22] Such incidental items included wild life which was not always real, but, in keeping with the artificial nature of the form, as in the case of Geoffrey Thorn's production of *Cinderella* at the Grand Theatre, Islington, for the season of 1896, merely "representations of hares, rabbits, squirrels, stags, foxes, pheasants, wood pigeons, etc."[23] In the same year at the Brixton, Frank Parker's production employed a panorama.[24] *Cinderella* enjoyed a number of independent productions in this and the following season, each offering its own brand of "incidental items" and trying its best not to repeat well-known and worn-out effects. As the years passed, increasingly extraneous specialties were added simply for the sake of their novelty. In 1899 at the Grand Theatre, Fulham, *Cinderella* included "Dainez's pony and dog circus."[25] Apparently the popularity which the pantomime-spectacle had achieved with the productions of Oscar Barrett could be maintained only by the intrusion of such superfluous items. Reaction or regression in this theatrical form might normally have been expected at about the time of the appearance of George Méliès, who, capitalizing upon the potentialities of the film strip, the camera, and the laboratory, was to bring a new lease of life to this type of nineteenth-century pictorial theatre.

The influence of the motion picture upon the staging of pantomime was felt soon after its arrival. Efforts were promptly made to extend its pictorialism. The production of *Dick Whittington* at the Parkhurst, London, on December 24, 1895, gave "brief visions of past pantomimes."[26] During the next year at the Royal Osborne, Manchester, in an apparent effort to stimulate attendance, it was announced that cinematic interludes were "to be introduced into the bill on Monday, and will remain there until the end of the run."[27] In the recognition that cinema could well satisfy the obvious taste for the pictorial novelties of the stage pantomime, the motion picture was annexed in the hope that it would bolster the pantomime's waning favor. The fairy-tale adventures of Dick Whittington and his cat, beginning with the frame-up in London, continuing with his flight and shipwreck off the coast of Morocco, his travels inland, and finally his triumphal return to Glasgow, provided the kind of opportunity for graphic illustration that could be so much better handled in the motion picture.

Now, while the pantomime-spectacle was, in a large sense, characterized by its exploitation of fantastic effects, the artificial conventions by which these effects were presented had been in the process of breakdown for a number of years, so that by 1899 certain effects had to be eliminated. The traditional closing transformation scene was not used in the 1899 *Whittington* at the Kensington Theatre and, at the time, it was openly feared that "the days of veneration for these ancient institutions are passed."[28] A more thorough realism in the stage picture had to be offered. In the Oscar Barrett production of *Whittington* of the same year, "a 'practicable' field of corn is cut"[29] before the audience, and the sequence of the ship at sea employed a seacoast panorama and a workable ship. "The Ship is a very solid affair. We have of it a three-quarter view, set diagonally across the stage, showing its stern, its deck and its three masts. Night falls, twinkling lights shine everywhere; the masts, the lines of the ship are illuminated in outline. With the dawn we see the coast of Africa passing before us." [30] That a more realistic pictorial production was given the artificial pantomimic form after the motion picture had been used to bolster the appeal of a pantomime bill is an interesting example of the early influence of the film upon staging methods.

The first attempt of George Méliès in the field of the pantomime, *Cinderella,* in twenty tableaux, was made in 1900. In 1901, Klaw and Erlanger imported the Drury Lane production of *Beauty and the Beast* to the Broadway Theatre, New York, where it opened on the fourth of November. It seemed that the motion picture had now driven the stage into an extravagantly elaborate production.

New York has never gazed upon such a bewilderingly lovely spectacle. The ballet of the seasons was a pageant of the most exquisite color effects, the weird dance of the witches in midair gave you gooseflesh and the final denouement when the enchanted palace was revealed in all its incandescent glory was so blazingly beautiful that, having quite run out of exclamation points, one felt like calling frantically for either smoked glasses or blinders. [31]

When this production went to Boston, its "succession of brilliant spectacles, in which fairies and witches and handsome princesses and princes and beautiful women who fly through the air and comedians who introduce some very modern vaudeville specialties, all mingle to make a bewildering ensemble." [32]

The presence of the film seems to have driven stage pantomime into new and unusual fields for spectacular novelties. For example, "a huge automobile arrived in jointed sections," [33] having somehow wormed its way into the fairy tale. There was so much scenery that "even the long cast is dwarfed by the succession of settings," [34] which, it was noted, "would take all of Boston Common if set up at one time to be pushed before the footlights on the surface of the stage." [35] But there was an inevitable futility in such a rivalry between the stage pantomime and the screen, for, although it may at first glance appear a paradox, it is significantly true that wherever the stage achieved a measure of success in this competition the smaller became its audience, simply because an elaborate stage spectacle could be accommodated in relatively few theatres. At the same time, in terms of quantity, speed, and variety of pictures and of magical effects, Méliès was easily able to surpass the most extravagant stage pantomime. And, of course, in the matter of productional costs as well as in the consideration of the size of the potential box office, the screen had nothing to fear from the competitive efforts of the stage.

And so when, in 1912, we find *The Sleeping Beauty* produced by Arthur Collins at Drury Lane, the pantomime stage seems to have capitulated this pictorial struggle to the screen. While in the past the book had served merely as a simple framework for the exhibition of elaborate spectacle, it was now developed for other values. The inability to proceed any farther in the spectacular direction brought about the introduction of certain compensations which would have been unnecessary ten to twenty years earlier, prior to the work of Méliès. The author now found it necessary to supplement the usual pantomime libretto "with a most ingeniously invented and humourously conceived sub-plot."[36] Previous elaborations upon the traditional fairy tale had been in the field of scenery, costumes, and magical effects. Collins' *Sleeping Beauty* marks a certain recognition that, productionally speaking, the pantomime-spectacle had conceded its pictorial basis to the film. The capitulation was by no means instantaneous. This play merely indicates the existence of a trend, since confirmed by time, which has seen the complete transfer of the pantomime-spectacle from stage to screen. With the gradual surrender of its basic source of appeal, the pantomime of nineteenth-century England and America vanished from the stage to reappear upon the screen, attaining, in the new medium, a continual improvement which has lasted even to the present day.

The first five chapters of this book have been concerned with the demonstration of the presence of a cinematic approach in the various branches of popular theatre in the century preceding the introduction of the motion picture. The implication has continually been that the history of the early film would fit neatly into this pattern of development, and that the cinema would find its footing as an art form simply by taking over the areas of the nineteenth-century melodrama, spectacle play, and pantomime-spectacle previously popular upon the stage. It was further implied that, in this way, the screen was to continue the entire cycle of the realistic-romantic theatre which stemmed from Garrick and of which these three dramatic forms were the significant part. There is hardly need at this time to present an objective history of the film. The story of the growth of the motion picture has been excellently treated by a number of critics and historians. These men have chosen not to relate this development in the cinema to conditions within the older theatrical forms. Hence, the truth of the ideas postulated in the part of this volume which has to do with the stage must hinge upon corroboration by significant illustration in the history of the screen. By reviewing the evidence, it may be possible to show the way in which stage and screen are historically linked. The relative aesthetic position of each during the period which saw their coalition may be established, the evolution of a theatrical cycle traced, and eventually a better understanding of the fundamental attributes of each of the two media may arise. And so we shift now from the story of theatrical practices in the years prior to and surrounding the early film to practices within the film itself, examining these in the light of the values we have thus far determined.

SIX

PHOTOGRAPHIC REALISM:
THE BIRTH OF THE FILM, 1895-1902

 The arrival of the motion picture as a full-fledged and autonomous art form may be dated with the presentation of D. W. Griffith's *The Birth of a Nation* in 1915. From the time of the first screenings of the Edison-Armat vitascope in 1895 and 1896 to the achievement of a cinematic art form in 1915 a period of twenty years elapsed—two decades passed before the technique of the camera and the photoplay achieved its selectivity, its unity of purpose, its dramatic emphasis, its interplay of episodes, transition, and dramatic climax, its aesthetics of pictorial composition, dynamic and static, in short, before it attained the status of an art form. Such basic devices as the cut-back, dissolve, fade-in, fade-out, pan, and close-up may have become useful techniques soon after the arrival of the vitascope, but their development for artistic and dramatic effect, for the integration of an aesthetic, dramatic, and pictorial whole did not come about for twenty years.

During these years the art of the motion picture lacked the development and refinement brought by D. W. Griffith, yet its acceptance as a medium of theatrical entertainment was immediate. If a connection exists between the nineteenth-century stage and the screen, it may be found in these early years.

The camera of itself has no more value as an artistic medium than has a typewriter. Both are recording devices. The value of the camera as a medium of entertainment may occur when it is used to photograph entertaining subjects. Its value as a medium of art does not come about until a manner or a technique of recording these entertaining subjects has been developed. The motion picture began as a simple recording device. Like other arts, it began with mere imitation, the pedantic pictorial reproduction of nature. It had no alternative, for until the development of artificial lighting with mercury-vapor lamps about 1906,[1] indoor work was impractical. Outdoor scenes, presenting no lighting problem, comprised the main body of films during these years. Here, amidst actual and natural surroundings, the cinema fell into perfect step with the realistic pictorial trends of current theatrical endeavor.

I. TOPICAL FILMS: SIMPLE PICTORIAL REALISM

When, on May 18, 1896, the vitascope was first shown in Boston, the first recorded critique of the motion picture by Mildred Aldrich made much of the realism of the pictures, proclaiming that the figures moved "almost as large as life usually, and, in some cases, larger than life, and in all cases, just as natural as life. . . even the changing expressions of the principals, is reproduced."[2] The motion picture had made its opening bid as a simple photographic device. As part of this exhibition, the *May Irwin Kiss,* taken from a current stage success, established the film as serious competitor of the stage. "The real scene itself never excited more amusement than did its Vitascope presentment and that is saying much."[3]

With this very first showing, realism in the theatre found a new medium. The Lumière brothers' film, *Arrival of the Paris Express* (1895), similarly, was such as might be "witnessed on a journey to or from the Riviera. . . it stands out with a realism that seemingly defies improvement."[4] There was surprise and pleasure that real scenes from life could be reproduced. Such simple topical screen subjects satisfied some of the thirst for naturalism in the theatre. These early films, often lasting less than a full minute, had simply to reproduce action of any kind. Upon this basis of pictorial realism, no matter how fleeting, the motion picture gained a foothold.

News events were hailed from the start. Pictorial reproduction of anything that moved seemed the only requirement. The demand for this kind of film was so great that as early as 1897, when films scarcely ever ran beyond fifty feet, Enoch Rector risked 11,000 feet to record the Corbett-Fitzsimmons fight at Carson City, Nevada. Any news was good news. No premium had yet been put on promptness by the pictorially inquisitive minds of the times. Sports formed a large category of topical films, including photographic reproductions of *The Henley Regatta in England, Feeding the Ducks at Tampa Bay, Spanish Coronation Bull-Fight, Filipino Cockfight*. Locale was always specified to heighten the realism of the pictures. Strange and foreign views, such as *In Busy Frisco, Shanghai from a Launch, In The Yellowstone, Sampans Racing— China*, were always in demand.

Railroad scenes were of two kinds, either simple views of trains in action or panoramic scenic views taken from trains in motion. The first type were much more spectacular and real than could be provided by current two-dimensional stage locomotives. *Bucking the Blizzard*, taken near Watertown, New York, during the great blizzard of 1899, shows the snowplow "pushed by two of the heaviest type of locomotives. . . throwing the snow with great velocity hundreds of feet through the air away from the tracks."[5] The second type, illustrated by such a film as *The Gap, Entrance to the Rocky Mountains*, used a rudimentary form of "trucking" camera for its spectacular pictorial effect. "The view, as if one were riding on the cow-catcher of a locomotive running at high speed, is one that even tourists riding over the line are not privileged to enjoy."[6] An entertainment scheme known as Hale's Tours and Scenes of the World exploited this type of pictorial realism. In 1903, Hale, an ingenious showman, recognized the theatrical possibilities of the topical film. He planned to transport his audience bodily as well as imaginatively into the midst of the scenery being shown. Using films of spectacular scenic splendor taken from observation platforms and cowcatchers of trains, he sought to increase the pictorial illusion by arranging his theatre "like the interior of a railway carriage; to make the journey more realistic, an additional effect was secured by the seats rocking from side to side when the carriage appeared to be rounding a corner. The outside of the theatre resembled the end of a railway carriage, upon twin rails, the attendant being dressed like a railway guard, complete with red and green flags."[7] Scenic illusion satisfied nineteenth-century hunger for pictorial theatre.

Films of fires, *The Burning of the Standard Oil Tanks at Bayonne, New Jersey; Fire-Boat, John M. Hutchinson;* and so on, provided the realism of positive identification as well as the sensational spectacles of buildings burning, apparatus in action, dangerous deeds, and risky rescues.

While railroad views had already begun to free the camera by "trucking" in the horizontal plane, a topical film, *A Perilous Proceeding,* heightened its realism by trucking vertically to show "workmen on a New York skyscraper descending from the roof by means of a derrick. This picture was taken by means of a special apparatus which enabled the camera to follow the men as they were lowered to the ground."[8] Camera techniques were already directed toward a greater pictorial realism. At the same time, war films opened new areas for the spectacular and the sensational. Not to sacrifice authenticity, the Biograph Company, "during the Spanish War, sent two expeditions to Cuba. The Philippine Campaign was covered by two separate expeditions; the War in China by two expeditions; the War in South Africa was covered by three operators who remained during almost the entire campaign."[9] Location filming became the early vogue. Biograph's *Assault on the South Gate of Pekin* was taken by an "operator on the spot."[10] The realistic, reproductional quality of these spectacular selections attracted audiences. An execution by hanging, filmed on the spot in Jacksonville, Florida, shows the victim "mounting the platform accompanied by several clergymen. The executioner adjusts the black cap and the noose about the prisoner's neck. The trap is touched and the body is seen to shoot through the air, and hang quivering at the end of the rope. A very ghastly, but very interesting subject."[11] Jailbreaks were staged on location. *The Escape from Sing-Sing,* filmed on twenty-seven feet, showed "the roof of the famous prison. Two convicts are making an attempt to escape. A guard shoots one; but is himself killed by an iron bar in the hands of the other who succeeds in getting away."[12]

Such topical films as these comprised one of the largest single categories of motion-picture material available during these early years of the cinema, from 1895 to 1902. The implication is obvious, namely, that the success of the early film as a medium of theatrical entertainment came directly from the advertised and actual realism of the pictures, supported by such values as fixed horizontal and vertical "trucking," and further enhanced by spectacular and sensational subject matter.

II. ACTION-TABLEAUX FILMS

The early film succeeded so well on its simple basis of realism and spectacularism that when the opportunity came to film pictures dramatically, to arrange a sequence of scenes for a dramatic effect, it was often entirely overlooked. In 1896, a special outdoor performance by Joseph Jefferson of *Rip Van Winkle* amidst the natural scenery of his summer home on Buzzard's Bay, Massachusetts, was recorded by Biograph on 219 feet of film. But instead of shooting this subject with a view toward an interesting and a dramatic continuity, it was filmed in eight episodes billed and sold as separate catalogue numbers: "No 45. *Rip's Toast*, 25 feet," or "No. 48. *Rip's Passing over the Mountain*, 26 feet."[13] Action-tableaux, such as this, were simply used as the photographically realistic versions of the same material that audiences were accustomed to viewing on the stage in the artificial conventions of the times.

Another early experiment with the episodic action-tableaux film, the Salmi Morse version of the *Passion Play*, filmed in 1897, followed the same pattern. Banned originally from the stage, it was played with scenery and costumes on the roof of the Grand Central Palace in New York and filmed on about two thousand feet. Twenty-six action-tableaux reproducing the course of the Passion, each filmed separately, could be projected continuously without clumsy interscene waits necessary upon the stage. The pictures moved rapidly from "The Jews and Pilate in the Temple" to "Christ before Pilate, Condemnation, Carrying the Cross, Crucifixion, Taken Down from the Cross, The Resurrection, The Ascension."[14] In this case, material had been lifted directly out of the theatre and had been given, from the important pictorial aspect, a presentation upon the screen superior to that of the stage.

The episodic-tableaux film gained in popularity both because of the impetus given by the work of George Méliès and because, in its crude way, this type of motion picture could tell a simple story. The story might be romantic, as in the two preceding instances; it might be fantastic, as in the work of Méliès; or it might possess the realism of the domestic stage melodrama, as in *The Downward Path* (Biograph, about 1901). To the staging of the melodrama, particularly in the provinces, the· pictorial realism of *The Downward Path* offered an undeniable threat. In this rudimentary film, five action-tableaux episodes,[15] each about thirty feet in length, each with a separate title, and each shown successively, were calculated to reveal the moral lesson in the career of a young country girl who succumbs to the temptations and becomes involved in the wickedness of the big city. The first of these, The Cheeky Book Agent, shows "the entrance of the tempter into the farmhouse in the shape of an agent. He makes love to the girl." Then follows the second scene, She Ran Away With the City Man: "She descends from her room by a ladder. Her father attempts to detain her, but the window sash falls on his head. The flying couple are pursued by the mother and a farmhand in their night clothes." With no interscene wait, the third episode, The Girl Went Astray, is shown: "The girl is now on the city streets. The book agent . . . is seen demanding money of her. Her aged father and mother . . . arrive just in time to witness the scene. They attempt to save the girl, but the brute knocks the father down, and drags the victim away." A title, The New Soubrette, flashes on, and she is now "in a bowery concert hall. She is under the influence of liquor and takes part in a scene of riotous abandon." Finally, the fifth episode, In Suicide Hall, shows her "deserted by her lover and left to her fate. Carbolic acid is her only resort." The moral is driven home. In a matter of minutes a story has been told with as much pictorial elaboration as would take nearly an hour on the stage of that day. The appeal of this method was so strong that other material was taken from the stage. *Ten Nights in a Barroom* was done in five episodes from the popular play. These action episodes were staged as motion-tableaux and photographed from a fixed position. The early film had taken both matter and method from the stage.

The success and popularity of this technique seem to have

been fairly well established by 1902. In the same year E. S. Porter made further progress with *The Life of an American Fireman.* But when later he filmed *Uncle Tom's Cabin,* he reverted to the episodic-tableaux method. Here he used a prologue, as introduction, with fourteen subsequent action-tableaux to tell the story. The pictorial sensationalism was enhanced by a "departure from the old method by dissolving one scene into another."[16] Material was taken from the nineteenth-century melodrama stage and, after the story had been "carefully studied and every scene posed in accordance with the famous author's version,"[17] the motion picture of *Uncle Tom's Cabin* proceeded to improve upon the spectacular aspects of the stage version through use of the dissolve linkage.

The first forward step in cinematic technique beyond the simple telling of a story was achieved by action-tableaux. This method which had originated in the nineteenth-century melodrama theatre was taken over directly by the film and improved upon. The material so frequently borrowed from the stage was always of the same realistic-romantic nature. The ability of the film to carry on the same type of production as the current melodrama stage was recognized long before it had achieved status as an art form.

III. STORYETTES

The length of films in the "storyette" category exceeded that of the topical subjects or the episodic-tableaux and offered a greater opportunity for the development of the pictorial tendencies of the nineteenth-century stage. In a film, *Personal,* directed by Wallace McCutcheon, Sr., the "chase," a clumsy technique of nineteenth-century melodrama theatre was, according to F. J. Marion of Kalem Pictures, accidentally filmed for the first time.[18] In the script, a French nobleman meets a bevy of prospective wives at Grant's Tomb. The author called for a deluge of affection upon the Frenchman. The actor personating the Frenchman, confronted by this tidal wave of impassioned femininity, disregarded the script and turned tail in his first bid for freedom. The girls made madly after him, spurred in the frolic by laughter of the studio crowd, over hedges, under park benches, all over the place. Director McCutcheon seized the moment, "panorama'd" the camera, and

followed the chase—now the girls, now the Frenchman. The un-
rehearsed pursuit was kept in and the film's length extended to
675 feet. The free "panning" of the camera throughout the chase,
adding to the realism and the sensationalism of the picture, had
unwittingly attempted a technique of the melodrama stage.

Ordinarily, however, this type of film was taken from a single
fixed position, using the same method as the action-tableaux but
telling a simple story in the single scene. Such a film as *The Dis-
appointed Old Maid* shows a burglar as he enters "an old maid's
bedroom by means of a window, and hearing someone approach,
crawls under the bed. The old maid enters and sits down to remove
her shoes. As she does so she sees the form of the man under the
bed. Delighted. . . she proceeds to lock the door, and drag him
out. . . To her chagrin. . . the man proves to be nothing but a
stuffed dummy."[19] The story is not told by the camera but is
simply recorded as written and played. This kind of material, dependent upon business and properties rather than upon language
or characterization, was in this fashion closely allied to the popular
stage.

The Maniac Barber falls into the same category, but depends
for its appeal upon camera trickery. It shows a customer entering
a barber shop and taking a seat.

> The barber places the cloth about his neck, sharpens his razor and
> then goes mad. He seizes a huge knife, cuts the man's head off, and
> takes it to a table some distance away. There he lathers and shaves the
> face, then taking the head back to the chair, he places it in its proper
> position on the trunk. The customer, thereupon, rises, pays his bill. . .
> and leaves the shop.[20]

While this material could hardly have been borrowed straight from
the stage or from life, its spirit, if not its fact, was akin to that of
the stage. In the film its performance was deft and realistic. In this
country, as in London, the film had begun to copy the stage even
prior to 1902. The scene and story in *Nabbed by the Nipper,*
filmed on twenty-six feet, are characteristic:

> Snow is falling on a deserted street as a woman enters with her child,
> urging her intoxicated husband to return home. A little matchboy

passes and offers the man a box of lights, but is driven by him from the scene. The bully knocks his wife down in the snow, and then staggers off. He is however foiled by the boy, who rushes on with his head down, into the man, and both roll over. The boy jumps up and shouts to a policeman, who takes the man into custody, as a Salvation lassie and her masculine helper enter the scene and assist the fallen woman and her child.[21]

Disregarding the incongruity of title, such material, thoroughly illustrative of nineteenth-century stage melodrama, was used by the film simply because, first, its appeal rested in pictorial illusion, and secondly, because this illusion could be treated more realistically by the film.

The ultimate development of the storyette within this first period in the rise of the film may be said to have come with *Uncle Pete's Pipe,* filmed in two scenes. The first shows

an old gentleman entering a store and purchasing a large stock of fireworks for the children. He smokes his long pipe as he starts off home.

The second shows him approaching the house, still puffing away on his big pipe. Just as he arrives home, a spark from the pipe sets the fireworks off, and there is a tremendous explosion. Neighbors rush in from every direction, a policeman calls an ambulance, which comes upon a run, and the poor old gentleman is carried off to the hospital. The realism of this picture is splendid.[22]

Events as they may have happened in real life were treated so as to form a sensational pictorial episode. In this quality, also characteristic of the popular nineteenth-century stage, is to be found the drama of the earliest film storyettes.

Exclusive of the work of Méliès, developments in the early motion picture, during the first seven years of its life indicate that (1) it was hailed from the start for its realistic pictorial quality rivaling and usually surpassing the stage, and (2) this quality was seized upon by early film makers, who, borrowing freely from the stage, enhanced the inherent realism of the camera by such early techniques as the "truck," the "pan," the "dissolve," and a rudimentary chase sequence. The cinema, through the period of the storyette, was continuing the current realistic-pictorial trends of the stage.

SEVEN

PICTORIAL FANTASY:
GEORGE MÉLIÈS

 Before his entry into motion pictures, George Méliès had been a professional magician and a caricaturist. He became interested in the "magical" properties of the camera, in its capacity for confounding trick effects. His aim from the start was to create fantastic and visually sensational subjects. He was not interested in reproducing the realism of life, but gained realism for his fantastic material by means of the camera. By 1900 he had exploited the trickery of the camera on over two hundred subjects, each about one-hundred feet in length and each, like *The Vanishing Lady, The Haunted Castle, The Laboratory of Mephistopheles, The Bewitched Inn,* and so on, showing "people disappearing magically, cut in half, flying through the air; apparitions taking horrible shapes, animals turning into human beings and human beings into animals."[1] Such a film as *The Devil in a Convent* illustrates his basic interest in the motion picture. The devil, followed by an imp, jumps from the font of holy water in a convent.

Both are transformed into a priest and choir boy. They then summon the nuns to service and while preaching change back to their natural shapes, frightening the nuns out of their wits. The devil then transforms the church to resemble Hell and the nuns flee for their lives. Many imps appear and dance wildly round the devil, but are finally driven off by the ghosts of departed nuns, leaving only the devil. Suddenly an apparition of St. George appears and in a struggle with His Satanic Majesty overcomes him, driving him off to Hell and ending the film with a cloud-burst of smoke.[2]

The visions of the nineteenth-century stage had at last taken life. The film, five years after its arrival, had improved upon the stock-in-trade effects of the pantomime-spectacle stage and upon such a basis advanced its initial aesthetic approach.

The general improvement in illusion over that of the stage came as much from productional techniques as it did from the camera itself. Such subjects as those just mentioned were filmed in the usual manner in a single scene played before a static camera. Méliès soon adopted the constructional form of Salmi Morse's *Passion Play*, discussed in the preceding chapter as the "action-tableaux" technique, calling it the method of "artificially arranged scenes." He, like his colleagues in both stage and screen, was striving toward a pictorial continuity. Unlike American producers, he made no secret of the fact that his scenes were "fake," devised from two-dimensional staging techniques of the current melodrama and pantomime stage.

This productional method included the use of backdrops painted in perspective reproduction of locale. Cornices, fireplaces, stoves, dishes, tiled roofs, bookcases, pictures, highlights, and shadows were all painted in the conventional stage manner. Fantastic effects and natural objects were similarly executed in two dimensions: seven-headed hydras, submarines, airplanes, enormous toads, Cinderella's carriage, caves, trees, moons, or train wrecks. These were then arranged with actors and possibly certain necessary three-dimensional properties in front of the backdrop and the action proceeded, as on a stage, before a fixed camera. In the construction of the setting, the effect, or in the staging, no attempt was made to achieve a pictorial realism beyond that of the conventional stage.

But while the inherent realism of the camera contrived to impart a preferable realism to this form, Méliès was not satisfied. To exploit and to heighten the pictorial illusion of his sensational and fantastic subjects, he utilized certain camera and laboratory techniques. "In his efforts to mystify and startle his audience Méliès evolved the fade-out, the overlap-dissolve, the double exposure and like expedients,"[3] thus leaving nothing fantastic to the imagination, and in this way improving upon similar attempts on the stage.

A pumpkin could be turned into a carriage, or the head of a man in a train wreck could be cut off at the neck.

Méliès, then, in terms of production and staging, simply continued nineteenth-century methods, carrying them, through his use of camera techniques, to a certain perfection. He went beyond the appropriation of nineteenth-century productional techniques. He borrowed material which formed the nucleus of the spectacle stage, both pantomime and historical, and found it particularly adaptable to his method of filming.

His first successful experiment with the long narrative film taken from the pantomime-spectacle stage was *Cinderella*. It was completed in 1900, and although filmed on 2000 feet, was released by Pathé in 900 feet. Twenty of the important episodes of the well-known fairy tale were selected and filmed in a series of action-tableaux. *Cinderella* introduced "devices of the stage. Elaborate settings, special costumes, carefully composed tableaux, professional acting, and many dissolving scenic effects, ballets and marches gave the film a theatrical grandeur that distinguished it above all its competitors."[4] Thus the competition being offered by Méliès to the realistic-romantic stage arose in this case from his elaboration of pantomime-spectacle material through ultrasensational pictorial effects.

With the success of *Cinderella*, many more of the fairy tales of the pantomime stage were filmed. In 1901, *Red Riding Hood* was done in twelve tableaux on 520 feet, and *Blue Beard* in twelve tableaux on 690 feet. These fantastic spectacles were related to the second category of Méliès' films. Using the same productional technique, this group aimed at realistic spectacle. In 1900, *Joan of Arc* was produced in twelve tableaux using "about 500 persons. . . all superbly costumed. . . with pictures of the greatest beauty in the production of which nothing has been economized."[5] The eighth scene, The Battle of Compiègne, became a

reproduction of a Battle of the Middle Ages. . . At the moment when the men-at-arms begin to demolish the palisades by means of axes, a draw-bridge is suddenly lowered, and a company charges out of the town. . . two Burgundian soldiers throw [Joan] off her horse. She is taken prisoner into the town and the drawbridge is closed. Furious, the

French captain orders reinforcements, and the picture terminates with a general assault and a furious battle. The bombs thunder from all quarters; men-at-arms climb turrets by ladders; the defenders shower projectiles and boiling pitch upon them and the archers shoot thousands of arrows making many victims.[6]

The success of this and others in the same class—*Robinson Crusoe, Gulliver's Travels,* both about 1902, and *The Damnation of Faust* in 1904—was achieved in a manner copied from nineteenth-century staging practice and thus marks the relation between the early screen and the stage.

This last subject, *Faust,* introduced still another type of Méliès production, that of original fantasy. It became Méliès' most successful form. Taking the legend of Faust, he developed it according to his own fantastical tastes. The twelfth of fifteen motion-tableaux shows The Nymphs of the Underworld, The Seven-Headed Hydra, The Demons.

In the midst of the falling water of the cascade there appear almost imperceptibly some naiads floating about in the air. . . They gradually fade away and in the water trickling down the cliff there appears a monster of a seven-headed hydra which twists restlessly about. This beast disappears and demons bearing torches. . . perform all sorts of capers. They set fire to the cavern. . . the water ceases to flow. Mephistopheles seizes Faust and both vanish into the ground.[7]

In this field of gothic grotesquery Méliès excelled. In 1902 *A Trip to the Moon* was filmed in thirty action-tableaux on 845 feet. It is significant that long films should have been first attempted with material which depended upon sensational pictures, upon the literal presentation of the fantastic. The many scenes of this and others of its kind often required no acting, the dramatic illusion arising simply out of the pictures. In *Fairyland,* which was photographed on 1040 feet, scene 13, entitled "Encountering a Tempest at Sea," used no actors. The "open ocean" appears:

The waves swell with rage; the sky becomes threatening, black clouds appear on the horizon and approach with marvelous rapidity. The galley rolls and pitches among the billows, scarcely making any headway. The storm bursts with fury, lightning illumines the sky, rain falls in torrents, the sea is overturned, the galley is half-swamped and is driven with terrifying swiftness against some cliffs which border the wild coast. (This tableau is one of the cleverest arranged for cinematograph.) The sea is represented by natural water agitated mechanically. The rain is likewise real water. . . the tableau has a marvelous appearance of reality.[8]

Shades of Dion Boucicault, Steele MacKaye, and the rest! In the following year, 1904, an imaginery trip to the sun, called *An Impossible Voyage,* was filmed. Méliès spent $7,500 for its fantastic effects, "employing all the known devices of locomotion—automobiles, dirigibles, balloons, submarines, boats, rockets, et cetera." A group of scientists departs the world. "At three hundred miles an hour they visit the rising run and the aurora borealis, pass through a solar eruption, get frozen in a heavenly embankment, are thawed out by an explosion and eventually land on earth again."[9] Its effects, of the same type as those of nineteenth-century pantomime-spectacle, were not only fantastic elaborations but, by virtue of the camera, were much more realistically presented. Méliès was both continuing and heightening the current realistic-romantic vogue in staging.

Méliès' original fantastic subjects were extremely popular. In the following year, *The Palace of Arabian Nights* used 1400 feet and thirty tableaux. Then came *An Adventurous Automobile Trip,* again exploiting trick effects. A policeman is struck by a car. "By a passage of the automobile over his body [it] is flattened out as thin as a sheet of paper. . . the King sets out leaving the work of pumping up the policeman to his original size to the numerous bystanders, but the latter became so animated in their efforts that they cause the poor unfortunate to explode."[10] This kind of spectacular trickery, far superior to that of the pantomime stage, naturally brought new converts to the nickelodeons. As the *New York Telegraph* proclaimed, on the morning of June 13, 1905, "Nothing funnier has been seen here in many a day. . . The thing is a scream."[11]

Méliès continued in this vein, but from about 1905 the popularity of his sensational trick effects wore off as the artificiality of "arranged" tableaux became ever more apparent. He sensed the unabated taste for realism, abandoned his "fake" methods, and produced an action-melodrama, *A Desperate Crime,* of the most sensational sort. This time he made special mention that the "drama is unfortunately real and we are giving a faithful and exact reproduction of it in all its details."[12] These details included an extremely realistic torture scene, a triple murder ending in robbery and arson, a gun battle between criminals and police, a great courtroom scene, and finally an execution by guillotine and a pauper's funeral. In the same year he tried another of the same type, *Robert Macaire and Bertrand,* using improvements in scenery, but retaining tableaux technique. Unable to compete with the new cinematic developments of Porter and his colleagues, he turned again to fantastic material in the next year, and, although he continued to make pictures until the outbreak of the war, he never regained his earlier prestige.

George Méliès brought to the film its first aesthetic approach. He recognized the realistic properties of the film and, at the same time, he realized that the camera, paradoxically, could proceed extravagantly in the creation of fantastic effects. His many camera and laboratory devices were all calculated toward the realistic presentation of romantic values. For instance, double exposure enabled him to show ghosts or visions without the clumsy apparatus of vampire traps, mirrors, or scrims; stop action made it easy to turn a pumpkin into Cinderella's carriage; with reverse action, gravity could be defied; fast or slow motion made clowns out of ordinary performers; the dissolve turned the traditional transformation scene into a special possession of the screen; and animation transferred all the grotesquery of gothic romance into the stock pile of cinematic effects. He borrowed both the method and matter of the nineteenth-century pictorial stage, and by use of the camera increased the realism of its spectacular stage forms. Méliès thus extended the life of the realistic-romantic cycle emanating from Garrick, and in this way helped to postpone the reaction which normally would have been expected at about this time.

EIGHT

MELODRAMA:
THE PHOTOPLAY, 1902-1913

 The photoplay, a series of situations pictorially developed not only to tell a story but so interlaced that this story became cinematically dramatic, had not found significant expression prior to 1902. It came in that year with E. S. Porter's *The Life of an American Fireman*. Its arrival did not mark a cessation of activity by George Méliès or by the makers of the simple reproductional episodes. Both felt Porter's competition and both exaggerated their individual qualities, Méliès, as we have seen, becoming more fantastic, and the makers of episodes more sensational. Thus, while the technique of Porter in the fourteen-minute, one-reel melodrama became the basic form in the decade from 1902 to 1913, it was not in extensive use until about 1906-1908, and even then films of this genre appeared on bills supported by the episodic films.

I. THE MELODRAMA

The physical conditions which controlled the filming of *The Life of an American Fireman* were no different from the conditions under which reproductional topical subjects or realistic storyettes were filmed. Porter's contribution came in the dramatic, or better, cinematic arrangement of such a series of reproductional topical subjects. From an already existing stock of such subjects, Porter developed a technique which gained for him the dominant creative position in the motion-picture industry prior to D. W. Griffith. Once this technique had been set up, the hundreds of pictures Porter produced were stereotypes; film after film repeated the pattern and method developed in *The Life of an American*

Fireman and crystallized in *The Great Train Robbery*. The industry followed suit, daring no great changes until about 1910.

The Life of an American Fireman was released on 425 feet. Pictorial realism and spectacularism were the main objectives. It aimed "to portray the life of an American Fireman without exaggeration and at the same time to embody the dramatic situations and spectacular effects which so greatly enhance a motion picture performance." To guarantee the authenticity of these spectacular effects, the "services of the fire departments of four different cities, New York, Newark, Orange and East Orange, New Jersey," were secured, "and about 300 firemen" appeared in the various scenes. It became "the first motion picture ever made of a genuine interior hitch."[1]

These authentic incidents filmed from real life were blended into a pictorial continuity by means of dissolve linkage. The scenes were arranged to present two parallel lines of action progressing simultaneously and providing, through their eventual intersection, culmination and climax. The first line opens with the fire chief asleep and dreaming in his office chair. The second line starts with a vision, a dream which comes to the chief, of a mother putting her child to bed. This scene dissolves to the ringing of an alarm at the neighborhood box. In this way the relationship between the two lines of action is quickly and firmly established. Consecutive scenes show the firemen asleep in their quarters above the engine house, waking, sliding down the brass pole, arranging the "genuine interior hitch," finally issuing from the engine house and dashing full speed through the streets, joining "countless pieces of apparatus." The film is cut to the scene of the fire. The engines arrive. Operations begin. In the meantime, the second line of action has advanced to the point where the woman and her child have been trapped in the burning building. The film dissolves to the interior to show them surrounded by flames, suffocated by heavy smoke. Here the two simultaneous lines of action meet as a fireman rescues the woman and child, providing a climactic finale.

The success of *An American Fireman* obviously depended upon the pictorial development of two lines of action, which, proceeding simultaneously, culminated to form the climax. Within this structural form were included such spectacular devices as the vision which introduced the second line of action, the dissolve linkage blending the scenes, and a change in camera position showing first the interior of the burning room and then its exterior as the action moves out the window with the rescue. Both the technical devices and the editorial pattern of this first photoplay were direct appropriations from the stage of nineteenth-century melodrama.

In the following year (1903), Porter followed his first success with *The Great Train Robbery*, filmed on 740 feet. The significance of this picture lay not only in its technique but also in the timeliness of its arrival. For at this point in the history of the film, audiences had begun to lose interest in pictures that simply moved. Managers found them helpful as "chasers" between vaudeville acts. This photoplay succeeded in reviving interest in the film. "It was shown that pictures were not yet dead, for one New York vaudeville theatre restored the pictures to their old 'headline' position, making *The Train Robbery* the featured attraction."[2] Coming, then, at a significant, if not crucial moment in the development of the motion picture, the technique employed by Porter sustained the popularity and insured the permanency of the medium.

Porter's aim in this photoplay seems to have been similar to that of the stage melodrama from which it was derived. But while the stage was impeded by a conventional method of production, the screen had at its disposal the reproductional powers of the camera, as well as its fluidity. Realism plus sensationalism in the presentation of its melodramatic material supported the cinema through this critical period in its early career.

Unlike *An American Fireman,* the scenes of *The Train Robbery* were contrived and rehearsed particularly for the purpose. Unlike the contemporaneous work of Méliès, the scenic conventions of the stage were combined with scenes filmed "on location." The quality of the film is entirely cinematic. Action is three-dimensional with a three-dimensional playing area. Movement is used toward and away from the camera, not simply in a plane perpendicular to its line of vision against flat, contrived scenery. The camera, on occasion, swings to follow the action. The chase scenes are altogether natural. Thus, while the fundamental quality of the film was wholly cinematic, this very quality was developed out of the constructional pattern and the pictorial approach of the nineteenth-century melodrama stage.

Porter made refinements in his original editorial technique. He began his story with a simple pictorial continuity. The robbers are shown entering the railroad telegraph office, forcing the operator to signal the engineer to stop his train for water, binding and gagging the operator, and departing to catch the now moving train. From the action in the office the continuity proceeds in a straight line forward to the watering tank, the train pulling out, and the robbers boarding it as it begins to move. At this point the camera leaves the robbers and cuts to a new line of action proceeding simultaneously in the interior of the mail car, where the clerk is busy at the safe. He hears a sound at the door, peers through the keyhole, and discovers the burglars trying to make an entrance. As they succeed, the two simultaneous lines of action meet to provide the first climax, where the clerk locks the safe, throws away the key, and is killed in the ensuing gun battle. Porter cuts quickly from this climax to another, proceeding simultaneously in the locomotive cab and tender, where more of the robbers are battling with the fireman and engineer. The fireman is knocked senseless, and the engineer is forced to stop the train and unhitch the locomotive. The scene is now cut back to the first group of bandits who in the meantime have lined up the passengers on the tracks and are "frisking" them. The next three scenes follow a simple pictorial continuity, showing three phases of the bandits' escape: the locomotive run, the race over the hills to the waiting horses, and finally the dash into the wilderness on horseback. This continuity is broken to flashback to the uncompleted line of action stemming from the original attack of the bandits upon the telegraph officer and their successful departure. The operator's daughter releases and revives him. He rushes out to give the alarm. The film cuts to a dance hall where a secondary action, "a lively quadrille," is in progress. This action is interrupted as the operator enters and alerts the men, who join the second branch of the main line of action. Again there is a cut across to the first branch of this main line, the robbers escaping. They are being followed by a posse, which they manage to outdistance and, in apparent safety, examine their loot. Suddenly they are surprised by the posse. A gun battle results, and in this simultaneous culmination of the two original lines of action, the bandits are killed.

The melodramatic editorial pattern of this film, deriving directly from that of nineteenth-century stage melodrama, was supported by photographic realism and pictorial sensations, the first by means of location shooting and the second through the use of such fluid and spectacular cinematic techniques as pictorial continuity, forward cutting, cross-cutting, or flashing back. These devices and the simultaneous development of a number of parallel lines of action became the platform upon which the future of the film was secured.

In the presence of such an effective pattern for the development of action melodrama, subsequent releases sought ever more sensational effects. *The Train Wreckers,* an Edison release of 1906 in 815 feet, used stock sensations of long theatrical standing.

The daughter of the switchman overhears a gang of ruffians who are planning to wreck the next express train. They discover and tie her to a tree and go ahead with their work. Her dog comes to her rescue and she sends him to fetch her father in the switch tower. She goes to the cross-ties placed there by the men, but cannot remove them. She uses her red petticoat and flags the train to a stop. But as soon as the train starts up again the blackguards blackjack her and tie her to the rails and leave her to her fate and escape on a hand car stolen from a neighboring road tool shack. A train is bearing down on the girl and the girl's lover is its engineer. He sees her, rushes down to the pilot and while the train continues madly on, he lifts her from the tracks to safety. The train is stopped and her father arrives. They uncouple the engine and start off after the villains. They overtake them and a pistol duel at top speed ensues with the villains all killed and some of the crew of the train.[3]

Against the realism of such sensational material the stage melodrama, attempting similar pictorial effects, could hardly hope to compete.

Porter's films reflected contemporary American life and commented upon current issues and interests. In *The Kleptomaniac* (1905), he protested a double standard of justice, one for the wealthy and another for the poor. At the same time he experimented further with cinematic technique in this picture. The first line of action, Mrs. Banker's shopping tour, her shoplifting, and arrest, is developed in a direct pictorial continuity without reference to the second line. Then the second line is introduced, showing a mother's theft of a loaf of bread to feed her starving children, and her subsequent arrest. These two lines which have no actual relationship in time or place are brought together at the police-court trial, where, by an acquittal of Mrs. Banker and a conviction of the poor mother, they serve to satirize justice. A final tableau shows Justice winking as she holds a pair of scales in which gold overbalances bread. By means of the camera, two physically unrelated lines of action are contrasted by relating each of them editorially to a third line. Thus experimentation with film construction evolved around the original pattern of parallel action.

The Ex-Convict (1905), another melodrama, again on a social theme, emphasizes social injustice by rapid contrast-cutting between the lives of an ex-convict and a wealthy manufacturer.

These techniques originally used upon the stage of the nineteenth century formed a simple editorial system which remained the basic photoplay construction to the time of Griffith. Changes or refinements did not come until 1910. It is significant that this motion-picture pattern grew directly out of the capacities of the camera in the hands of an artist untrained in the methods of the stage. Porter's borrowing of the methods of the melodrama stage appears unpremeditated and accidental. It would seem, on the other hand, that the technique of the motion-picture camera was intimately related to the stage of the nineteenth century, for its product, in Porter's theatrically untutored hands, fell automatically into the dramatic patterns of the melodrama.

Talent from the stage appeared later, but in the meantime the industry continued to build considerable success upon the melodrama-photoplay technique demonstrated by E. S. Porter. To the sensationalism of this method, effort was continually made to add realism and authenticity. *A Desperate Encounter between Burglar and Police* "accurately depicts scenes and incidents of a noted crime in New York City in which a well-known police officer was killed. The scenes were enacted over the very same ground, and the same night-watchman and the same policeman who took part in the real tragedy are seen in the picture."[4] with such "on location" filming of episodes out of real life, the melodrama of the film sought to outdistance that of the stage.

Toward the end of the nineteenth century a secret organization of citizen vigilantes, in the manner of the Ku Klux Klan, existed in the Middle West. They were known as the White Caps. Porter sensed that the activities of such a group would lend themselves to cinema, and sensed, too, that the film would gain conviction through the authenticity of its source. This filming, as many others of the time, achieved the three qualities which have, from the start, recommended the motion picture. It "portrayed, in a most vivid and realistic manner, the methods employed by the 'White Caps' to rid the community of undesirable ctizens. . . As a soul-stirring melodramatic production, it is undoubtedly the finest picture that has ever been offered to our customers and the public, while the photographic qualities and beautiful moonlight and early morning effects must be seen to be appreciated."[5] Realism, action-melodrama, and spectacle joined hands in these early films.

That these attempts were successful in meeting an audience need of which the stage, in 1905, was falling short is nicely phrased in a review of a stage play, *Zorah,* given at Proctor's Fifth Avenue Theatre. Edison had just released *Stolen by Gypsies,* a simple melodrama.

Yesterday, between the second and third acts, there was a wait of over half an hour, during which the audience was treated to an intensely interesting motion picture, entitled *Stolen by Gypsies.* There was so much human interest to this little story, and its climaxes came so thick and fast, as it followed the child from the moment it was stolen up to the hour of its rescue a year later in the gypsies' camp, that it made *Zorah,* by comparison, seem rather stilted and stagey.[6]

The conventions of realism of the legitimate stage were apparently in the process of breakdown, and the screen, with its unfailing reproduction of real life, was moving into the breach, taking over a ready-made and waiting audience. By 1909, Walter Prichard Eaton reported, "Popular [stage] melodramas, since moving pictures became the rage, have decreased fifty percent in number."[7] While the stage melodrama lost its audience, that of the motion picture expanded. Eaton found himself pondering, even in 1909, "that in New York City alone, on a Sunday, 500,000 people go to moving picture shows. . . you cannot discuss canned drama with a shrug of contempt. . . Eighty percent of present day theatrical audiences are canned drama audiences. . . Four million people attended moving picture theatres, it is said, every day. . . 7000 canned drama theatres."[8]

In the words of Montrose Moses, the melodrama "has flourished on the screen because one of its chief characteristics was a dependence on variety of background, quick shifting from one place to another, water and land effects, three-dimensional situations which called into play all the athletic powers of the players. These demands could be met and even amplified on the screen."[9] The stage had originally met the same needs with a clumsy and conventional staging method. The screen, with the fluidity and authenticity of the camera, could easily surpass the stage at its own game.

Before the single-reel photoplay was superseded by the feature film during the period beginning in 1913, a series of Boucicault melodramas was screened. Filmed on two or three reels, these were ordinarily released in single-reel episodes, but were nevertheless experiments with the longer film. Again the melodrama served as basis for further progress. The series included *Kathleen Mavourneen* (1911), *The Colleen Bawn* (1911), *Arrah-na-Pogue* (1911), *The Shaughraun* (1912), *The Octoroon* (1913), and *Kathleen Mavourneen* again in 1913. All but the first and last were filmed by Sidney Olcott for Kalem Studios on location in the "authentic" backgrounds of Ireland. It is not at all surprising that the Boucicault melodrama should have been taken into the films. For these plays, by virtue of their dependence upon external effects, as well as by virtue of the values inherent in their dramatic style, were prime cinematic material.

The photoplay form exploited by E. S. Porter found its largest expression in the field of the "western" film. This soon "became the most popular form of entertainment ever known, although [it] did not reach the heights of success until 1909-1910."[10] In a typical week in 1908, a large distributor handled only eighteen pictures which were not westerns.[11] In the same year the cowboy, a fresh, romantic hero, was introduced to the American audience in the Broncho Billy series. But the pattern of the western retained the techniques set up originally by Porter in *The Great Train Robbery*.

And so, in looking back over the establishment of the melodramatic photoplay, it may be seen first of all that Porter's technique came at a critical point in the rise of the early film to insure the permanency of the medium. This technique grew out of a pictorial continuity of separate but related dramatic episodes strung together to tell a story. Through the flexibility of the camera, two or more lines of action were developed pictorially in the same film. These parallel lines of action, usually occurring simultaneously and culminating in a single climax, were either developed simultaneously by cross-cutting, or separately by simple pictorial continuity. Visions were used to suggest a simultaneous event in one or the other of these parallel lines. These editorial techniques were used to integrate episodes staged as action-tableaux usually "on location." For the most part played before a fixed camera, there are instances of the camera's moving to follow the action. Similarly, the position of the camera might be changed in the course of a scene to show the same action from a different vantage point with a shift in dramatic emphasis. The whole of this development in cinematic technique was imbued with the authenticity of photographic realism.

E. S. Porter's subject matter also came from the immediate realities of American life. The successes and setbacks of the policeman, burglar, factory worker, slum mother, clerk, country girl, mechanic, drunkard, artist, farmer, and politician were all cinematized. Thus the melodramatic technique, rooted in realism, became the second basis for the cinema's bid for permanence. With both its romantic quality and its realistic illusion it continued the realistic-romantic theatrical cycle, demonstrating a technique similar to that of popular melodrama and borrowing material directly from it.

II. COMEDY-SLAPSTICK

With the decline of popularity of the "trick" film comedy of George Méliès, slapstick became the significant comic form. The film *Personal*, discussed by F. J. Marion as the earliest photoplay,[12] was a comedy. The basic situation of this was farcical[13] and provided an opportunity for the broad, burlesque style of chase sequence. The bevy of fervent would-be wives madly after a frightened little "French" fortune hunter made for broad business. It was such overdone comic business that characterized early screen comedy. Lacking dialogue, the comedy of character and wit were difficult if not impossible to achieve, and film comedy naturally took on burlesque values. There were those who already felt that laughter "should not be too much at the mercy of mere mechanical devices, of waterhose, and dust-shoots and interminable masses of sticky dough, and ice-cream that covers the actor's face as with whiskers."[14] But there was no suggestion as to how, in the absence of these contrivances, laughter might be elicited. This pictorial, surface technique employed in screen comedy was rooted in the very nature of the silent camera as it was in the basic premise of the popular nineteenth-century pictorial stage. Both forms were enhanced by the addition of physical stage effects.

Personal was the first of a long line of successful screen comedies, all based upon and extending these same qualities. The most obvious instance of slapstick arising out of exaggerated business was that of the practical joke. *Mrs. Smither's Boarding-School* (Biograph, March 28, 1907) starts with pupils making a dash for the Professor's bedroom where they carry out all sorts of practical jokes, tying his clothes into knots, filling his hat with ashes, nailing his shoes to the floor, and so on. Comedy of external effects was synonymous with the early motion picture.

As in *Personal*, a farcical or even fantastic premise might be used to bring about the burlesque buffoonery. In *The Love-Microbe* (Biograph, 1907), an erudite Professor Cupide extracts a love microbe from a pair of lovers. He injects this into various anti-pathetic couples. The miraculous results give rise to all sorts of ludicrous clowning. *The King of the Cannibal Islands* (Biograph, 1908) tells the story of Heine, a henpecked refugee from his wife's flying pots and pans, who puts out to sea, is shipwrecked and cast upon a cannibal island. He soon becomes king and when his testy spouse overtakes him she is thrust alive into the steaming stew pot and cooked for lunch. These films, obviously enough, relied upon the pictorial hence realistic presentation of the burlesque style of comic business resulting from the original fantastic or farcical premise.

The difference between the trick film of the Méliès type and that which combined fantasy with farce was not great. There was always a strong temptation to exploit the "trick" values of the camera for laughs. *The Snow-Man* (Biograph, February 19, 1908) did just that. The film opens

outside the schoolhouse and a furious blizzard is raging. . . made up of generous quantities of sawdust. The legs, arms, torso and head of the Snow-man were fashioned of fluffy, white cotton, each a separate part, and were hidden under drifts of sawdust. . . marked so that the children could easily find them. One youngster pretends to mould of saw-dust an imaginary leg, but in reality is hunting the buried finished one, on locating which, she surreptitiously pulls it from beneath the sawdust. In this way, finally, all the parts of the Snow-man are. . . put together, revealing a beautiful Snow-man.

Then the Good Fairy of the Snows who all this time has been dream-ing in the silver crescent of the moon, looking for all the world like the charming lady of the Cascarets ads, is given a tip that the children have finished their Snow-man. . .

From her stellar heights, by means of a clumsy iron apparatus she is lowered to earth. (Sadly crude it all was, but it thrilled the fans of the day.) With her magic-wand the Good Fairy touches the Snow-man and it comes to life. Predatory Pete now comes along, sees Mr. Snow-man, and feeling rather jolly from the consumption of bottled goods, he puts his pipe in the Snow-man's mouth, and when he sees the Snow-man calmly puff it, in great fright he rushes off the scene, dropping his bottle, the contents of which the Snow-man drains. In the resultant in-toxication the Snow-man finds his way into the schoolhouse. Finding the schoolhouse too warm, he throws the stove out the window. Then he throws himself out the window and lies down to "sleep it off."

When the children return the following morning, the Snow-man, who is still sleeping, frightens them almost into convulsions. Then the picture really got started—the chase began. . . in front of a stationary backdrop that pictures a snowdrift. The actors standing off-stage ready for the excitement, come on through the saw-dust snow, kicking it up in clouds, eating it, choking on it, hair, eyes and throat getting full of it. Back and forth across this one "drop" the actors chase. On one run across, a prop tree would be set up. Then as the actors were supposed to have run some hundred yards at least on the next cross, the prop tree would be taken away and a big papier-mache rock put in its place. That scene being photographed, the rock would give way to a telegraph pole and so on until half a dozen "chases" had been staged before the one drop.*[15]

The theatrical illusion presented here, and that offered by the stage in the years preceding and surrounding the early film, were similar. Both depended upon pictorial realism. It is obvious that the screen could achieve a greater and more flexible realism in the treatment of such fantastical effects as the Snow-man's smoking, drinking, becoming intoxicated, throwing the stove and himself out the window, and so on, than could the pantomime or music-hall stage.

This style of external-effects comedy developed, with many elaborations, into the slapstick of the silent film. To the flying stoves, drunken snow-men, boiling wives, "energized" loafers, artificially inflamed couples were added the gamut of mechanical effects characteristic of the work of Mack Sennett.[16] The basis for its success, save for an added "girl-appeal," remained the same.

John Bunny[17] sacrificed the appeal of fantasy and trickery and added his peculiar genius in comic pantomimic characterization to the usual pattern of farcical situation and burlesque buffoonery. In *The Autocrat of Flapjack Junction* (Vitagraph, 1913),[18] for instance, Bunny, cast as a boardinghouse keeper, is desperate over the competition of a widow who is a rival in the same business. He rushes into the forest to commit suicide, but instead rescues a band of chorus girls in distress. In return they patronize his boardinghouse, restore his business standing, and in the end make it possi-

---

* From *When the Movies Were Young* by Linda A. (Mrs. D. W.) Griffith. Copyright, 1925, by E. P. Dutton and Company, Inc., and quoted with their permission.

ble for him to marry the widow. Thus, while Bunny's contribution was highly individual, it does not alter the relationship between this form and the stage.

The whole field of early film comedy, then, using the same storytelling technique which had been developed by Mr. Porter for the melodrama, based its appeal on (1) the fantastical-farcical premise, and (2) the resultant broad business and burlesque buffoonery. The success of this external-effects type of comedy grew out of the ability of the camera to realize these two values pictorially. A general similarity in the concept of comic theatrical illusion existed between this type of film comedy and that of the nineteenth century pictorial stage. A tangible relationship can be found between this early slapstick film, the music-hall burlesque, and the pantomime.

III. THE AMERICAN TRICK FILM

While George Méliès' method in the trick film was simple, direct, and objective, American producers in attempting this same type of film added a new realism. Through the proper editorial arrangement, the fantastical trick elements could be introduced subjectively; they could be shown to the audience as if through the eyes of the actor experiencing the fantasy. In this way the fantasy became a personal, subjective experience of the audience and not the simple observation of trick effects. This resulted in an increase in the realism of camera fantasy and thus in an extension of the popularity and dramatic effectiveness of the form.

For instance, Biograph's *The Tired Tailor's Dream* (1907) opens with the tailor going to sleep and dreaming. The audience, imaginatively partaking of his snooze, sees his brush, chalk, square, and suits of clothes come to life. The fantasy gains in realism through its subjective treatment. In *The Princess Nicotine* (Vitagraph, 1909), by Blackton and Smith, a pipe smoker dreams. Again the spectators enter his dream subjectively as fairies emerge from his tobacco box, eluding his grasp through a series of transformations into roses and other objects. These transformations, significant devices of the pantomime-spectacle stage, gained realistically and sensationally through the technique of the camera and an editorial treatment which presented them as subjective experience.

Probably the best of these comic fantasies was Porter's *Dream of a Rarebit Fiend* (Edison, 1906). An attempt was made to thrill the spectator by sensational fantasy subjectively presented. The dream of the rarebit fiend becomes the audience's personal experience. As the camera sways and reels we see the walls reeling as if we were the dreamer. Furniture, clothes, and other properties take life. When the sleeping dreamer sails out of his bed and into the midnight sky, it is really the audience dream-flying. Devils drum a pitchfork rhapsody on our own skulls, a weathervane catches us dropping through space, whips us into a drunken twirl and through the roof of the dreamer's house, where he wakes to find himself in bed. This fantastic material gained in the impression of reality conveyed to the spectator by virtue of an editorial technique which imbued it with the quality of subjective experience. Produced at a cost of $350, this film created effects which would have cost thousands upon the stage and which would have relied greatly upon the acceptance of conventional treatment.

Domestic trick-film production, then, besides contributing a subjective approach to fantasy, utilized all the values of sensational spectacle, transformations, visions, and so on, that Méliès had exploited, and which belonged, in both form and spirit, to the fabric of the nineteenth-century pantomime-spectacle stage.

IV. EARLY SPECTACLE FILMS

The early motion picture leaned heavily on the appeal of spectacle. These films generally used the episodic-tableaux technique derived from the stage and were not done in the style of the photoplay exploited throughout this period by E. S. Porter. *Parsifal* (Edison, 1904), employing the "same talent, scenery and costumes used in the original dramatic production,"[19] shows in a spectacular manner, entirely reminiscent of the nineteenth-century stage, "the magic castle of Klingsor, a place of fantastic outlines illuminated with a dim unholy light. . . The whole castle sinks and in its place rises the magic garden full of tropical vegetation and luxurious wealth of flowers. . . One after the other [the Maidens] slip away and return in the guise of living flowers."[20] This manner of production reproduced on the screen the representational spectacle of the stage. The stage spectacle had thus been recognized in these early years as a source for screen material. The new medium met the same audience that had patronized the romantic spectacle of Kean, Phelps, Barrett, Irving, and the rest.

Attempts were naturally made to improve upon the methods of the stage. In the case of outdoor spectacles, filming on location was always the most popular and successful method. Longfellow's *Hiawatha* (Bioscope, 1903) used twenty scenes, all episodic-tableaux, but all authentic. It was filmed on location and was enacted by North American Indians of the Ojibway tribe at Desbarets, Ontario.[21] The reproductional realism of this type of spectacle was obviously impossible on the stage. Similarly, *An Acadian Elopement* (Biograph, 1907) showed "the Normandy of the New World, with its blossomy fields, and lanes shaded with masses of pendulous foliage, colored with ephemeral clusters of wild flowers."[22] On the other hand, spectacles calling for indoor photography and indoor settings were limited by productional facilities. Indoor photography was not a practical procedure until 1906, and in the next few years only the three pioneers, Edison, Biograph, and Vitagraph, established indoor studios. Set construction was still two-dimensional and extremely simple. Scene painters and designers, gradually recruited from the theatre, used sets consisting mainly of "flats" much like those of the stage.

These productional limitations did not exist in costuming. *The King's Messenger* (Biograph, 1908), employing the single-reel photoplay technique, was "laid in the seventeenth century, and the costumes, while historically accurate, are most lavishly elaborate."[23] Attempts such as these were paving the way for the colossal and authentic feature-length screen spectacle.

In the meantime, film makers conscientiously utilized the methods of the pantomime-spectacle stage, surpassing them in fluidity as in realistic illusion through use of the camera. In *Dorothy's Dream* (Urban and Bioscope, 1903), principal scenes of seven of the best known fairy-tale pantomime-spectacles were combined. The girl dreams. "The good Fairy appears, gradually taking shape from a nebulous mist floating in the air; she waves her magic wand over the little dreamer and causes to pass in review, visions of the principal scenes of *Dick Whittington, Robinson Crusoe, The Forty Thieves, Cinderella, Aladdin and the Wonderful Lamp, Blue Beard* and *Red Riding Hood.*"[24] While visions and transformations were directly borrowed from the stage, the ability of the screen to handle as many as seven principal scenes in a few minutes eclipsed the clumsy, conventional machinery of the stage. Releases such as *Dorothy's Dream* or *A Christmas Dream* (Bioscope, 1903), which packed "twenty scenes with dissolving effects, tricks and spectacular tableaux, snow-scenes, ballets, night effects and marches"[25] all into 528 feet or six minutes, indicate the extent by which the screen could outrival the spectacle stage even with its own weapons.

The current dramatic stage, too, with its spectacles of historical and religious nature, provided material for the screen. *Ben Hur* was done as a single-reel dramatic spectacle by F. A. Rose and Sidney Olcott for Kalem in 1907. In this early filming of the popular novel, while the stage might possibly have surpassed the screen version in lavishness of setting, it could not provide a more realistic climax, for this climax was the famed chariot race in the Circus Maximus of ancient Rome. Disregarding any personal preferences in this instance of the early rivalry between stage and screen, the significant conclusion is that such a rivalry had arisen and that, by virtue of the competition, the realistic-romantic theatrical cycle experienced an extension beyond the point at which reaction would normally have been expected.

With the making of longer films, the popularity of the appeal of spectacle in motion pictures was again demonstrated, for it was in this area that experiments were attempted. In 1909-1910, J. Stuart Blackton filmed *The Life of Moses* for Vitagraph in five reels. Authenticity was guaranteed by the Reverend Madison C. Peters, an authority on Hebrew history. Released in five separate reels or as a unit, this picture marks a step toward the feature-length film made on the basis of spectacle.

The first aesthetic approach to cinema, that of M. Méliès, was founded on spectacle, artificial and fantastic; the second aesthetic development, that of the photoplay form of E. S. Porter, exploited action-melodrama; and now the third great advance, that of the feature-length film, was being heralded for its realistic spectacle. Melodrama and spectacle were obviously the two dramatic qualities so fundamentally cinematic that they served as bases for experiment and progress. While the melodrama had established and defined the screen audience, competition for this audience "centered on display and exaggeration of sets, mobs and dramatic action."[26] In the production of *Napoleon, the Man of Destiny* (Vitagraph, 1909), Blackton "spent three months in France searching records and archives to secure unimpeachable historical accuracy of details. The country was ransacked for furniture of the period, and the staging of interior scenes. No less than £6,000. were sunk in this enterprise."[27] Backed by such authenticity, spectacle moved into an ever-more significant position in film output. This position was clinched when famous players of the stage saw suitable material for their appearance upon the screen in the feature-length spectacle.

Sarah Bernhardt and Lou Tellegen appeared in *Queen Elizabeth* in 1912. It was filmed by Louis Mercanton in four reels complete with stage scenery and business. Sarah not only took her curtain call on the screen, but her final plop into a pile of pillows directly toward the camera as the climax of the death scene, seems nearer slapstick than drama. Despite its many technical and aesthetic shortcomings, and despite the danger of its extreme length, Adolph Zukor, sensing the strong taste for the historical spectacle film, purchased the American rights with Daniel Frohman. On July 12, 1912, it was exhibited as the first feature film of the Famous Plays with Famous Players. Shown in full length, it was nevertheless a great success. The epoch of the feature film had thus been introduced by the foreign spectacle film.

The Battle Hymn of the Republic (Vitagraph, 1911), under the direction of Larry Trimble, provides an excellent illustration of how thoroughly popular theatre had sacrificed its imaginative and poetic conception through the course of the realistic-romantic theatrical cycle; how this pictorial theatre, in its never-ending quest for the sensational, had sunk, in the early spectacle film, to a new low in "literalism." Events associated with Julia Ward Howe's composition of the poem were spectacularly depicted as titles were

57. *Le Royaume des fées,* a George Méliès-Star film (1903).

58. *Le Royaume de Neptune,* a George Méliès-Star film (1907).

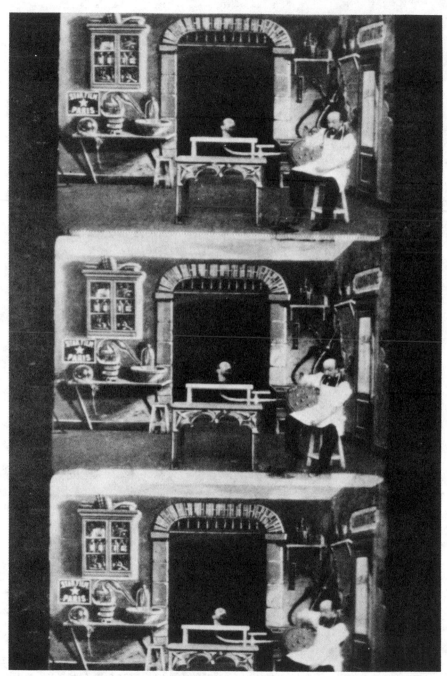

59. *L'Homme à la tête en caoutchouc,* a George Méliès-Star film (1902).

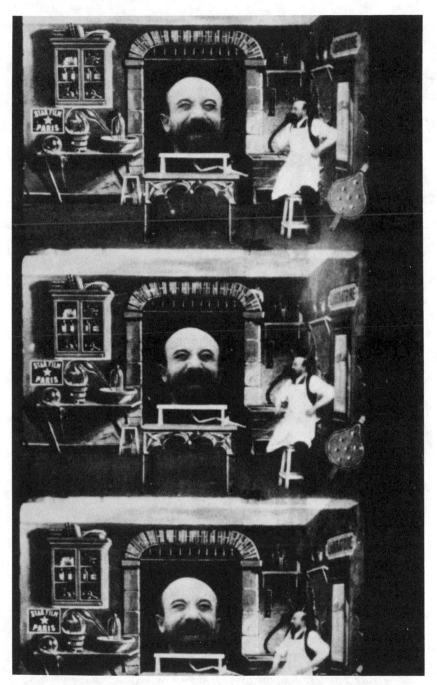

60. *L'Homme à la tête en caoutchouc,* a George Méliès-Star film (1902).

61. *Uncle Tom's Cabin*, the play produced by William Brady (1901).

62. *Uncle Tom's Cabin*, the play produced by William Brady (1901).

63. *Uncle Tom's Cabin,* the film directed by Edwin S. Porter (1903).

64. *Uncle Tom's Cabin,* the film directed by Edwin S. Porter (1903).

65. *Edgar Allan Poe*, directed by D. W. Griffith (1909), with Linda
Arvidson and Herbert Yost.

66. *Fighting Blood*, directed by D. W. Griffith (1911), with Blanche Sweet
and Lionel Barrymore.

67. *The Count of Monte Cristo,* directed by Colin Campbell for Selig (1912), with Hobart Bosworth.

68. *The Count of Monte Cristo,* produced by Famous Players (1913), with James O'Neill.

69. *The Prisoner of Zenda,* directed by Edwin S. Porter and Daniel Frohman (1913), with James K. Hackett and Beatrice Beckley.

70. *The Squaw Man,* directed by Cecil B. De Mille (1913), with Dustin Farnum and Red Wing.

71. *The Nightingale,* written and directed by Augustus Thomas for Ethel Barrymore's screen debut; an All Star Company film (1914).

72. *A Good Little Devil,* produced by Paramount (1914), with Mary Pickford and Ernest Truex.

73. *Enoch Arden,* directed by D. W. Griffith (1911), with Frank Grandin and Linda Arvidson.

74. *Enoch Arden,* directed by D. W. Griffith (1911), with Wilfrid Lucas.

75. *Judith of Bethulia,* directed by D. W. Griffith (1913), with Mae Marsh and Robert Harron.

76. *Judith of Bethulia,* directed by D. W. Griffith (1913).

77. *The Last Days of Pompeii*, produced by Ambrosio (1913).

78. *The Last Days of Pompeii*, produced by Ambrosio (1913).

79. *Cabiria*, directed by Pastrone and Guazzoni for Italiana-Film (1914).

80. *Oliver Twist*, directed by James Young (1916), with Marie Doro, Tully Marshall, Raymond Hatton, and Hobart Bosworth.

81. *Madame DuBarry*, directed by Ernst Lubitsch (1919), with Pola Negri and Henry Liedtke.

82. *The Count of Monte Cristo*, directed by Emmett J. Flynn for William Fox (1922).

83. *The Count of Monte Cristo*, directed by Emmett J. Flynn for William Fox (1922).

84. *Orphans of the Storm,* produced by United Artists (1922).

85. *Orphans of the Storm,* produced by United Artists (1922).

flashed upon the screen. From scenes of President Lincoln, despondent over the lack of response to his last call for troops, and of a mother refusing to let her son join, the scene moves to Julia Howe asleep at midnight, rising in a trance and writing at a table by the bed.

The pictures that might possibly have passed before her mind during the trance are thrown upon the screen. . . "Mine eyes have seen the glory of the coming of the Lord"; a gracious picture of the nativity. . . "I have seen him in the watchfires of a hundred circling camps" and "They have builded him an altar in the evening dews and damps" —for these are given symbolic pageants of the Holy Sepulchre crusaders. . . Just before the overthrow, the line is projected upon the screen: "He hath loosed the fateful lightning of his terrible swift sword." Then the heavenly host becomes gradually visible upon the air, marching toward the audience, almost crossing the footlights. . . "Our God is marching on." . . . Then comes a procession indeed. It is as though the audience were standing at the side of the throne at Doomsday looking down the hill of Zion toward the little earth. There is a line of those who are to be judged. . . barbarians. . . Caesar. . . Dante. . . Richelieu. . . Napoleon. Many people march toward the strange glorifying eye of the camera, growing larger than men.[28]

The theatrical value of the film apparently rested in the pictorial explanations of the words of the poem; imaginative participation departed in favor of graphic exposition.

Yet the success of spectacle in the film justified increasing production costs. *A Tale of Two Cities* (Vitagraph, 1911), done in three reels, each released separately or as a unit, cost $20,000.[29] *Cinderella,* a favorite of both the pantomime-spectacle stage and of the early Méliès film, was produced by Selig in 1911 in three reels, ninety-nine scenes, and a cast of three hundred. In the 1913 production of *Dick Whittington and His Cat,* a $12,000 sailboat was burned for a spectacular climax.[30] Sidney Olcott's productions never lacked for authenticity. In 1912 *From the Manger to the Cross* was filmed for Kalem on location in Palestine.[31] Scott's *Ivanhoe* was done on location at Chepstow Castle, England, in 1913 by Herbert Brenon for Imp Studio. Now, while many of the spectacle films which fall into this 1902-1913 period were produced in a number of reels, they were still largely distributed and exhibited as single-reel subjects. Yet the authenticity of these single-reel spectacles, coupled with the fluidity of their cinematic technique, outstripped stage spectacle and at the same time pointed the way toward the arrival of the feature-length film. Thus this early film form assimilated the pictorial techniques of the nineteenth-century realistic-romantic stage and popularized them to the point where they now led the way into the elaboration of cinematic art.

This discussion of the film during the years from 1902 to 1913 has not included the work of D. W. Griffith which fell into this period, nor of certain foreign influences manifest at about this time. We have nevertheless been able to see that action-melodrama and authentic-spectacle provided the two greatest single sources of appeal for the early film; that action-melodrama had insured the permanency of the medium and that spectacle had already indicated a basis for the feature film and foreshadowed the immense expansion soon to be felt within the motion-picture industry; that these two types of film, while relying largely upon pictorial realism and authenticity, were essentially of a romantic nature, and that the trick film and early screen comedy, although of secondary importance, fell within the same pattern. Thus the screen during the years from 1902 to 1913 had usurped the place of the stage melodrama, the pantomime-spectacle, and the realistic-spectacle, and in this way had continued and heightened the realistic-romantic phase in the theatre of the nineteenth and early twentieth centuries.

NINE

REALISM AND ROMANCE:
D. W. GRIFFITH

 D. W. Griffith entered motion pictures in 1907. He began as author and actor, writing a number of scripts this first year and appearing in Porter's *Rescued from an Eagle's Nest* (Edison, 1907). Born in the South in 1880, he was openly exposed from childhood to its romanticism and sentimentality. "The sentimental bias implanted in Griffith by his father (a former Confederate colonel) was reinforced by the boy's love of poetry in the Victorian manner."[1] He became an actor in the provincial theatre of the South, playing in residence or touring with the sentimental and sensational melodramas of the period. He took this theatre seriously enough to plan his career as playwright in its manner, and had gained some recognition for his play, *A Fool and a Girl*, presented in Washington and Baltimore in 1907. Having spent his conditioning years in close and constant contact with this romantic theatre, Griffith suddenly found himself in the position of writer, actor, and director— a creative artist in the most realistic art medium ever known. He was reluctant at first to jeopardize his standing in the legitimate theatre, but he gradually recognized that the screen might enable him to achieve in a much more realistic manner the same romanticized concepts with which he had been involved on the stage. He accepted his first directoral assignment with the Biograph Company in 1908.

Productional conditions were still poor at this time. Progress since Porter's *Train Robbery* was negligible. *The Snow-man*, produced at about the time of Griffith's entry into motion pictures, is indicative of the methods in use. Indoor photography had not become practical until 1906. The delay in productional progress was partly due to the furious strife over patent rights in which the industry was embroiled from 1897 to 1908. This condition was eliminated on January 1, 1909, shortly after Griffith's debut as a director. On this date the Motion Pictures Patents Company was formed by the seven American manufacturers, Edison, Biograph, Vitagraph, Lubin, Kalem, Essanay, and Selig; the two French firms of Pathé and Méliès; and finally the distributor, Kleine. This organization, which became known as the "trust," pooled all patent claims and agreed to issue no further licenses, thus removing the padlocks from the cameras and paving the way for progress on a peaceable basis. The industry assumed the cloak of dignity and respectability.

This legal reorganization called for productional and aesthetic reforms. Frank Woods, an early film critic, "now set about to criticize the pictures with the same seriousness with which he would have criticized the theater. He bought books about Indians and let the producers know there was a difference between the Hopi and the Apache and the Navajo."[2] Griffith was forced into high standards of productional realism, for early screen criticism followed stage patterns.

His first release, *The Adventures of Dolly* (Biograph, July 14, 1908), borrowed a melodramatic subject previously treated by Porter in *Stolen by Gypsies* and used a similar editorial structure. It was an outdoor film, hence pictorially realistic. To this realism Griffith added his own romantic touch. In the Porter film, Dolly had been accidentally found and recognized by her former nurse years after her kidnaping, and then simply rescued from the gypsies by the police. But in the Griffith picture, the gypsies hid her

in a water cask, put it on their wagon and sped away. As they pass over a stream, the cask falls off the wagon and into the water where it is carried by a strong current downstream, over a waterfall, through seething rapids, finally to enter the quiet cove of the first scene. Fishing boys hearing strange sounds from the cask break it open and discover Dolly. Soon she is safe in the arms of her overjoyed papa and mama.[3]

To the hard-edged melodrama of Porter, Griffith began by adding a fuller pictorial development, both sentimental and romantic.

With such romantic material he began to refine Porter's editorial approach with techniques directed toward a more thorough realism. In his filming of *For Love of Gold*, from Jack London's romantic melodrama, *Just Meat*, he made progress in the realistic presentation of character. Previous to this, the usual method for revealing the mental reaction of a character had been with a double-exposure "dream balloon" flashed above his head. Griffith eliminated this conventional technique by cutting down the editorial unit from a full scene "take" to a single "shot." The climactic scene in this picture, showing two thieves dividing their latest plunder, developed out of the fear of each that the other suspected a double-cross. Suspense and drama arose over which would first succeed in getting rid of the other, and how. This was, in its small way, the beginning of a long line of psychological thrillers, since the thieves managed to poison each other's coffee. Dramatic climax was developed through the use of a single "shot" within the scene "take." Instead of playing the entire scene before a stationary camera, with action proceeding as if on a stage, both actors visible at once, and with "dream balloons" coming to the aid of their pantomime, Griffith shifted his camera to shoot one or the other as the dramatic focus demanded. Where whole scenes had been the previous editorial unit, single shots were used here. The result was greater realism in the presentation of character and a more fluid cinematic continuity.

This use of the single shot as editorial unit had a still further effect. By eliminating all distractive elements at the moment when the reaction of the individual character became the significant dramatic value, it reduced the necessity for exaggerated acting and overplaying. Restraint in acting, hence greater realism of character, became possible.

With this start toward a more realistic treatment of character and toward a smoother and more articulate editorial pattern, Griffith sought next to improve the realism of the photography itself through an aesthetic approach to lighting. In *Edgar Allan Poe* (Biograph, 1909), he achieved a three-dimensional quality, therefore greater realism in photography, with the use of light and shade. It is of interest, too, that this new photographic realism was again coupled with a subject straight from the heart of nineteenth-century romance, dealing, as it did, with Poe's *The Raven* and incidents in the poet's baroque and abnormal life. The need for this realism in photography led Griffith into further successful experiments with lighting. In *A Drunkard's Reformation* (Biograph, 1909), he photographed fire burning in a fireplace in a darkened room. The weird, grotesque effect, with its ephemeral shadows and fugitive figures, created a startling and realistic illusion on the screen. In *Pippa Passes* (Biograph, 1909), he discarded the usual editorial form of melodrama and in a simple, direct story leaned heavily upon the pictorial appeal of his realistic lighting. Morning, Noon, Evening, and Night, the four parts of the film, were realistically filmed. And while Browning was the most rarified dramatic stuff up to date, it was reported that "the adventurous producers who inaugurated these expensive departures from cheap melodrama are being overwhelmed by offers from renting agents."[4] The appeal of simple pictures realistically presented by means of the new developments in film lighting equaled the box-office draw of melodrama.

This advance in realistic photography was followed by further progress in the articulation of motion-picture syntax and in realistic character portrayal. A one-reel version of *Enoch Arden,* rechristened *After Many Years* (Biograph, 1908), sacrificed both melodramatic structure and the usual chase sequence. Much of its success came out of the editorial technique. It was the first film to use the "close-up" to reveal more realistically than could the full shot what was going on in the minds of the characters. The visualization of a state of mind arose out of the manner in which the close-up was worked into the fabric of the film. For instance, from a close-up of Annie brooding in her seaside cottage over the fate of her long-departed Enoch the camera dissolves to a shot of Enoch shipwrecked on the desert island. The juxtaposition of these two strips of film suggested to the spectator a psychic relationship between the two which, with its reduction of spatial limitations, was not only a marvel of pictorial realism but marked the beginnings of subjective revelation of character in the cinema.

The Lonely Villa (Biograph, 1909) indicated further advance in the realism of the pictorial medium with a cross-cutting technique which left little to the imagination of the audience. A husband leaves wife and children alone in their remote villa to drive twenty miles away to fetch his mother. Robbers break into the villa. The husband's car breaks down. He calls his wife on the telephone just in time to hear her terrified cries before the wires are cut. Between these parallel lines of action a cross-cutting technique, new in its rapidity and dynamic development, was employed. Both lines of action were transferred to the screen exactly as they were progressing. The visual impact of the rapid-fire succession of "takes" developed a dynamic crescendo of suspense which was relieved only at the breaking point by the husband's last-minute arrival to effect a rescue. This cross-cutting technique was repeated in *The Lonedale Operator* (Biograph, 1911), heightening the melodramatic values through facile and realistic pictorial presentation and thus perfecting the technique employed many years before in the melodrama of the stage.

Griffith worked continually to increase graphic realism. It seems that every refinement in editorial technique was associated with this desire. In *Ramona* (Biograph, 1910), he combined the long shot with the full shot and the close-up. This of itself marked progress toward a fluid cinematic structure. But at the same time the underlying significance of this development is that each type of shot was devoted to that special purpose which seemed "right" or real in view of the dramatic value of the particular scene being filmed. The vantage point of the camera was changed in the same way that an ideal spectator, wishing to gain a real view of the action without being distracted, would change his position. The technique of photography joins here with that of editing to cast off elements of conventionality and to attain a truer realism. Action was now shown as an ideal spectator would wish to see it had he actually been present.

With the use of the full shot, more restrained acting had become possible than in the early filming of a full scene before a static camera. Similarly, the close-up allowed for more realistic acting than did the full shot. In *The New York Hat* (Biograph, 1912), this refinement in the articulation of the camera made possible a break away from the broad, stereotyped, robust, and artificial pantomime of the earlier films.

Griffith ever sought new methods and fresh areas. The Biograph Company, on the other hand, was more conservative. Experiments, innovations, and improvements were welcomed as long as they were successful and as long as they remained in the areas of editorial technique and camera articulation, for here no productional investment was necessary. Longer films, with costly production, were as yet unproved and here Biograph opposed the genius of Griffith. He succeeded, despite opposition from the company officials, in refilming *Enoch Arden* in two reels in 1911. He defied the policy of Biograph in this case on the basis of a film which relied as much on the spectacle appeal of California backgrounds as upon the popularity of a well-known stage subject.

It was becoming increasingly difficult to add new and more realistic refinements to the editorial structure established by Porter. Griffith began to look in new directions. Editorial and photographic advancements had been achieved; productional expansion appeared to be the next logical step. His first attempt at a longer film had been stymied by the conservative Biograph policy, which forced a single-reel release of the two-reel version of *Enoch Arden*. Consequently, his next attempt at a spectacle film, *The Battle* (Biograph, 1911), retained the single-reel form but involved a larger pictorial conception, employing hundreds of soldiers fighting in trenches, on the run, on the march, suggesting what was later to be fully developed in *The Birth of a Nation*. Large-scale spectacle became a part of the fabric of the melodramatic photoplay.

The psychology of a bevy of village lovers is conveyed in a lively sweethearting dance. Then the boy and his comrades go forth to war. The lines pass between hand-waving crowds of friends from the entire neighborhood. These friends give the sense of patriotism in mass. Then as the consequence of this feeling, as the special agents to express it, the soldiers are in battle. By the fortunes of war the onset is unexpectedly near to the house where once was the dance.

The boy is at first a coward. He enters the old familiar door. He appeals to the girl to hide him, and for the time breaks her heart. He goes forth a fugitive not only from battle, but from her terrible girlish anger. But later he rallies. He brings a train of powder wagons through fires built in his path by the enemy's scouts. He loses every one of his men, and all but the last wagon, which he drives himself. His return with that ammunition saves the hard-fought day.

And through all this, glimpses of the battle are given with a splendor that only Griffith has attained.[5]

This combination of spectacle and melodrama was so successful, and the treatment in this short picture so popular, that even after the feature-length film had been established, *The Battle* was reissued June 11, 1915, four years after its original production.

In 1912 the second significant American spectacle film and the first to recognize the challenge of current European spectacles was produced. This was Griffith's *The Massacre* (Biograph, 1912). Again the enlargement of the scope of film melodrama was attained through the addition of spectacle. Again a romanticized historical subject was reproduced with realism. Custer's last stand came to life. On the West Coast, far from the dingy offices of Eastern film magnates, cries for budget reduction fell unheard. Hundreds of cavalrymen and scores upon scores of Indians were unleashed. Costumes and sets reached a new high for lavishness in American films. But the release came too late, for new European spectacles of a more magnificent scale had already reached American exhibitors and Griffith's *Massacre* passed unnoticed in the crowd.

Within the single-reel form Griffith had aimed, first of all, at heightening the realism of the camera, of acting, and of the production; secondly, toward a refinement and articulation of the melodramatic cinematic syntax originally demonstrated by Porter; and thirdly, at an enlargement of the pictorial and productional conception of the film through the addition of spectacle. Throughout the last years of this single-reel development, the influence of the foreign film was being felt and it must have reached Griffith, for, either under its stimulus or in his own creative spontaneity, he had begun to offer a certain competition to European importations. A steadily increasing stream of historical spectacles shows an early recognition of the cinematic possibilities of this form. *The Slave* (Biograph, 1909) was a melodrama set in Roman times, supported by "a series of most beautiful pictures of the Romanesque type."[6] In the following week came *The Mended Lute,* with a great deal of authentic spectacle

based on the life and customs of the American aboriginals. . . Much thought and time were given the many details, and we may claim that as to costumes, manners and modes of living, it is more than reason- ably accurate, these details having been supervised by an expert. . . The subject as a whole is a combination of poetical romance and dra- matic intensity, the canoe chase being the most picturesque and thrill- ing ever shown.[7]

The addition of historical spectacle to melodrama was con- sciously taking place in a large body of the Biograph output. *The Death Disc* (1909) exploited historical costumes of the Cromwellian period; *The Call to Arms* (1910) was a story of the Middle Ages with picturesque period paraphernalia and background; *Wilful Peggy,* of the early days in Ireland; *The Oath and the Man,* of the French Revolution; *Rose o' Salem Town,* of Puritan witchcraft; *Heartbeats of Long Ago,* of fourteenth-century Italy; *The Span- ish Gypsies,* of sunny Andalusia, and so on. A full series of Spanish and Mexican films was produced. Browning's *A Blot on the 'Scutcheon* was produced with complete costumes in 1912. *Lena and the Geese* (1912) went to old Holland for its locale. Two reels were devoted to *A Pueblo Legend* (1912), authentically spectacular and filmed on location in Old Pueblo of Isleta, New Mexico. Cos- tume plates and shields, weapons and accessories were loaned by the Museum of Indian Antiques at Albuquerque.[8] The success of these authentic historical spectacles on the screen demonstrates the continuation by the film of the approach and the manner of the nineteenth-century stage.

Griffith's romanticism was as evident in his choice of players as in his subject matter. Lewis Jacobs has observed that "all his heroines—Mary Pickford, Mae Marsh, Lillian Gish, Blanche Sweet —were, at least in Griffith's eye, the pale, helpless, delicate, slim- bodied heroines of the nineteenth century English poets."[9] It was this same romantic bias which, when added to the stimulus sup- plied by the success of lavish European spectacles, suggested the subject for an early attempt at supremacy in the field of the spectacle film.

Working in comparative secrecy in the town of Chatsworth, far from the Los Angeles film colony, Griffith began production in 1912 of a Biblical spectacle. In the following year he completed *Judith of Bethulia*, the first American four-reel film designed for feature-length exhibition. The picture was not released until 1914, and in the interim Griffith's association with Biograph had terminated. His reckless extravagance in this production led the company to request his resignation as director. The balm of appointment as producer-adviser in the productions of newer directors was insufficient to prevent his complete separation from Biograph and his immediate entrance into the Majestic-Reliance Company.

Judith of Bethulia borrowed its material from the scriptural spectacle of the same name by Thomas Bailey Aldrich, currently successful upon the stage. Needless to say, the stage production, impeded by physical limitations, was dwarfed by Griffith's screen version. An entire army of Assyrians, authentically garbed and marshaled in the manner of the period, was thrown against the city walls. The production involved feats of engineering.

Between two mountains was the location chosen for the great wall against which Holofernes hurls his cohorts in vain attacks. Eighteen hundred feet long, and broad enough to permit of the defenders being massed upon it, the wall rose slowly until it was a giant's causeway connecting the crags on either side. Within, a city sprang up, in whose streets take place some of the most thrilling scenes in the picture. Beyond it, in the valley, was pitched the great armed camp of the Assyrians. In the chieftains' tent alone were hangings and rugs costing thousands of dollars.[10]

This was the most expensive production Biograph had yet attempted. Great numbers, more than one thousand people and about three hundred horsemen, were marshaled. The monstrous scale of the conception did not interfere with the development of details and authentic properties.

The following were built expressly for the production: a replica of the ancient city of Bethulia; a faithful reproduction of the ancient army camps embodying all their barbaric dances; chariots, battering rams, scaling ladders, archer towers, and other special war paraphernalia of the period.

The following spectacular effects: the storming of the walls of the city of Bethulia; the hand-to-hand conflicts; the death-defying chariot charges at break-neck speed; the rearing and plunging horses infuriated by the din of battle; the wonderful camp of the terrible Holofernes, equipped with rugs from the Far East; the dancing girls in their exhibition of the exquisite and peculiar dances of the period, the routing of the command of the terrible Holofernes, and the destruction of the camp by fire.[11]

Vachel Lindsay, in his excellent description of this film, has pointed out that the structure of this spectacle employed an editorial form utilizing four sorts of scenes. There were scenes showing (1) the particular history of Judith and Holofernes; (2) the wooing of Naomi by Nathan; (3) the streets of Bethulia massed with the people in their sluggish mass movement; and finally, (4) scenes of the assault, with camp and battle scenes interpolated, to unify the continuity.[12] Spectacle had, at the cost of $32,000,[13] assumed the salient position and melodrama existed only as a means for exploiting spectacle. And it was through editorial patterns demonstrated in the melodrama that the preceding four types of scenes were integrated. The story of Judith and Holofernes and the courtship of Nathan and Naomi were subsidiary to the spectacle and derived their dramatic stature and significance from the spectacle. Nathan and Naomi, for instance, "are seen among the reapers outside the city or at the well near the wall, or on the streets of the ancient town. They are generally doing the things the crowd behind them is doing, meanwhile evolving their own little heart affair."[14] This heart affair of two black and white figures flickering across the screen gained its dramatic power through editorial association with the huge, spectacular environment and with the masses whose mob mind could be visually dramatized upon the screen. Naomi and Nathan transcended the personality of mortals. Their own little personal drama, woven into the vast tapestry of the spectacle, gained thereby an emotional significance which far exceeded the possibilities of simple chase melodrama. The limitations of conventionalized character portrayal were removed by an editorial pattern involving elements of spectacle. When Naomi is rescued by her sweetheart, Nathan, this "act is taken by the audience as a type of the setting free of all the captives."[15] Judith similarly derives her stature from Bethulia, and Holofernes achieves his dramatic identity as the personification of the Assyrian army. Thus, through a clever editorial form, the dramatic as well as the pictorial scale of the cinema was extended. Spectacle values had become absolutely necessary to the development of the silent motion picture. And it was a recognition of these values that had prompted Griffith's entrance into the feature film with *Judith of Bethulia.*

With the arrival of the feature film came improvement in the use of musical accompaniment. Stage melodrama and early screen melodrama had, of course, both used musical accompaniment to the action. It had been stereotyped, direct, and bold in its intention, oftentimes the impromptu creation of the pianist or organist bred to the work. For *Judith,* however, a complete musical accompaniment with specific predetermined cues was provided.

Open with *Maritana* (Wallace) until Judith in Prayer:
Then *The Rosary* (Nevin) until she leaves woman with child:
Then *Maritana* until "The Army":
Then *William Tell* (Rossini) the last movement. Play this to end of reel:
Then *Pique Dame,* overture (Suppe) all through:
Then *Poet and Peasant,* overture (Suppe) until "Water and Food Famine":
Then *Simple Aven* (Thome) until "The King":
Then *Peer Gynt*—Suite II, opus 55 (Grieg) until Judith has vision:
Then *Woodland Sketches I & II* (MacDowell) until she dons fine clothes:
Then *Lament of Roses* (Sonnakolb) until "The King":
Then *Peer Gynt*—Suite II, opus 55 (Grieg) until end of reel.[16]

Music, an integral part of nineteenth-century melodrama and spectacle, was utilized here by the screen in the same fashion. The quality of the music, obviously enough, was calculated in its naïve way to heighten the intensity of the scene.

Through the work of D. W. Griffith in the period from 1908 to 1913, motion pictures progressed from single-reel storyettes and topical episodes to successful experiment with the feature-length spectacle film. Griffith had come to the films with a rich background of Victorian romanticism both in the theatre and in his general approach to life. Without sacrificing any of his strong romantic bias, he developed the realistic capacities of this medium to serve in the exploitation of his romantic conceptions. Whatever progress Griffith made in the development of a cinematic syntax had always been motivated by his quest for a greater and more fluid screen realism, whether for character portrayal, scenic production, or narrative development. In this way, he pioneered in the evolution of a technique for this new art form, which was originally derived from the forms of the nineteenth-century stage but which succeeded in eliminating the restrictions and conventions with which this stage had been fettered.

In the search for greater realism Griffith carried this editorial development to a point beyond which improvement was difficult. And at about this time the influence of foreign spectacle films was being felt in this country. Responding to these two coincidental conditions, Griffith made his first attempt at a feature-length film on the basis of a spectacular production with *Judith of Bethulia*. He took his material directly from the stage and surpassed the stage in its production. In this way, presenting a romanticized historical spectacle in an authentic and lavish fashion within the melodramatic cinematic structure, Griffith produced the first American four-reel photoplay. He appears, then, as the strongest and most successful of the early screen continuators of nineteenth-century melodrama and spectacle, of realism and romance.

TEN

SPECTACLE:
THE FEATURE FILM

The influence of the foreign film upon the work of American producers during the significant years of the fusion of stage and screen came in three areas. The first of these, that of the fantasy, was the contribution of George Méliès. A second influence appeared with the slapstick farce of Max Linder. But it remained for the feature-length foreign spectacle film to jar the well-seated popularity of the domestic single-reel melodrama.

I. FOREIGN INFLUENCES

By 1908 the French development of the spectacle film growing out of the work of Méliès had become a full-fledged influence. French producers, notably Pathé, undertook elaborate filmings, with scenery on an extensive scale, lavishly mounted, "toilfully rehearsed, carefully acted,"[1] far in advance of current American production. They had discovered that the scope of cinema in terms of spectacle was unlimited and that its proper exploitation would yield a commensurate return.

Even within the single-reel form foreign experiments had emphasized the values of spectacle. With the increase in the length of the film, new titles appeared in this category, those of Pathé achieving a further distinction. The subject, for example, of *Nero and Brittanicus*[2] (Pathé, 1913), was simple enough: the poisoning by Nero of his stepmother in the struggle to become ruler of Rome. Nevertheless, three full reels were given to it and the release was in color. Spectacle added stature to the thrill of simple melodrama. With such productions, screen spectacle was "established

and developed by the firm of Pathé Frères." Striking historical subjects combined "gorgeous mountings" with "melodramatic episodes," and, to enhance realism, many of the scenes were "enacted
in their natural surrounding."[3] These foreign spectacles encouraged a host of Shakespearean filmings as well as other historical
pieces in the United States. But when, in 1909, Vitagraph released
Les Misérables in four reels, separately exhibited, Pathé retaliated
with a twelve-reel production. In the 1902-1913 period, the French
spectacle film usually surpassed the American.

But if the French surpassed the American, they, in turn, were
excelled by the Italian. When *The Last Days of Pompeii* was done
by the Italian firm, Ambrosia, in 1908, it was filmed in one reel. In
1911 Ambrosia made it again in six reels. In the same year Pas-
quali released an eight-reel version. In 1911 *The Crusaders* was
filmed by the Cines Società Italiana in four reels with a cast of five
hundred and a production schedule of five months. Italian domination of spectacle film during this early period was established by
Quo Vadis? and *Cabiria.* The success of these two pictures was directly reflected in American production.

Quo Vadis?, produced in 1912 by Cines Società Italiana, was
filmed in eight reels to be exhibited continuously as a feature-
length picture. Coming at a time when American distributors
looked askance at anything above 1000 feet, it is significant that
such a daring experiment was made in the name of spectacle. It
was shown in this country as a feature film at the Astor Theatre,
New York, on April 21, 1913, and was received less for its worth as
a play than for the excellence of its individual pictorial episodes.

Massive pillars stood in front of the house of Vinitius and through
the open doors of Petronius' chamber the spectators glimpse a garden
rich in foliage and the white ornamentation of marble figures. The
orgies of the court in Nero's palace proceed with a degree of natural-
ness which would never have been possible on the stage. The crowd in
front of the palace as Rome burns, the emperor hearing with astonish-
ment·their imprecations, and the sight of Petronius turning their affec-
tions once more to Caesar—these episodes were accomplished with a
vivid flash impossible to the dramatic stage.

It was of course the burning of Rome which most fully revealed the
capacity of·the pictures to indicate spectacle. Through streets swept

by smoke and flame rushed panic-stricken people. Houses tottered and crumbled about them as the flames advanced relentlessly. With striking reality is the burning of the city represented, and the later views of the charred and ruined buildings added their effectiveness to the scenes.[4]

The influence of this film upon the development of the American motion picture was manifold. By transferring a current stage spectacle to the screen with a lavishness far in advance of the best effort of the stage, it marked the end of the stage spectacle and at the same time indicated the direction which the film could most successfully follow. Its success at the box office ushered in the epoch of the feature film. By 1914 this picture alone had "exerted a greater influence in creating the plethora of stage plays on the screen than any individual achievement of the cameraman to this day."[5] The formula for the successful feature film, through adaptation of stage material, was distinctly defined by this same film. "*Quo Vadis?* singularly is the one erstwhile stage success to completely eclipse as a photoplay its theatrical vogue."[6] Feature films adapted from the stage in areas other than that of spectacle appeared risky ventures. It is small wonder that the stage spectacle soon went the way of the stage action-melodrama.

Cabiria, the second of the influential Italian productions, was filmed by Giovanni Pastrone in 1913 for Italiana. The screen story had been written especially for the production by d'Annunzio. It filled twelve reels and ran for nearly three hours. D'Annunzio supervised the production, insisting on full-scale replicas of complete buildings for the sake of authenticity.[7] It was first shown in this country at the Knickerbocker Theatre, New York, on June 1, 1914.

Constructionally, *Cabiria* presented a looseness which weakened its dramatic effect. "We jump with ease across the Mediterranean, or plunge from daylight into moonlight."[8] At the same time, this looseness contributed to the introduction of a great number of spectacular episodes where "the background and mass-movements must stand as monumental achievements in vital patriotic splendor."[9] The drama of character-conflict existent in the book may have been buried beneath the continuous surge of scenic glories, but the dramatic impact of the spectacle, inexhaustible, lavish, and gigantic, was overwhelming. The cinema had imbued static scenic spectacle with a dynamic dramatic personality far beyond the potential of individual characterization at that time.

> The principals do not carry out the momentum of this immense resource. The half a score of leading characters, with the costumes, gestures, and aspects of gods, are after all works of the taxidermist. They are stuffed gods. They conduct a silly nickelodeon romance while Carthage rolls on toward her doom. They are like sparrows fighting for grain on the edge of the battle.[10]

Screen spectacle presented forces in conflict whose significance, by virtue of a clever editorial pattern, surpassed that of mere human beings.

After seeing "the marvelous siege of a Carthaginian city in *Cabiria*," Walter Prichard Eaton, referring to the already extinct stage melodrama, again wailed "that the spectacles will go the same way," for "not even on the Hippodrome stage could such an effect be achieved."[11] The success of such foreign spectacle films forced American producers into feature pictures of the same type. As in the previous case of the screen melodrama, success was achieved because the audience was ready. It merely required diverting from the legitimate to the film houses, and apparently this was no longer difficult. By bidding for this spectacle audience, the screen continued the realistic-romantic cycle in staging, carrying it to a peak beyond that reached upon the stage.

II. THE EARLY FEATURE FILM IN AMERICA

The challenge offered by *Queen Elizabeth, Cabiria*, and *Quo Vadis?* was accepted by the single-reel spectacle film and subsequently by the first American feature-length picture, D. W. Griffith's *Judith of Bethulia*. The popularity of *Judith*, continuing for a number of years after its original issue, indicated the security of box-office support for the spectacle film and for a feature-length policy. The financial backing, however, for such expensive productions and the distributional organization for their exhibition was lacking for some time after the release of *Judith*. The transition from single-reel melodrama to feature-length spectacle could not take place overnight.

Gradually distribution difficulties were surmounted and new producers entered the field. Adolph Zukor inaugurated his "famous plays with famous players" policy in 1913 with *The Prisoner of Zenda,* starring James K. Hackett. Lasky, Goldfish, Friend, and De Mille organized the Feature Play Company in 1914, and in the same year Klaw and Erlanger contracted with Biograph for the filming of their stage successes. Griffith pursued his own course in feature-film production. Hobart Bosworth and Garbutt organized Pallas Pictures for this same purpose. Moresco followed, and finally W. W. Hodkinson organized Paramount Pictures Corporation in 1913-1914 in order to guarantee to these independent producers a satisfactory distribution for their multi-reel pictures. In this way, by assuring exhibitors a supply of feature films as secure as that of the "trust's" single-reel films, the problem of distribution was solved. Exhibitors could now change horses in mid-stream.

Next came the problem of suitable theatre buildings for the showing of feature pictures. The increased length of these films canceled the rapid audience-turnover principle of the nickelodeon. Increased production costs could not be met simply by an increase in the price of admission to the nickelodeons. Large motion-picture houses had to be built or taken over from the stage. Audiences to fill these houses had already been found by the metropolitan exhibitors of the foreign spectacles, and the movement of the film from the nickelodeon to movie theatres mushroomed in the next few years. "By February, 1916, approximately 21,000 remodeled or entirely new movie theatres were in operation, and by 1917 the nickelodeon had become an antique." [12] With the new movie theatre came a still newer audience. This audience, marshaled by the appeal of the foreign and domestic feature spectacles, had, for the most part, previously patronized the legitimate theatre and now demanded entertainment on the same level.

The coming together of a number of such forces, namely, the arrival of a new audience, the influence of the foreign spectacle film, the movement into larger film houses, the entry of theatre directors into the film, the increase in the length of the motion picture, the increase in productional costs, and so on, was exerting a cumulative and dynamic influence upon the industry. Transitions, no matter how gradual, were inevitable, and film producers found themselves turning more and more to the legitimate theatre for material. The aesthetic values governing the borrowing of this material from the stage and its subsequent treatment upon the screen would further define the relationship between stage and screen in the early years of their fusion.

Audiences, long accustomed to picture plays, were at first satisfied with nothing more than a photographic copy, camera fixed and static, of a stage presentation. Such pictures indicate an area in which the screen sought to compete with the stage without offering any contribution beyond that of more rapid and fluid scene changes. *The Miracle* (1913) was filmed from Max Reinhardt's $250,000 staging of the spectacle in Germany. Similarly, *America* (1914) was photographed directly from a performance on the stage of the New York Hippodrome. Films of this kind, while not comprising a large category, indicate recognition by film makers of the motion-picture appeal of stage spectacle.

In addition to that of spectacle there were two other classes of material borrowed directly from the stage. Plays were drawn from the new drama of the late nineteenth-century dramatists' revival and from the melodrama stage. In the first group, where the dramatic values arose from dramaturgy, character, theme, and dialogue, failure resulted. In the second group, where action-melodrama and realistic spectacle were the two main sources of appeal, success was apparent. The early feature film had already been well adapted for the realistic treatment of romantic material drawn from the nineteenth-century stage. It is not surprising that the camera should have been more successful with the realism of externals than with that of internals.

In 1915 Ibsen's *Ghosts* was filmed by Majestic with Henry B. Walthall and Mary Alden. According to Vachel Lindsay's description of this film,[18] the producer suffered under no misapprehension. He recognized that the play, as constructed by Ibsen, could not be simply transferred to the screen. Neither Ibsen's dynamic dramaturgy nor the profundity of his character and thematic concepts were to be translated by the screen technique of that day. Ibsen's play, without benefit of title alteration, was transformed into action-melodrama. The events of Mr. Alving's life prior to the opening of the play were all pictured. The previous sins of the father were acted out. Characterization was altered and all sense of dramatic proportion lost. Pastor Manders became a caricature. Engstrand was turned into a man of respectability with an income. The twenty great situations of Ibsen disappeared, and when Oswald, with the symbolic headaches, writhes in agony upon the floor, "A hairy arm with clutching demon claws comes thrusting in toward the back of his neck."[14]

These "ghosts" visually presented lost all of the emotional and spiritual significance of the original treatment. On the screen they became nothing more than sensational and melodramatic trickery, a caricature of Ibsen's intention. And when, according to the customary melodramatic film structure, it became necessary to deliver a closing emotional punch, a chase sequence was introduced. "The boy and his half-sister are in their wedding-clothes in the big church. Pastor Manders is saying the ceremony. The doctor [an addition] charges up the aisle at the moment people are told to speak or forever hold their peace."[15] Ibsen's ironic climax has turned into a suspense sequence over whether the boy will get the girl or whether Manders will arrive in time to "wise them up." Then for the final "lift," the impact upon the characters of the play of Manders' revelation that boy and girl are really brother and sister is attempted visually as "four able actors have the task of telling the audience by facial expression only, that they have been struck by moral lightning. They stand in a row, facing the people, endeavoring to make the crisis of an alleged Ibsen play out of a crashing melodrama."[16] Apparently the cinema knew only one manner: that of melodrama.

Underlying this failure upon the screen of drama dependent upon the realism of subjective character portrayal were the limitations imposed upon acting by the camera. Griffith had made some progress toward a more real style of acting. Cecil B. De Mille, fresh from the stage and the Belasco approach, brought with him to the screen the utter restraint and understatement of Belasco's technique. His influence in this direction and away from the broad pantomimic style of his predecessors began with his first production, *The Squaw Man* (1914), and was developed subsequently in *The Cheat* (1915), and so on. The better class of actors coming into the films from the stage sponsored this new "realism" in acting. Paradoxical as it may seem, however, this so-called new "realism" in acting, characteristic of the period from 1913 to 1919, was as conventional in its own way as the single-reel style of pantomimic elaboration and overplay. This "realism" carried restraint to the point where all emotion was expressed by means of a "long, level stare," which might signify "keen analytical mind or congenital obtuseness; cold hate or hot passion; warm friendship or sullen enmity; indomitable determination or a touch of hay fever."[17] Restraint, for the audience of the early feature film, was the epitome of realism in acting. Actually, it was more conventional than real and automatically set up a barrier against any attempt at realistic characterization. Character on the screen tended to remain impersonal.

This condition in acting was not only at the root of the failure of screen adaptations of the new realistic problem drama of the late nineteenth century, but was also a fundamental factor in the screen success of stage melodramatic spectacles. The concept of character in screen melodrama or spectacle gained its dramatic value either through large-scale, rapid, and vigorous action or through elaborate spectacle. In other words, character became dramatic on the screen through the visual presentation of external actions, places, or events rather than through the dynamics of deliberation resulting in action. Screen character had become a symbol of certain elements of action, melodrama, and spectacle. This conventionality in acting drove the film farther into melodrama and spectacle as the only two sources through which character could achieve dramatic significance upon the screen.

Further attempts with Ibsen on the screen met the same failure as had *Ghosts*. In their mad scramble for any successful stage material that might have been available, film producers sometimes lost sight of basic screen requirements. How, for instance, can Ibsen's ironic overtone in *Peer Gynt* be photographed? The Moresco

Company tried to capture it, but their filming of this play in 1915 received severe criticism: "When Peer drives his old mother in a reindeer sled up to Saint Peter at Heaven's gate, the trip is made in Peer's elfin imagination, and suggested to the audience by the power of the actor's art and poet's words. The poor camera man attempted to photograph it and achieved something supremely ridiculous."[18] The great new drama of the last century lost its power through pictorial illustration and explanation. Subjective emotional and spiritual experience, conflict between minds and moral codes, struggles of the soul—these the camera could not translate. If the essence of the drama of Ibsen and his colleagues was dialogue, theme, and character, that of the photoplay was action and spectacle. For the screen, internal realism was out and external realism was in. And while, in their early rush for stage material, film producers may sometimes have overlooked this limitation, the public and critics soon called it to their attention.

The drama of Ibsen and many problem-playwrights of the nineties had nothing in common with the silent cinema. On the other hand, the single-reel photoplay used techniques similar to those of the nineteenth-century stage melodrama, and stage spectacle was successfully transferred to the screen. In 1916, there were "still about one hundred ordinary films and twenty-five long feature films released every week by the various distribution agencies."[19] Because competition necessitated a rapid output of films, producers were forced into a repetitious story formula, illustrated, for the feature film, by such a picture as Colin Campbell's production of *The Spoilers* (Selig, 1914). Taken from the novel by Rex Beach and filmed in nine reels, it became the first so-called American super picture. It inaugurated the opening, in April of that year, of Mark Mitchell's new Strand Theatre. Employing a traditional melodramatic editorial structure, every opportunity was taken to enhance spectacle values.

There are, in The Spoilers, inspiriting ocean scenes and mountain views. There are interesting sketches of mining-camp manners and customs. . . But the chase rushes past these things to the climax, as in a policeman picture it whirls past blossoming gardens and front lawns till the tramp is arrested. . . The pursuit progresses without St. Vitus dance or hysteria to the end of the film. There the spoilers are discomfited, the gold mine is recaptured, the incidental girls are won, in a flash, by the rightful owners.[20]

Under the influence of the foreign spectacle pictures, the length of this film was increased and its pictorial emphasis heightened, but melodrama was not sacrificed. The combination of spectacle and melodrama in the early feature film was recognized and acclaimed by its contemporary critics. "The melodrama may be cheap; yet it does not disturb the cultured mind as grossly as a similar tragic vulgarity would on the real stage, because it may have the snowfields of Alaska or the palm trees of Florida as radiant background."[21] Spectacle glorified melodrama.

The Biograph Company in 1913, after Griffith's departure, negotiated a feature-film policy with the stage firm of Klaw and Erlanger, under which the latter's stage successes were to be filmed by Biograph for future release. Biograph, still conservative, relied upon the proven appeal of the film and attempted full-length melodramas which had been successful upon the stage for years. Success on the screen came automatically. *The Woman in Black* (Biograph, 1914), in four reels, was "an old time melodrama that still plays to crowded houses, doubly thrilling in pictures because all the action takes place before the audience."[22] Such material, employing stereotyped characters simply for the sake of vigorous and rapid-fire action and using a contrived plot for the sake of its strong situations, lent itself to cinema. Furthermore, the technical devices in construction and staging which such plays exploited were originally conceived along cinematic lines. In the following week a screen version of the old Augustin Daly favorite, *Under the Gaslight,* was released. Here "the unusually strong plot is enhanced by the rich variety of spectacular scenes possible to the camera."[23] These nineteenth-century stage melodramas soon deluged the screen. *The Romance of a Poor Young Man* was released on November 21, 1914, and in the same year *East Lynne, The Lady of Lyons, The Ticket-of-Leave Man, The Lights o' London,* and many others. Boucicault was successful and popular in the early feature film. Adolph Zukor's first production was *The Prisoner of Zenda.* Others, such as *The Count of Monte Cristo,* followed. The novel went successfully from stage to screen. Ouida's *Under Two Flags* was both staged and screened. In 1915 it made "a colorful picture, remarkable for the beauty of its settings, for the wealth of atmosphere. . . The sandstorm in the desert is in itself enough to distinguish the production as something out of the ordinary."[24] The early work of De Mille, with *The Squaw Man, The Virginian, The Girl of the Golden West,* and *The Warrens of Virginia,* all in 1913-1914, embodied the same combination of melodrama and spectacle.

The elaboration of sensational and spectacular physical effects in these melodramas included battle scenes, horse races, firing squads, train wrecks, boat races, and so on. It is no wonder that the screen, in taking over material which was originally conceived as if for the motion picture, was able, in its presentation, to supersede the stage. De Mille's production of *Cameo-Kirby* (1914) relied for its effect upon a race between two side-wheelers with the explosion of one in midstream. The exploding-boat effect had been used by Boucicault in his staging of *The Octoroon* back in the sixties and seventies. At that time it had been created along conventional lines. De Mille conceived a much more realistic illusion of the race and explosion at a much lower cost by filming it in miniature. A tank was built, forty feet long, six feet wide, and a foot deep.[25] A simple board construction covered roughly with a waterproof tarpaulin was all that was necessary. Paddles at the side kept the water in motion, and the two little side-wheelers, eighteen inches long, were controlled by wires under water.

Their smokestacks belched forth what were supposed to look like terrific clouds of smoke, while lights showed in cabin windows and people could be seen indistinctly on deck: they had to be seen indistinctly since they were made of cardboard and stood not more than an inch high. On the far side of the tank hung a painted canvas drop showing the distant shore, again not too distinctly.
The camera traveled closely alongside the two boats as they moved down the tank, first one, then the other being ahead until they neared the end of the tank, when a property man pressed a button and a small charge of powder blew one of the boats to pieces.[26]

In 1920, Griffith's famous *Way Down East* depended upon the same graphic realism of spectacular effects.

All the exteriors were to be real, not studio-contrived. In March when a blizzard conveniently came along, the snowstorm scenes were filmed at Mamaroneck, assistants hanging on the legs of the cameras to prevent their being whirled away by the wind, and Miss Gish having to be thawed out at intervals. The ice scenes were then shot at White River Junction, Vermont, under peculiarly uncomfortable circumstances.[27]

A realism impossible to the stage had been achieved. "Not once, but twenty times a day, for two weeks, Lillian floated down on a cake of ice."[28] Shooting on location provided an authentic pictorial presentation upon the screen of the same effects which had been presented conventionally upon the stage.

The exploitation of productional aspects was rapidly accepted by both producers and public. When De Mille produced *Carmen* in 1915 with "genuine sets instead of the painted, flat scenery usual at the time,"[29] he was credited by Walter Prichard Eaton with one "of the most successful pictures of the season."[30]

Similarly, Thomas Ince's *The Italian* (1915), a study of immigrant life in the slums of New York, achieved its dramatic power through spectacle.

The first part, taken ostensibly in Venice, delineates the festival spirit of the people on the bridges and in gondolas. It gives out the atmosphere of town-crowd happiness. Then comes the vineyard, the crowd sentiment of a merry grape-harvest, then the massed emotion of many people embarking on an Atlantic liner telling good-by to their kindred on the piers, then the drama of arrival in New York. The wonder of the steerage people pouring down their proper gangway is contrasted with the conventional at-home-ness of the first-class passengers above. Then we behold the seething human cauldron of the East Side, then the jolly little wedding-dance, then the life of the East Side, from the policeman to the peanut-man, and including the bar tender. . .

The hero represents in a fashion the adventures of the whole Italian race coming to America: its natural southern gayety set in contrast to the drab East Side. The gondolier becomes boot-black. The grape-gathering peasant girl becomes the suffering slum mother.[31]

From these pictorial elements the story and its type characters gained their dramatic significance. Their stature came in direct proportion to that of the spectacle.

While aesthetic progress in the film had come about through the spectacular elaboration of productional aspects, costs were embarrassing. Griffith's *Judith of Bethulia,* filmed for $32,000, frightened the Biograph Company back into its conservative action-melodrama policy. Pioneers were nevertheless available. Universal spent a reputed $100,000 on the six-reel Biblical film, *Samson and Delilah* (1914). Griffith, no longer with Biograph, was attracted by Thomas Dixon's successful stage melodrama, *The Clansman,* dealing with the South, the Civil War, and the Reconstruction period. Eager to challenge the success of European spectacle films, Griffith was excited by the spectacular productional opportunities of the play. Mutual refused to finance the production in the scale of Griffith's conception. A new corporation was formed under the name of Epoch Films, and *The Clansman* was filmed in twelve reels at the cost of $100,000. Released in 1915, it ran for forty-five consecutive weeks in New York alone, and within the next few years grossed $18,000,000. This production, rechristened *The Birth of a Nation,* was a phenomenal artistic as well as financial success. Its methods expressed an ultimate in motion-picture achievement, clarifying the antecedents of the film and forecasting its future.

The Birth of a Nation embodied three qualities which were responsible for its success and thus exerted a significant influence on the art of the film: (1) full utilization of the action-melodrama editorial technique, (2) great authenticity in setting and in acting, and (3) spectacle on a colossal scale. One quality supported the other, and in the mutual assistance the whole arose to a new level in cinematic expression.

In editorial technique Griffith did not alter his methods; he merely intensified them. Cutting in all directions, backward, forward, and across, transitions through clever camera devices, dynamic use of productional values and of the camera to build the scene and to control the over-all development of dramatic intensity, all were brilliantly welded to surpass Griffith's previous efforts. His use of the single shot as an editorial unit was recognized for its effectiveness in development of climax by Henry MacMahon, early screen critic of the *New York Times.* "Every little series of pictures, continuing from four to fifteen seconds, symbolizes a sentiment, a passion or an emotion. Each successive series, similar yet different, carries the emotion to the next higher power, till at last, when both of the parallel emotions have attained the swift shock of victory and defeat."[32] With such an intensively developed editorial technique, Griffith spared no effort to achieve realistic and spectacular melodrama.

The authenticity and scale of graphic values Griffith now knew to be the greatest appeal of motion-picture spectacle.

Sets were all constructed according to elaborate research which had been conducted for some time previous to starting work on the picture. The result of this research was the installing of the first research library in the picture business. All properties such as weapons, uniforms, furniture, costumes and also personal characteristics of leading characters like Sumner, Grant, Lee and Abraham Lincoln were carefully modelled on the best obtainable data in which every effort was made to have the picture authentic as an historical document.[33]

The care exercised in preparations for the production bore fruit. For instance, the assassination of Lincoln at Ford's Theatre,

with the play *Our American Cousin* going forward on the stage, is shown in careful accordance with the historical accounts of it. How Lincoln's guard left his post to get a view of the play; how Booth waiting in the rear of another box, slipped through the door in the interval and fired at the President as he watched the play, all are seen. Booth's leap to the stage and his escape in the sudden excitement are faithfully portrayed.[34]

It was this sort of thing that audiences trained in the melodrama and the spectacle of the nineteenth century now looked for and expected in the film. And it was this sort of thing that the film could best do. In the war scenes of *The Birth of a Nation* this facility was spectacular. "Troops charging, artillery trains galloping, flags waving, shells bursting over barricades, the flow of battle over a field miles in length, are shown in full detail; and immediately after the excitement of the charge there is the sight of trenches full of torn and mangled bodies."[35] The illusion of authenticity in this daring motion picture, treating with realism the racial problems of the South from the clansman's bias, moved people "to cheers, hisses, laughter and tears, apparently unconscious and subdued, by tense interest in the play; they clapped when the masked riders took vengeance on negroes, and they clapped when the hero refused to shake the hand of a mulatto who had risen by political intrigue to become lieutenant-governor."[36]

The authenticity given its production resulted in such a realistic illusion that controversies immediately sprang up. Harvard's President Eliot condemned its "tendency to perversion of white ideals."[37] Race riots occurred in Boston. The *New York Evening Post* labeled it "An appeal to race prejudice," and in the same breath explained this appeal as "a thrilling historic spectacle of battles and life of the days of the Civil War, and an explanation of Southern feeling in the reconstruction days in defense of the Ku Klux Klan which terrorized negroes during that period."[38] But on the following day, the Reverend Thomas B. Gregory defended the film on the basis of its authenticity against all charges of exaggerated and malicious propaganda. "I know it is true," he said, "because I lived through the actual realities themselves. . . I am prepared to say that not one of the more than five thousand pictures that go to make up the wonderful drama is in any essential way an exaggeration. They are one and all faithful to historic fact, so that looking upon them, *you may feel you are beholding that which actually happened.*"[39] The italics are my own to draw attention again to the fact that while Griffith exploited both melodrama and spectacle it was the authenticity of his production that enlarged its emotional power. By virtue of this quality, long-past truths, melodramatically treated, appeared as current actualities. If the popularity of the film had been secured in 1902 on the basis of simple melodrama, its establishment in 1915 as a full-fledged and autonomous art form came through the fusion of authentically spectacular production with this melodramatic structure. This fusion, when we consider, for instance, the poor reception given *The Clansman* at the Liberty Theatre, New York, in 1906, superseded similar activity in spectacle and melodrama on the stage.

In 1916 Griffith continued in the manner of *Judith of Bethulia* and *The Birth of a Nation* with *Intolerance*. The Wark Producing

Corporation was especially formed for its production. The original single-thread conception of *Mother and the Law,* intended as a satire on contemporary legal injustice, was enlarged to become an elaborate condemnation of hypocrisy, prejudice, and intolerance in four different eras. Four parallel stories were developed. The original story of only contemporary interest was given dramatic stature by the clever editorial integration of three other stories spectacularly treated: one dealt with the Fall of Babylon, the second with the Christ Legend of Judea, and the third with the Massacre of the Huguenots on St. Bartholomew's Eve. It was another instance of spectacle coming to the aid of melodrama.

Money was plentiful after the success of *The Birth of a Nation* and Griffith spent lavishly. The payroll reached $12,000 per day. Babylonian walls reached three-hundred feet in height; elaborate streets in Paris, New York, and Judea were duplicated in full scale. For the magnificent banquet scene at the Feast of Belshazzar, $250,000 was spent. Three-hundred-thousand feet of negative were exposed. Costs rose like the driven snow. Griffith bought out his alarmed backers. A total outlay of $1,900,000 was finally reported.

The picture was released on September 5, 1916, in thirteen reels. Griffith had started with the single story of the slums, the mother, strikes, gangsters, and prisons. Its appeal was that of contemporary problem drama; its theme focused directly upon the present, and its treatment was melodramatic. The addition of the three complementary stories served to carry the film out of the present and to color it with a significance beyond that of temporary interest. And each of these stories was, in itself, a spectacle. In other words, through the addition of three parallel spectacles, the simple melodrama was raised far above its original level. The young wife rushing to save her unjustly condemned husband from the gallows was entirely melodramatic and of only contemporary importance, but its dramatic and thematic significance was lifted out of all time and presented as an eternal verity through the intercutting of the culminating events of the other three spectacles: Christ struggling toward Calvary, the Babylonian mountain girl racing to warn Belshazzar that his priests had betrayed him, and

the Huguenot fighting his way through the streets on St. Bartholomew's Day to save his sweetheart from massacre by the French
mercenaries. The melodrama of *Intolerance* achieved its dramatic
significance and thematic stature through graphic integration with
breath-taking spectacle, thus bringing to a culmination the melodramatic editorial syntax emanating originally from the popular
nineteenth-century stage and demonstrated years previously by
Porter in *The Great Train Robbery*.

But in these very virtues there is to be found a fault which
stemmed from the conscious overemphasis of spectacle in *Intolerance*. The theme was sometimes lost in the "abrupt hail of
images," [40] which hammered the sensibility cruelly with their overwhelming magnificence and scale. Griffith's fatal mistake was one
of excess, so that the film's four-part story was "much like listening
to a quartette of excellent elocutionists simultaneously reading
novels by Arnold Bennett, Victor Hugo, Nathaniel Hawthorne
and Elinor Glyn." Who won was unimportant. It was a great
show, but to assimilate it "at a sitting result[ed] in positive mental
exhaustion." [41] The story and its universal theme, the struggle
against prejudice and intolerance, were blurred by those "interminable battle scenes"; the spectacle had turned upon itself and
often devoured Griffith's thematic conception. Nevertheless, the
film remains as eloquent testimony of the acceptance by the screen
of the methods of the legitimate stage spectacle, and of how this
quality was developed through melodramatic editorial structure in
an attempt to give the melodrama a greater dramatic and thematic
significance.

Although *Intolerance* was not the financial success that *The
Birth of a Nation* had been, producers and audiences remained in
agreement regarding the position of spectacle in the cinema. Under
the aegis of Thomas Ince, the western spectacle-melodrama attained new eminence, setting a pace for the expanding industry
with such productions as James Cruze's epic *The Covered Wagon*
in 1923. Adventure spectacle of a somewhat different sort was used
in such outstanding motion pictures as *Treasure Island* (1920),
and in the 1922 version of *The Count of Monte Cristo*. Documen-
tary spectacle, in a sense historical spectacle, found superb screen

expression in King Vidor's *The Big Parade*. Cecil De Mille added sex, glamour, and the bath to spectacle yet managed to exploit its previously defined religious themes with such films as *The King of Kings* (1923) and *The Ten Commandments* (1924). Fred Niblo's *Ben Hur* (1925) set something like a record for productional extravagance in this genre. Spectacle, with its great box-office appeal, having provided an opening wedge for the introduction of the feature film, now pointed the way toward aesthetic and financial expansion. When once its formula had been established, the simple necessity of quantity output made repetitions of the successful pattern inevitable.

Three instances of this formula, all of them dealing with plays taken from the stage and produced in films, illustrate its significance in the relationship between stage and screen, and show how, in the field of melodramatic spectacle, the screen not only superseded the stage of the nineteenth century but naturally surpassed all similar efforts during the early twentieth century. These examples are *Treasure Island* (1920), *The Count of Monte Cristo* (1922), and *Ben Hur* (1925).

In April of 1920 the Maurice Tourneur filming of *Treasure Island* was released. The review of the Boston showing clarified for the new feature-film audience the essential advantage of the motion picture. How, for instance, could the stage offer, with any degree of truth or realism, the scenes so vividly portrayed upon the screen:

> Two pirates in a death struggle with the thumb of one slowly gouging out the eyeball of his mate. . . two gentlemen of fortune killing a third before a deep blue background, and racing down to the sea waving their blood-stained cutlasses. And last a whole ship's company dangling in the wind from the yards of their vessel—black bundles against a vivid blue sky. . . A buccaneer is pinned to the cabin door by a knife through his chest, and there he hangs stiff and dead with a blood spot widening on the door behind him.[42]

In the realistic presentation of this romantic material the screen excelled. In attempting the production of such material the stage exceeded its capacities, and either fell short in its realism or resorted to conventional practices. During the opening decades of the twentieth century it was the screen which furthered the trend of nineteenth-century realistic pictorial staging. The stage had long exhausted its potential in this area and, now in the doldrums of transition, climbed temporarily aboard the film's bandwagon.

In 1922 Fox produced *The Count of Monte Cristo,* a screen version of the play which had been treated as simple melodrama in a stage production at the Broadway Theatre in New York in 1848, and which had been toured day in and day out by James O'Neill over the entire country during the last part of the century. In 1900 Leibler and Company, cinema-wise, added a lavish spectacle production to the melodramatic plot. It is significant that Mr. Tyler, production manager of the 1900 Leibler staging, commented at the time of the film's release: "I can realize that William Fox has probably accomplished on a tremendous scale what we tried to do with the limited facilities of painted scenery and calcium lights."[43] The superiority of the screen version of this nineteenth-century stage favorite came from its

wealth of pictorial and dramatic detail that no power of the illustrator of books could possess or a dramatist achieve in the spoken word.

Even a momentary introduction of Napoleon Bonaparte had a punch to it in a few views that gives some of the touch of real history so characteristic of the books of Alexandre Dumas. . .

It is in its vast amount of pictorial detail of real and not simulated things that makes this film one of the real achievements of the modern screen. Many of the scenes in the first part were made in the streets and along the waterfront of Marseilles, the scene of the opening chapters of the book. It was the real Chateau d'If that the audience saw. It was on a real island off the coast of Italy that John Gilbert as Edmond Dantes, found himself after he had made his escape from the fortress. . . the underwater photography showing the remarkable escape of Dantes from the fortress stood out as a fascinating bit of film detail of an unusual nature.[44]

Attempts at spectacular realism on the stage could never have hoped to equal those of the early screen. And conversely, that the stage of the nineteenth century had attempted such material at all is an excellent indication of how cinematic the approach to theatrical production had been fifty years prior to the film's arrival.

The promises implied by these two films and all previous screen spectacles were climaxed by *Ben Hur* (Metro-Goldwyn-Mayer, 1925). "When a photoplay leaves one feeling it to be the only possible medium that could fully tell the story it unfolds, there can be little doubt of its success."[45] The material for *Ben Hur* was taken from the early-century stage success. Three years were consumed in its filming. Hampton reported the cost to have been $4,500,000, while *Variety* claimed $6,000,000. Directed by Fred Niblo with M. Guissart at the camera, it starred Ramon Novarro, Francis X. Bushman, Betty Bronson, and Carmel Myers. Première took place at the George M. Cohan Theatre on December 30, 1925. It was such an excellent example of all the qualities that had characterized the successful feature film to date that contemporary critics quickly reported:

The amazing thing about *Ben Hur* is that the films have been so late in discovering it, for it belongs quite peculiarly to the province of the movies, and *it has everything that was once considered the sine qua non of the successful film.* It has pageantry, romance, a religious glamour, and, what is perhaps even more, the chariot race, which to one who never saw it done, *seems utterly impossible outside of the films.*[46]

These *"sine qua non"* features of the successful film arose out of a production so spectacularly colossal

that a great shipyard at Leghorn was taken for the construction of Rome's fleet and Golthar's pirate galleys, that the vessels constructed were practical triremes, some of them of ocean-going proportions, that a bonus was paid to each sailor for extra minutes spent on the doomed fireship, and that the last scene shows them diving off the blazing hulk in droves; that these scenes were filmed on a "huge floating platform." It is set forth that an army of sculptors carved the massive figures to adorn the race course, and that another army of mechanics laid out a hundred-acre area and built around it the Circus Maximus.[47]

And so on and on; even the Wise Men were led "not by one star alone but by whole constellations shooting across the sky."[48]

The stage treadmills of the chariot race gave way to a formidable display.

A mighty amphitheatre sets the scene, a really remarkable bit of spectacularism as even the sceptic will admit. Thousands of spectators bank the race course. No need for the program to set forth statistics; the size of the gathering is apparent. Half a hundred horsemen clear the way for the chariots. And then the race itself: twelve chariot teams, four horses to each, all of the steeds black except the milk-white chargers of Ben Hur. A thrilling race it is, with the chariots slewing around the turns in clouds of dust, with first one team and then another in the lead, with the horses straining at the traces, with the piling up of one driver and his horses in a preliminary disaster, and the destruction later of three—or were there four—others in a mass collision. Even the sceptic. . . agrees that *the stage version of the race, thrilling though it may have been, must have seemed tame compared to this.*[49]

The line of romantic spectacles deriving from the archaeological stagings of Planché, thence of Charles Kean at the Princess', Irving at the Lyceum, and their many colleagues seems to have reached its zenith with this production. Iris Barry, reviewing the film later that year for *The Spectator*, speaks eloquently of its spectacular scale.

There has never been a film to equal it in magnificence of setting. City walls, public buildings, private houses, columns and colonnades are all ten times larger than anything the world has ever seen. . . There is a real poetry of size and opulence in the film. Antioch looks like a city of giants in the morning of the world. The dismal pinnacles of rock among which the exiled lepers are moving haunt the imagination with their huge greyness. . .

At the chariot races we look at only one section of the amphitheatre but still we see a crowd of fifty thousand souls receding to the sky. The chariots race like lightning, we almost feel that the horses are pulled round in mid-air as they take the corners of the track.[50]

A peak in the theatrical cycle beginning originally with David Garrick and coming up through the productions of the actor-managers of the nineteenth century to David Griffith had been confirmed with this 1925 release of *Ben Hur*.

The spectacular production naturally smothered the acting. "None of the acting is acting at all; it is mere participation in moving tableaux vivants, a sort of breather between the smashing spectacles which are the chief matter of the picture."[51] The film made no claim beyond that of spectacle. A Boston daily,[52] in fact, itemized the "tableaux vivants" and the time of their appearance on the screen in the following manner:

Matinee		Evening
2:35	The Star of Bethlehem	8:35
2:40	Jerusalem Restored	8:40
2:59	Fall of the House of Hur	8:59
4:29	The Last Supper	10:29
4:50	Reunion	10:50

Apparently the melodrama of the play was less important than the spectacles and served simply as a frame for the hanging of the pictures, which, in the tradition of the nineteenth century, were heightened by the music of an especially devised score by David Mendox and William Axt.[53]

These last three feature films indicate rather conclusively that the photoplay, in borrowing material from the stage, surpassed the stage in melodramatic action and in spectacle because of the scale, authenticity, and number of pictures possible to the cinema. B. B. Hampton has noted, "Audiences had given their greatest approval to sumptuous costly productions; less expensive pictures had not usually been highly successful. . . Bigness—elaborateness—sumptuousness—lavishness—these seemed to constitute the elusive 'quality' the public wanted."[54] In *Ben Hur* the film had achieved a new level on this second great and permanent platform for rivalry with the stage; namely, spectacle. Walter Prichard Eaton thought it wise to forecast in this case, too, that, as with the old-fashioned melodrama which disappeared from the stage to reappear upon the screen, "it is more than likely that the old-fashioned spectacular play will fall more and more into disrepute."[55] It was upon this basis that the future of the feature film was assured. When the obstacles in the way of its cinematic production and exhibition were finally hurdled, the spectacle play sprang from the stage to the screen and, finding its ultimate expression in the new medium, gradually abandoned the old.

Feature films in the early years had taken much of their material directly from the stage or directly from the novel which, in many cases, had previously been adapted to the stage. This material had been of two sorts. The first, the drama of the school of Ibsen and the late-century dramatic revival, depended upon the internal and subjective realism of character, dialogue, idea, and passion, as well as upon the dynamic dramaturgy synonymous with the work of these playwrights. It failed upon the screen of the early feature film. The second kind of material provided by the stage depended upon the appeal of external realism, that of spectacle and action-melodrama with its loose, episodic construction. It succeeded upon the screen.

Thus, while both the stage and the screen spectacle and melodrama were similar expressions of the realistic-romantic phase in the arts of theatre stemming from Garrick, the screen carried this cycle to a much higher level than was possible upon the stage of the times and thus postponed or canceled the beginnings of reaction to this theatrical cycle already evident in the stage of the early twentieth century.

ELEVEN

FROM GARRICK TO GRIFFITH

Mildred Aldrich's review of the first motion-picture exhibition in Boston has suggested an inquiry which has shown that between the stage and the early screen there was more similarity than difference. The cycle of realistic-romantic theatrical expression which had found its roots for the English-speaking stage in David Garrick ultimately reached its peak with the work of David Wark Griffith.

A connection between stage and screen was suggested even before the cinema made its appearance. A preliminary investigation into the chronological aspects of the invention of motion-picture machinery disclosed that progress in this chain of development occurred simultaneously with advances in the realistic-romantic theatre emanating from Garrick. For instance, interest in the reproduction of motion was revived in 1824 with P. M. Roget's paper, *The Persistence of Vision,* and by 1832 animated pictures had been achieved with J. F. A. Plateau's phenakistoscope and S. R. von Stampfer's stroboscope. This initial period coincided with that rise in the pictorial theatre of realism and romance indicated by the stagings of J. R. Planché, the acting of Edwin Forrest and Edmund Kean, and by the drama of J. S. Knowles, Victor Hugo, and George Gordon Byron.

The second surge toward the photographic reproduction of motion did not develop for over twenty years. In 1853 Baron Uchatius projected Plateau's phenakistoscopic pictures. A series of inventions followed in rapid order, culminating in 1861 with Coleman Seller's kinematoscope which related the zoëtropic principle to that of still photography. This second period coincided with a second great period in nineteenth-century realistic-romantic activity marked by the theatrical work of Charles Kean and the American Booth, the literary achievements of Thackeray, George Boker, Dumas *père,* and so on.

The culminating phase in the development of the projection of the photographic reproduction of motion and the culminating nineteenth-century phase in the realistic-romantic cycle of pictorialism in the theatrical and literary arts were both inaugurated at about the same time. On April 25, 1864, du Hauron made application for a patent which we are told anticipated the entire scheme of the motion picture. For the next three decades one step followed close upon another until, in 1895, the continuous projection of reproduced motion was demonstrated. In 1865, a year after du Hauron's patent application, the Bancroft-Robertson company opened at the Prince of Wales's. This final phase in the cycle of nineteenth-century theatre which saw the pictorial combination of realism and romance found such other outstanding exponents as Augustin Daly, Steele MacKaye, André Antoine, the Saxe-Meiningen group, David Belasco, Henry Irving, the Moscow Art Theatre, and so on. It included the entire dramatic revival of the nineties as well as a host of novelists among whom George Eliot, Thomas Hardy, Robert Louis Stevenson, and Rudyard Kipling are particularly representative. Thus the peak of Victorian aesthetic activity, with its highly pictorial bias in the arts of staging, the drama, and the novel, coincided with the final phase in the invention of the motion picture.

The relationship suggested by these chronological parallels is significant. It would suggest the well-known adage, "Necessity is the mother of invention." The motion picture, like the realistic-romantic expression in the arts, was deeply rooted, even during its long period of incubation, in the social needs of the times. The obvious implications would still those untutored critics who maintain that cinema arrived simply when the necessary technical knowledge and equipment were available. Cinema was not born simply with the invention of Eastman's celluloid film nor with the arrival of the motion-picture camera; the need for cinema had been felt as early as 1824, and its conception and early development occurred simultaneously with analogous advances in the theatre of realism and romance. Both responded to the same popular "tension," the same aesthetic preference. The facilities were products of the need, and not the need of the facilities. Cinema, in the aesthetic and sociological sense, was closely related to the realistic strivings of David Garrick.

In addition to the implied sociological relationship, the overall chronological pattern between the development of the reproduction of motion and the realistic-romantic theatre suggests an immediate aesthetic partnership. Within the large pattern, smaller cycles of progress in each of the two lines of activity appeared simultaneously. This revelation prompted a reëxamination of nineteenth-century theatre, particularly during the latter half of the century. A distinct aesthetic kinship between stage and screen became apparent as theatrical values, developed upon the stage of the nineteenth century, were transferred to the screen during the years of the recognition, acceptance, and growth of the new medium.

The early popularity of the screen and its establishment as an art form were the result of activity in four distinct areas previously attempted upon the stage. The first of these areas, nondramatic and purely pictorial, that of the reproductionally painted panorama, found immediate and permanent expression upon the screen in the topical film episode. Subsequently, the stage panorama disappeared. The second, represented in the film by the work of George Méliès, provided the screen with its preliminary aesthetic approach. Méliès' technique was that of a series of "artificially arranged scenes," each played before a static camera and interlaced with a rudimentary dissolve linkage. This method, as well as his choice of subject matter, made no pretense at realism but exploited the fantastic values of stage pantomime-spectacle. A gradual decline in the popularity of this artificial stage material upon the screen stimulated the quest for another aesthetic approach.

E. S. Porter insured the permanence of the new medium as an art form with his demonstration of a syntax for the one-reel melodrama. Porter's method became the great screen pattern for about ten years, roughly from 1902 to 1912, and upon this formula a screen audience was developed which secured a financial footing for the industry. Within the single-reel form, D. W. Griffith, taking over Porter's approach, strove, through editorial syntax and camera and productional techniques, to heighten the realistic illusion of the film. At the same time, his choice and treatment of subject as well as his choice and direction of players had a strong romantic tinge. Coming under the influence of the early foreign spectacle films, he added spectacle to melodrama with great success, even within the single-reel form.

The fourth area represents the final phase in the establishment of an art for the silent feature picture. About 1913, developments within the growing industry led to the introduction of the feature film. Material was borrowed from the stage. When it depended upon qualities of objective realism, upon the values of spectacle or melodrama, for instance, it succeeded on the screen. When its attributes were those of a subjective realism, as in the plays of Ibsen, failure usually resulted. Thus the fourth step in the development of cinema, that of the feature film, succeeded upon the addition of spectacle. The fantastic pantomime-spectacle, the melodrama, and the realistic spectacle, in that order, each a branch of that graphic approach to the theatre emanating from Garrick, were the three dramatic forms upon which the success of the screen as a medium of art and entertainment was established.

The cinematic characteristics of the popular stage of the century were most evident in stock melodrama. This form required the presentation of a series of stage pictures for the development of the narrative, managed either through a continuous flow of these pictorial episodes in a single line of action, or, more frequently, depending upon a cross-cutting or flashing-back between parallel lines of action, and employing methods of scene changing analogous to the film dissolve or the fade-out and fade-in. This constructional pattern with its implicit cinematic characteristics was eventually used by E. S. Porter in setting up the fundamental editorial technique of the motion picture.

Nineteenth-century melodrama owed its success not only to its cinematic construction and to its spectacular handling of scenery, but, in a considerable way, to the sensational values embodied in these stage pictures. If a practical cliff or tower were presented, you may be sure it would be used for a climactic leap; if a sea cave were shown, a drowning would occur; railroad tracks meant a last-minute rescue from a thundering locomotive; if a buzz saw appeared, the villain would surely use it for his dirty work; if a prison were shown, an escape must be made; horses raced, cannon roared, pistols spat, and sabers flashed, steamboats burned and trains exploded; bears jigged, Indians danced, snows stormed, winds wailed, mountains avalanched, pigs squealed, schooners were shipwrecked, and "headers" into real or artificial water were "a sure way of getting an audience." All manner of spectacular effects were dragged in to provide climax in this pictorial dramatic form.

Unfortunately, this cinematic pattern and its sensational pictorial conceptions depended to a great extent upon conventional staging. A survey of productional methods in general use during the years surrounding and prior to the arrival of the cinema, specific productional techniques demonstrated in the Harvard promptbooks, and the physical equipment of both metropolitan and provincial theatres of the period indicates that the largest part of the audience patronizing melodrama at the time of the arrival of the motion picture was accustomed to conventional stagings. Spectacular scenic realism, possible upon metropolitan stages, was by no means widespread. Irving, Belasco, and MacKaye were outstanding because of the very realism of their spectacular productions; but the melodrama, strongest single root of cinema, was more a provincial than a metropolitan form, and hence retained its conventionality long after realistic reforms were felt in the cities. The introduction of single realistic items of a sensational nature often destroyed the illusion of an otherwise stock production, and therefore barely alleviated the burden of conventional staging.

General discard of these conventions was impossible to nineteenth-century stage melodrama, for its success depended upon pictorial speed. In turn, pictorial speed depended upon the counterfeit conventions; hence, melodrama and scenic realism were incompatible under the inadequate staging facilities available in "that more integral part of the theatre of yesterday."

With the growing taste for scenic realism, the conventional staging methods which controlled the presentation of melodrama eventually broke down. It is not to be wondered that W. P. Eaton in 1909 should report that the production of stage melodramas had decreased at least 50 per cent since moving pictures became the rage. In the face of the breakdown of the conventions, the screen naturally assumed values which had been the backbone of stage melodrama. Screen melodrama became a simple continuation, upon the new basis of photographic realism and camera technique, of the specific dramatic techniques and spectacular pictorial aims which had existed upon the stage even prior to the middle of the century and which had been amply demonstrated by such productions as those of Dion Boucicault, or of Augustin Daly's stage manager, John Moore. Here, of course, is where a certain inadequacy has been felt in Lewis Jacobs' otherwise excellent treatment of the development of the American film. As has been noted, while Jacobs gives entire credit to E. S. Porter for distinguishing motion pictures from other theatrical forms, it has been quite clear that Porter merely translated into the photographic idiom of the screen the mid-century aims of the melodrama branch of the nineteenth-century theatre of realism and romance.

While stage melodrama lost its audience almost at once to the film, spectacle drama ran a somewhat different course. Spectacle was, from the start, and by definition, one of the basic elements of the film. Yet it was not exploited as such in any great way until such productions as *Quo Vadis?*, *Cabiria*, *Judith of Bethulia*, *The Birth of a Nation,* and so on, that is, until about 1912-1915. In the intervening years, roughly from 1895 to 1910, stage spectacle had reason to survive, for, while both melodrama and spectacle utilized the pictorial approach with all its cinematic implications, the spectacle drama succeeded in discarding many of the outworn staging conventions. Under the influence of the reforms of the sixties, seventies, and eighties, realistic pictorial developments in the spectacle play were not sacrificed to speed, variety, and sensation.

This holds true for the field in general as well as for the special work of Irving, Belasco, and MacKaye, whose productions became the embodiment of spectacular stage realism approaching the photographic ideal. The limited facilities of many provincial theatres impeded the full and realistic presentation of spectacle, hence this form became primarily a metropolitan theatrical expression occasionally reaching audiences in the larger provincial centers. Thus, the trend toward the pictorial drama, which had sprung from the stagings of Garrick, Loutherbourg, and Capon, and which had been further developed by Charles Kean, was purged of the conventionalities of the period by the realistic reforms of the Bancrofts, the Saxe-Meiningen, Augustin Daly, and the Théâtre-Libre of Antoine, eventually leading to Irving, Belasco, and MacKaye, and subsequently, upon the screen, to D. W. Griffith. The age hungered for the real as well as the spectacular. While the introduction of realism into spectacle drama may have extended the life of this form, its ultimate expression was to be realized through the invention of the motion picture.

Realistic spectacle drama, synonymous with theatrical success in the nineties, moving from stage to screen, provided the third basis for progress in motion-picture technique. The stage, however, having developed an audience for this type of production over a long period of time, and with great expense and care, was altogether unwilling to yield this audience to the screen without contention. Fortified by the success of pre-cinema staging improvements, highly realistic and spectacular productions, the logical property of the screen, were being offered on the stage even after the film had demonstrated its superiority in this area. The success of these presentations decreased as that of the screen spectacles increased. It is of incidental interest, too, that, in this exploitation of spectacle, the stage found much material in the novel that would lend itself to pictorial production. The screen, in its turn, immediately took over the same or similar material from the stage and with subsequent filmings further eclipsed the spectacle stage. Apparently the motion picture was much better qualified to film the novel than the theatre was to stage it, and, in this way, the cinema tended to deprive the stage of a certain source of its dramatic supply.

And so, while this pictorial theatre had been striving toward the cinematic ideal during the entire span of the nineteenth century, offering, by the success of its example, stimulation to the invention of the motion picture, the presence of insurmountable physical limitations eventually made further progress impossible. A platform for the development of the art of the film had been set up as the cycle of graphic staging attained its zenith. Conditions in the arts seldom remaining static, evolutionary reaction was normally to have been expected at about the time of the introduction of the motion picture. But in picking up the thread of realistic-romantic theatrical production at the very pinnacle of its expression and carrying it into a still higher level, the film postponed this reaction. In its turn, the stage sought less a new approach than, in the effort to regain its audience from the nickelodeons and the glamour palaces of the film magnates, an elaboration of the old one. Cinema came to fill an existing need and at the same time, paradoxical as this may seem, served to upset the anticipated course of theatrical development. Reaction had been in the air. It had been suggested by the work of William Poël in England and by the varied experimentation with new methods in the early century "producers' theatre." But the popular stage reverted to its pattern of the nineties as the methods of Belasco retained their favor, and the stage of the early century sought to outrival the screen upon its own terms.

The popularity of panoramas during the closing decades of the century provides distinct evidence of the aesthetic taste for motion pictures. The influence of this form cannot be specifically measured. It can only be recorded that the first of the pictorial forms to disappear from the stage upon the arrival of the film was the panorama. Soon stage melodrama gave way before the onslaught of E. S. Porter and D. W. Griffith in the same way that the pantomime-spectacle disappeared before the success of M. Méliès. This latter development appeared, at first glance, a contradiction, for the cinema on the one hand had been recognized for its realistic values, while the pantomime was a fantastic form. The inconsistency was resolved by the direct connection between the work of Méliès and that of the pantomime stage.

Pantomime-spectacle, throughout the nineteenth century, was a conventional form, both in the method of its staging and in its subject matter. Its presentation epitomized fantastic and spectacular values. As long as these qualities plus a certain novelty in "magical" effects were maintained, the conventional staging counterfeits retained their popularity.

At the same time this form appeared to possess cinematic qualities. Like the melodrama its narrative was developed by a single direct pictorial progression or by cross-cutting between parallel pictorial progressions alternately staged. This cinematic conception resulted in the use of certain motion-picture techniques. Transformations were of significant value in the fabric of pantomime and presaged such ordinary screen techniques as the dissolve, the fade-in, or the fade-out. Stage magic, prime stock-in-trade of this form, unfrocked by the naïve and clumsy machinery of the nineteenth-century stagehouse, cried out for the kind of sleight of hand which was to prove so accessible to the motion-picture camera and the film strip. As in the melodrama, the scenic vantage point—camera position as it were—was shifted during action in progress, thus dividing the dramatic unit into a smaller pictorial episode or "take." And in the manner of the silent film, dialogue was unimportant while the chief emphasis moved toward the visual aspects, more so in pantomime than in melodrama.

While realism may have been far from primary consideration in the staging of such fantastic, traditional, and familiar material as that of the pantomime, the realistic reforms of the sixties, seventies, and eighties had an influence upon the spectacular strivings of metropolitan productions. By the early and middle nineties a peak had been reached in the realistic presentation of these conglomerate fantasies with the productions of Oscar Barrett. Subsequent versions of the same pantomimes fell into a repetition of his patterns and effects. It appeared that further progress in the elaboration of this dramatic form was impossible to the stage.

In supporting the rise of the pantomime to its late-century perfection, theatre audiences very likely, directly or indirectly, offered a certain stimulation to the forces behind the development of the motion picture, for strangely enough, at the very time of the peak of the success and popularity of the Barrett productions, the cinema made its appearance. The motion picture was quickly recognized for its ability to satisfy the same aesthetic tastes as the pantomime and was soon included in some pantomime bills.

Because conventionalism of one kind or another was permissible in the pantomime, it has been suggested that the need of the pantomime stage for the motion picture was less for the sake of realism than for novelty, spectacle, and its capacity for theatrical magic. This contention was borne out at once by the work of George Méliès whose pictures, borrowing material directly from the pantomime stage, embodied all sorts of new, fantastic, and spectacular camera trickery.

Once the stage had felt the competition offered by M. Méliès, it pursued the rivalry with larger and more spectacular productions. This attempt was useless, of course, for any success in this direction automatically restricted its audience. Productional costs were increased but the potential audience was decreased. In entering such a competition with the screen, the pantomime-spectacle stage committed a kind of theatrical hara-kiri. Eventually there was capitulation, and the stage turned to a development of plot values, yielding the field of spectacle in the pantomime to the screen. Reaction in this branch of the realistic-romantic theatre which seemed imminent in the nineties was postponed by the cinema. The film showed an early facility in this field and after several years of competition between stage and screen, domination of the form by the screen seemed inevitable. And so the pantomime passed, in this way, from stage to screen, reaching, in the new medium, a greater perfection and elaboration which has continued, even to the present day, in the many productions of its natural heirs and successors, the forerunners and colleagues of Walt Disney.

Thus the melodrama, the spectacle, and the pantomime-spectacle, conceived and produced in cinematic terms during the entire course of the realistic-romantic cycle, had been moving in a direction which, by the turn of the century, would normally have met reaction had not the cinema appeared to continue and extend each of them, the one by George Méliès, and the other two by E. S. Porter, D. W. Griffith, C. B. De Mille and others. Having thus stimulated the arrival of the motion picture, the theatre of realism and romance was soon caught up in its own web and each of the dramatic forms which found successful expression in the cinema soon disappeared from the stage. The development of the popular stage, prior to the advent of cinema, into an entertainment medium akin to the screen and satisfying the same aesthetic preferences was most thoroughly carried out in the work of a certain triumvirate: Henry Irving, David Belasco, and Steele MacKaye.

The productions of these three represent the ultimate phase in the rise of realistic-romantic theatre during the nineteenth century and mark the peak beyond which reaction might have been expected. MacKaye's work attained a colossal reproductional level in his Spectatorium and Scenitorium just before the appearance of the motion picture. No similar or equivalent expression was attempted upon the stage after the successful debut of the screen. Irving's work reached the height of its popularity at the Lyceum about 1895. Soon after, his management failed since new backers would no longer sponsor his methods. David Belasco was more successful than Irving and seems to have offered his most reproductional stagings even after the arrival of cinema. He succeeded in competing with the screen upon its own terms because he exploited certain productional aspects not always possible in the early film.

The quality of the theatrical output of this triumvirate is of particular significance in the aesthetic relationship between stage and screen during the years of the fusion of the two forms. Henry Irving's approach to theatre, for instance, was entirely productional. This characteristic, evident in his staging of melodramas, was much more fully exploited in the presentation of Shakespeare and other historical pieces. Shakespeare, whether in comedy, tragedy, or chronicle play, never wore fancier dress.

The cinematic characteristics of the stock-melodrama pattern, with its flash-backs, visions, tableaux, sensations, pictorial continuity, and cross-cutting, were, of course, incorporated into his melodrama stagings, but were supported by realistic stage pictures. The attempt was constantly made for a reproductional kind of realism moving toward the photographic ideal. While this continually created difficulty in the handling of such cinematic devices as the instantaneous scene shift, with dissolve or fade-out and fade-in effects, the Lyceum and other metropolitan stages, elaborately equipped and staffed by large crews, managed extraordinary results.

Shakespeare and the historical drama provided Irving the greatest supply of material for the staging of realistic spectacles. Here all the sensational pictorial devices of melodrama were worked out with great care and an elaborateness known best to Irving: witches melted in and out on foggy heaths; castles dissolved into courtyards; barges appeared to float through rainbows; action progressed continuously from one locality into another as scenery changed amid simultaneous exits and entrances; the Friar's cell dissolved into darkness as the barred entrance to the tomb of the Capulets moved into misty view only to be replaced by the crypt, hewn in solid rock, which grew before the eyes. All manner of pictorial contrivances were employed, steam curtains and lighting effects playing no small part, and one picture flowing imperceptibly into the next. In these sequences, settings achieved the realism of actual reproduction of fact or fancy. In the re-creation of fact, archaeological studies and field trips supported three-dimensional reconstructions or skillful paintings of scenes as they may actually have appeared in the period specified by the script. Built-out, architectural setting played a large part in the work of Irving, as an exact duplication of time and place was attempted.

This quality was also true of properties. Real apples fell from trees; collars were studded with real diamonds; costumes reproduced original textures and fabrics, as well as colors and patterns; solid hillsides were thick with bushes of whitethorn; snow had to be kicked aside to gain stage footing; horses plunged and armies marched. The categorical realism of details was as reproductional as the over-all scenic approach. Expense was rarely spared, and productional costs in the interests of pictorial realism reached as high as $150,000. Weekly expenditures went to $10,000, as Irving sought the photographic ideal. Plays were attempted which had no further hope for success than through the pictures with which they were embellished.

In the staging of fancy, science was called upon for the realistic and spectacular presentation of imaginery, grotesque, or supernatural sequences. To the magic of the conventional vampire trap were added such techniques as gauzes and steam curtains for mysterious dissolve effects, new and ingenious electrical devices for sparkling swords and flashing sabers, and so on. Rainbows were meticulously fabricated, assembled, painted, and lighted for new translucent effects; Excalibur rose mystically from the mere; supernatural hands were boldly luminous; bouquets "fresh from Elysian fields," visually realized, were wafted on ethereal breezes.

For this photographic realism, whether of fact or of fancy, Henry Irving surrounded himself with the ablest of the reproductional scene painters: Hawes Craven, Joseph Harker, Walter Hann, T. W. Hall, W. Cuthbert, and William Telbin, supported by artists Edward Burne-Jones, E. A. Abbey, and Sir Lawrence Alma-Tadema. In the interests of archaeology he employed James Knowles, Alexander Murray, and the staff of the British Museum. Nothing was spared in the quest for the photographic ideal of the motion-picture camera.

Stage direction, both in its handling of individual character interpretation and in mass groupings, movements, and tableaux, supported and augmented the pictures achieved through scenery, lighting, costumes, and properties. The acting of Henry Irving and Ellen Terry was notable for its pictorial bias, its selection, and its emphasis of visual images, details of business or of pantomime, comparable to certain "montage" values of screen acting.[1] Into the solid, architectural, and mobile phases of the settings, masses of supers were maneuvered for great visual effects. Street fights were waged on bridges; entrances, en masse, were made from below stage as up a hill, or from the flies as down a mossy path cut into a solid hillside; gondolas slithered through crowded and dimly lighted canals and under bridges, and so on. Plastic and three-dimensional settings were devised as much for their potential in the arrangement of vivid groupings and action values as for their intrinsic pictorial quality. And the smallest detail, both in setting and in stage direction, was pre-planned for its graphic effect.

In keeping with the visual quality of setting, costuming, and stage direction, lighting achieved a new importance. Unusual and sensational effects were realistically presented. Rainbows now glowed with all colors of the prism; Stygian courtyards blazed with the glow of fiery torches; sunset faded into twilight and sunrise into dawn as the twenty-four-hour cycle was authentically staged.

To this the finest musical accompaniment was added. The classics were freely used, and Sir Arthur Sullivan was often engaged for original composition, orchestration, and choral arrangement.

In these ways the work of Henry Irving marked a need for the photographic ideal of the film ten years or more before its arrival. His many productions all attempted a motion-picture kind of theatre, and his success may very likely have exerted a certain stimulation upon the development of the cinema, for the original showings of the Edison vitascope coincided with the zenith of the popularity of Irving's pictorial theatre.

Henry Irving, then, stands as a steppingstone between the two main lines of the popular nineteenth-century theatre of realism and romance emanating from Garrick and culminating in the cinema. He took over the lines of the melodrama and of the spectacle. These two dramatic forms had, in attaining a mid-century peak with the work of Dion Boucicault and Charles Kean, respectively, continued earlier traditions. Henry Irving, in his turn, brought the mid-century achievements to a still higher level, which was eventually capped by the motion picture and D. W. Griffith. That Irving's productions moved to the very threshold of cinema during the development of the final phase in the invention of the mechanics of the motion picture would suggest that both Henry Irving and the cohorts of Thomas Edison sought to fulfill the same aesthetic need, namely, the need for the picture-play in motion. The cinema appeared when the theatrical need for the photographic ideal was greatest.

Once the film had made its appearance, Irving's productional methods were undermined. His management at the Lyceum failed since backers would no longer sponsor his approach. Then, in an effort to meet the pictorial challenge of the screen he attempted, in a new theatre, a $150,000 production of *Dante*. It ran for only eighty-two performances. This represented failure on the pictorial stage and provided a preview of capitulation to the film. Having presaged and influenced its development, Irving found himself, ironically enough, being plagued into provincial confinement by the inroads of the new medium.

That a group of these outstanding pictorial theatrical producers should have appeared simultaneously with the culminating phase in the achievement of the motion picture could hardly have been a chance occurrence. This group, as well as the forces behind cinema, responded to the same sociological "tension" and sought to satisfy similar aesthetic tastes. Of the triumvirate, Irving, Belasco, and MacKaye, who epitomize the approach to theatre in the century preceding cinema, Belasco, whether as producer of melodrama, historical spectacle, or the drama of intimate realism, appears to have benefited most directly from the realistic reforms of his predecessors. Less a reformer than a continuator, he carried existing staging methods to a cinematic level. To the spectacle, the melodrama, and the drama of intimate realism, Belasco imparted his peculiar talent for the literal and the pictorial. For the cinematic conceptions contained within each of these fields he provided a cinematic productional quality.

The arrival of the motion picture presented Belasco a formidable rival. He was forced to entrench his position. He selected and eliminated. He sacrificed the use of a large number of locales to the cinema and sometimes found that flash backs and vision sequences belonged more properly to the screen. Speed in the shift of solid, three-dimensional scenery he achieved by the elevator stage, installed in his renovated theatre of 1902, and by temporary wagon stages. But scenic speed was no longer a prime essential of the stage and this, too, he gave over to the film. On the other hand, he recognized, either consciously or unconsciously, that the screen could not follow him into two areas of his pictorial, reproductional theatre, namely, in the staging of interiors, particularly those dependent upon subtle lighting values, and in plays built around the restrained, naturalistic, David Warfield style of acting. These two areas, heritages from the Robertsonian reforms, Belasco continued to exploit and to elaborate even into the years of the silent feature film, and until the screen itself succeeded in discarding its own conventionalisms.

Thus, at a point when we might have expected a complete and successful reaction to the romantic pictorial approach of nineteenth-century theatre, the arrival of the cinema upset expected trends and forced Belasco into greater and more specialized efforts in the same old photographic directions. By careful selection, Belasco succeeded in spite of the cinema. Thus the film might now be considered a cause and no longer an effect. It had now become a force contributing to the continuation of the reproductional pictorial method in the theatre of realism and romance even after reaction might normally have been anticipated. Under its pressure Belasco was driven to the extreme of transferring a portion of a Childs Restaurant to the stage of his theatre. In its influence upon the early twentieth-century popular stage, particularly that of America, the cinema can be seen extending the realistic-romantic theatrical phase by at least twenty years, into and beyond the period of World War I.

To the one of this triumvirate whose career was cut short by death even before the appearance of the film must be conceded the creation of the most cinematic staging of the nineteenth century. From his earliest connection with the theatre, Steele MacKaye had demonstrated a thorough agreement with the pictorial mode of the Garrick cycle. His approach to theatre was altogether graphic, but sought to overcome the counterfeit conventional methods for handling the thrilling spectacular sequences of melodrama through the invention and introduction of a number of staging devices. Such machines as the sliding stage, the elevator stage, and the floating stage sought to eliminate two-dimensional scenery by providing means for the storage and rapid shifting of solid, three-dimensional settings. His luxauleator, illumiscope, colourator, cloud-creator, or nebulator all strove to heighten the visual illusion through advanced use of electric lighting. His silent unfolding announcer sought to eliminate dialogue, while his proscenium adjuster provided a method for controlling the size of the picture frame automatically to accommodate either a close-up, medium, or panoramic view. This inventive genius in the physical setting of the play was coupled with the sponsorship of a system of acting which, if carried to the conclusion of its basic premise, would have eliminated the need for the vocal illusion, for dialogue, completely. The actor would have become utterly subservient to the demands of MacKaye's scientifically created stage picture, and theatrical production would have assumed the quality of a silent film. These various inventions, plus a severe version of the system of Delsarte, were combined in his Spectatorium (incomplete), 1893, and his Scenitorium, 1894. Here, with his many scientific devices, electrically harnessed, he succeeded, just two years before the arrival of cinema, in staging a centrally controlled "motion picture-in-the-round," thus demonstrating beyond any possible question that the aims of nineteenth-century popular theatre were identical with those of the moving pictures. Here the central operator might exercise an editorial domination over the production analogous to that of the cutting-room. Within the few years of his short career Steele MacKaye had envisioned and achieved on a restricted scale the pictorial stage production of *The World Finder,* surpassed only by such later spectacle filmings as *Intolerance, The Birth of a Nation, Ben Hur,* or *The King of Kings.*

Audiences immediately identified the cinema, from its first showings, with the nineteenth-century vogue of pictorial theatre. It was readily established as the most realistic medium yet available to the theatrical arts. The stage might represent reality but the motion picture could photograph it. Going beyond the realism of the stage, and armed with the authenticity of moving pictures, romanticism moved into new levels and fresh areas upon the screen. Now a part of the realistic-romantic theatrical cycle, the screen extended, through the work of D. W. Griffith, the values which had grown out of the original staging reforms of Garrick. The pictorial-representational methods of Garrick and the nineteenth-century stage were superseded by the pictorial-authentic methods of Griffith. A one-hundred-and-fifty-year pattern in theatrical method had been traced.

The cinema, by doing so much better the selfsame things which had been the aim and objective of the popular nineteenth-century theatre, became the most widely patronized and effective art force in the world, the prime source of popular entertainment, as well as one of the most powerful propaganda weapon ever in the hands of men. By seizing upon methods and patterns in existence for nearly a century before its arrival, cinema secured its footing and in 1937, when Hollywood alone produced over four hundred pictures, achieved the distinction of hypnotizing into emotional and intellectual acceptance a goodly part of its daily audience of 20,000,000. Such has been the ultimate consequence of the *zeitgeist* of the eighteenth and nineteenth centuries which supported the realistic reforms of David Garrick and encouraged the revival of interest in the phenomenon of the persistence of vision. Whether the realistic-romantic cycle which began with Garrick has spent itself with the great screenings of Griffith has yet to be determined. The cinema, to be sure, did extend its length and did carry it into a higher plane. But there has been no second *Intolerance;* and *Ben Hur,* marking a pinnacle in the lavish productional spectacle, is already more than twenty years old.

NOTES

NOTES

The large number of newspaper articles and reviews which I have used are referred to in the Notes by date and name of the paper in which the articles appeared, whenever identification was possible. Many of these clippings I found in the Harvard Theatre Collection, where they are filed under the name of the play to which they refer. I have tried to describe in some detail the promptbooks in the Harvard Theatre Collection, and have included call numbers so that they may be easily found by anyone wishing to consult them. The abbreviation HTC has been used throughout the Notes to indicate the Harvard Theatre Collection.

Unless otherwise indicated, the motion-picture catalogues (*Edison Catalogue, Star Films, Méliès Catalogue, Bioscope-Warwick Catalogue,* and so forth) and most of the other motion-picture publications cited were found in the Museum of Modern Art Film Library.

I am indebted to the following persons or publishers for permission to quote from copyrighted material: Mr. Percy MacKaye for selections from his book, *Epoch: The Life of Steele MacKaye;* the Macmillan Company for selections from *Personal Reminiscences of Henry Irving* by Bram Stoker; Mrs. Elisabeth C. Lindsay for selections from *The Art of the Moving Picture* by N. Vachel Lindsay; and E. P. Dutton and Company, Inc., for selections from *When the Movies Were Young* by Mrs. D. W. Griffith.

INTRODUCTION

1. B. J. Lubschez, *Story of the Motion Picture* (New York, 1920), p. 10.

2. For the history and description of various inventions in the development of motion pictures given in the paragraphs below, see Terry Ramsaye's article "History" under "Motion Pictures," *Encyclopaedia Britannica* (14th ed., 1946), XV, 855-856; Lubschez, *Story of the Motion Picture,* pp. 10ff.; F. A. Talbot, *Moving Pictures; How They Are Made and Worked* (Philadelphia, 1914), chaps. ii-iv; Robert Grau, *The Theatre of Science* (New York, 1914), pp. 30ff.;

and Maurice Bardèche and Robert Brasillach, *The History of Motion Pictures,* translated by Iris Barry (New York: W. W. Norton and Co., and the Museum of Modern Art, 1938).

3. Described by J. R. Planché in *Recollections and Reflections* (2 vols.; London, 1901), I, 52-57.

4. Waldemar Kaempffert, "Invention as a Social Manifestation," chap. ii, p. 21, in C. A. Beard (ed.), *A Century of Progress* (New York, 1935).

5. Lubschez, *Story of the Motion Picture,* p. 51.

CHAPTER ONE

1. M. J. Moses, *The American Dramatist* (Boston, 1917), p. 307.

2. G. H. Leverton, *The Production of Later Nineteenth Century American Drama* (New York: Teachers College, Columbia University, 1936), p. 8.

3. *New York World,* November 17, 1872.

4. A. A. Hopkins, *Magic: Stage Illusions and Scientific Diversions, Including Trick Photography* (New York: Munn and Company, 1897), p. 255.

5. *Ibid.,* p. 256.

6. *Ibid.,* p. 255.

7. Walter Emden, "Theatres," *Building News,* XLIV, 350-352 (March 1883).

8. Julius Cahn, *Official Theatrical Guide*, I (New York, 1896-97), 120. The population figures given below are taken from this volume.

9. *Ibid.*, I, 389.

10. *Ibid.*, I, 315.

11. *Ibid.*, I, 433.

12. Leverton, *Nineteenth Century American Drama*, p. 21n.

13. Cahn, *Theatrical Guide*, I, 389.

14. *Ibid.*, I, 238.

15. *Ibid.*, I, 665.

16. *Ibid.*, I, 386.

17. *Ibid.*, I, 245.

18. *Ibid.*, I, 626.

19. *Ibid.*, I, 591.

20. Hopkins, *Magic*, p. 255.

21. Emden, "Theatres," pp. 350-352.

22. Cahn, *Theatrical Guide*, I, 433.

23. *Ibid.*, I, 336.

24. *Ibid.*, I, 85.

25. *Ibid.*, I, 169.

26. *Ibid.*, I, 235.

27. *Ibid.*, I, 242.

28. *Ibid.*, I, 243.

29. W. H. Crane, "Some Developments of the American Stage During the Past Fifty Years," *University of California Chronicle*, XV, 213 (April 1913). In this article, Crane gives further interesting evidence concerning the inadequacy of stage setting during this period. Speaking of one of his earliest performances, about 1863, he writes: "For the historical correct reproduction of a gorgeous domicile of Bourbon luxury, we played before a pair of flats—technically known as center door, fancy chamber—while two badly painted wings banked in the scene at either side of the stage and two wilted borders above represented the ceiling" (p. 211).

30. Percy MacKaye, *Epoch; The Life of James Steele MacKaye* (2 vols.; New York, 1927), II, 11.

31. *New Orleans Picayune*, February 5, 1880.

32. William Winter, *The Life of David Belasco* (2 vols.; New York: copyright, 1918, by Jefferson Winter), II, 245.

33. *Nashville Republican Banner*, January 23, 1874.

34. See previous references in this chapter to methods of lighting in various provincial theatres. John H. McDowell, in his article, "Historical Development of the Box Set," *The Theatre Annual*, *1945*, discusses the introduction of gas lighting, (p. 74, n. 4) and electric lighting (p. 76, n. 1) in British, European, and American theatres.

35. Winter, *Belasco*, II, 246.

36. Hopkins, *Magic*, p. 298.

37. *Ibid.*, p. 299.

38. *Ibid.*, p. 302.

39. *Ibid.*

40. Franklin Fyles, "Behind the Scenes During a Play," *Ladies' Home Journal*, vol. XVII, no. 5, p. 7 (April 1900). This article was the seventh in a series entitled "The Theatre and its People."

41. Olive Logan, "Secret Regions of the Stage," *Harper's New Monthly Magazine*, XLVIII (1874), 637.

42. Hopkins, *Magic*, p. 304.

43. *Ibid.*, pp. 303-04.

44. Logan, "Secret Regions of the Stage," p. 637.

45. Dion Boucicault, *The Octoroon*. Bound manuscript copy, marked on the title page, "The property of Henry Willard's, Howard Athenaeum, Boston, 1863." A program included at the front has the names of all players cut out and the name of one C. Wilkinson penned in as Colonel Pointdexter. Prompt copy thoroughly marked for effects, cues, some ground plans, all entrances, exits, tableaux, and so forth. HTC, call number TS 3469.201.

46. Dion Boucicault, *The Octoroon*. This promptbook, marked on the title page in handscript, "Prompt copy, Owen Fawcett, Jan. 23, 1867," is in five acts, the first four being a hand-marked prompt text published by Thomas Lacy (London), and the last in manuscript. It is very likely that the sensational fifth act, appearing here in manuscript, is Fawcett's own contrivance, for the original Boucicault version was published in only four acts. Several printed programs which are included show that Fawcett played Samuel Scudder in the following productions: August 1, 1867, Baltimore, Maryland; March 4, 1865, Winter Garden, New York; 1868, Walnut Street Theatre, Philadelphia; November 20,

1869, Walnut Street Theatre, Philadelphia. HTC, call number TS 3469.202.

47. Hopkins, *Magic*, p. 305.

48. *Ibid.*, p. 299.

49. Lavinia Hart, "Behind the Scenes," *Cosmopolitan*, XXIII (1880), 472-486.

50. Hopkins, *Magic*, p. 274.

51. Logan, "Secret Regions of the Stage," p. 637.

52. *Ibid.*

53. Hopkins, *Magic*, p. 304.

54. *Ibid.*

55. Gustave Kobbé, "Behind the Scenes of an Opera House," *Scribner's Magazine*, IV (1888), 454.

56. Both quotations in this paragraph are from Fyles, "Behind the Scenes," p. 8.

57. Hopkins, *Magic*, p. 309.

58. *Ibid.*, p. 308. My italics.

59. *Ibid.*, pp. 304-05.

60. Leo Waitzkin, *The Witch of Wych Street; a Study of the Theatrical Reforms of Madame Vestris* (Cambridge, Mass.: Harvard University Press, 1933), p. 22.

61. T. E. Pemberton, *The Life and Writings of T. W. Robertson* (2 vols.; 2d ed., London, 1893), I, 206.

62. McDowell, "Historical Development of the Box Set," p. 80, quoting E. W. Mammen, *The Old Stock Company School of Acting* (Boston, 1945), p. 30.

63. McDowell, "Historical Development of the Box Set," pp. 80, 82.

64. E. Grange and X. de Montepin, *The Corsican Brothers*, adapted from a novel of M. Dumas. This prompt copy, fully marked and interleaved, is a Samuel French printed version and is marked with the name of J. Moore on the cover. John Moore was prompter at the Bowery Theatre, New York, at the time of this play's production there on April 21, 1852. He also played the role of Boissec in this production and of Orlando in another whose program is included. There are manuscript sides for both Boissec and Orlando inserted but unbound in the rear cover. HTC, call number TS 2138.25.

65. *Nashville Republican Banner*, January 23, 1879.

CHAPTER TWO

1. W. J. Thompson, *A Race for Life.* A manuscript in the author's hand. The first page is marked: "First produced August 27, 1883." HTC, call number TS 3559.50.

2. Dion Boucicault, *Arrah-na-Pogue.* There are several versions of this melodrama in the Harvard Theatre Collection. The sketches for the staging of the sensational escape scene are taken from the DeWitt publication (HTC, call number DAL 966, 1.5) as produced at the Theatre Royal, Dublin, in November, 1864, and at the Princess' Theatre, London, in March, 1865. Another combination prompt and manuscript copy (HTC, call number TS 3055.45) is "as originally played in Dublin, Nov. 1864." Still another in manuscript (HTC, call number TS 3055.51) is marked "Owen Fawcett's copy . . . 1868."

3. *New York Herald*, July 13, 1865.

4. *Ibid.*

5. *Illustrated Sporting and Dramatic News* (London), September 12, 1891.

6. *The Era* (London), March 10, 1888.

7. *Philadelphia Item*, January 5, 1892.

8. *Boston Transcript*, January 7, 1896.

9. From an undated review of *Arrah-na-Pogue* appearing in an Oakland, California, newspaper (HTC).

10. Charles Dickens, *David Copperfield*. This adaptation, called *Little Emily*, is apparently by George F. Rowe, for the title page of the manuscript promptbook reads: "Little Emily by George F. Rowe." HTC, call number TS 3388.500.

11. *Boston Post*, October 7, 1890.

12. From a review of *Little Emily* [*David Copperfield*] taken from a Boston newspaper (HTC).

13. From a review of *Little Emily* in an unidentified London [?] newspaper (HTC).

14. *Boston Transcript*, February 12, 1907.

15. *New York Daily Advertiser*, May 20, 1874.

16. *New York Telegram*, May 20, 1874.

17. Charles Dickens, *Oliver Twist*. The George Almar adaptation, first performed in London on November 19, 1838, at the Royal Surrey, and in New York (with Charlotte Cushman) on February 7, 1839, was used throughout the century. In 1905 J. Comyns Carr provided a fresh version for Beerbohm Tree. The Almar version was used, with extensions, by John Moore when he staged this play for Augustin Daly in 1874. Moore, according to the *New York Times and Advertiser* in reviewing this production, staged the play at the old Broadway Theatre on June 24, 1869. When Daly took over the Broadway, renaming it Daly's Fifth Avenue, Moore remained as prompter and stage manager, and played Grimwig in the production. His manuscript promptbook is now on file in the Harvard Theatre Collection (call number TS 2478.307).

18. *Philadelphia Record*, May 7, 1895.

19. *New York Times*, May 15, 1895.

20. *Boston Advertiser*, December 25, 1894.

21. *Ibid.*

22. *New York Herald*, May 20, 1874.

23. *New York Telegram*, May 20, 1874.

24. Both quotations are from a review of *The Great Train Robbery* (HTC).

25. *The Era* (London), undated. See under *The Great Train Robbery* (as above).

26. *Boston Transcript*, October 1, 1912.

27. See Chapter One, note 59.

28. *Illustrated News* (London), February 28, 1852.

29. Both quotations are from the *Boston Weekly Transcript*, January 14, 1883.

30. *The Weekly Music and Drama* (New York), January 13, 1883.

31. *Ibid.*

32. *Ibid.*

33. *Ibid.*

34. *Boston Evening Transcript*, October 14, 1895.

35. At Laura Keene's Theatre, New York, March 29, 1860; in Boston, September 3, 1860; and at the Adelphi, London, September 17, 1860.

36. Dion Boucicault, *The Colleen Bawn*. The manuscript promptbook is fully marked, with running time also indicated for Act I (55 minutes) and Act II (50 minutes). This promptbook embodies staging principles in use during this period (1860-1900). HTC, call number TS 3121.50.

37. *The Era* (London), February 1, 1896.

38. From the manuscript promptbook. See note 36, above.

39. Published in the *New York Dramatic Mirror*, September 27, 1890.

40. *New York Daily Tribune*, March 30, 1860.

41. *Boston Evening Transcript*, November 8, 1887.

42. "Dear Harp of My Country," *Saturday Review* (London), February 1, 1896, p. 122.

43. Austin Fryers, "Bill of the Play," January 31, 1896. This review is otherwise unidentified. See under *The Colleen Bawn* (HTC).

44. *Boston Transcript*, January 21, 1896.

45. *Boston Herald*, January 21, 1896.

46. See Chapter One, note 41.

47. *Forbidden Fruit and Other Plays by Dion Boucicault*, edited by Allardyce Nicoll and F. Theodore Cloak (Princeton: Princeton University Press, 1940); Vol. I of *America's Lost Plays*.

48. Allardyce Nicoll, *A History of Early Nineteenth Century Drama, 1800-1850* (2 vols.; Cambridge, England: Cambridge University Press, 1930), I, 37n.

49. *Ibid.*, I, 37.

50. *Ibid.*, I, 36.

51. *Ibid.*, I, 37.

52. Dion Boucicault, *After Dark; or, Neither Maid, Wife nor Widow*, published by DeWitt "As first performed at the Princess's Theatre, London (under the management of Mr. G. Vining), on Wednesday, August 12, 1868." HTC, call number DAL 966,1.5.

53. From the DeWitt version.

54. From the DeWitt version.

NOTES

55. From a review of *After Dark* (HTC).
56. J. F. Daly, *The Life of Augustin Daly* (New York, 1917), p. 75.
57. Augustin Daly, *Under the Gaslight*. The promptscript, marked on the cover "G. W. Wilson," used the printed version by Samuel French (see HTC, call number DAL 117,7.65), and is interleaved with prompting and production directions. HTC, call number TS 2696.350.
58. See Chapter Eight, p. 184.
59. From a review of *Under the Gaslight* dated March 16, 1896 (HTC).
60. In a review by Charles Crozier in *The Era* (London), January, 1844.
61. Dion Boucicault, *Formosa; or The Railroad to Ruin*. Stage directions in the printed production version "As first performed at the Drury Lane Theatre, London, under the management of Mr. F. B. Chatterton, on Thursday, August 5, 1869." This book also includes ground plans. HTC, call number DAL 966,1.5.
62. A. B. Walkley, *Playhouse Impressions* (London, 1892), pp. 193-197.
63. *New York Sunday Dispatch*, October 19, 1858. My italics.
64. The two quotations describing this production are from a printed version of Dion Boucicault's *Pauvrette* published by Samuel French (French's Standard Drama No. CCXXIX), "As performed at the principal theatres." The outside cover of the book bears the name "Geo. Riddle," and the speeches of Count Maurice are checked. George Riddle was a member of the Boston Museum company in 1875-76. HTC, call number DAL 966,1.9.
65. Review of the London production of *Peep o'Day* (HTC). My italics.
66. Edmund Falconer, *Peep o'Day* (New York: Samuel French, n.d.). The prompt copy is heavily annotated; two playbills are inserted for a performance at the Broadway Theatre, New York, January 17, 1868, with Mrs. D. P. Bowers as Kathleen. John Moore was stage manager at the Broadway during this period. HTC, call number TS 2512.50.
67. The Moore property list included "A Mattress to catch bridge," thus muf-

fling the sound of the real crash on stage, preventing damage to bridge and stage, and utilizing the "crash machine" as the bridge plunged into the gully.
68. *The Times and Messenger* (New York), June 10, 1866.
69. Charles Dickens, *Our Mutual Friend*. The manuscript promptbook, marked "Geo. F. Rowe," is fully annotated for production. G. C. Odell, *Annals of the New York Stage* (New York: Columbia University Press, 1927-1945), VIII (1936), 15, credits Rowe with this adaptation. Rowe also played the role of Wegg in this production. HTC, call number TS 3494.650.
70. *Boston Transcript*, January 9, 1906.
71. *Ibid.*, February 12, 1907.
72. *New York Dramatic Mirror*, December 11, 1897.
73. *New York Evening Post*, January 6, 1897.
74. *The Era* (London), August 22, 1887.
75. *Boston Post*, April 9, 1899.
76. *Boston Herald*, September 19, 1899.
77. Dutton Cook, *Nights at the Play; a View of the English Stage* (2 vols.; London, 1883), I, 59-60. My italics.
78. *New York Times*, May 17, 1887.
79. Review of *The Odds* dated April 4, 1902 (HTC).
80. *Boston Times*, March 15, 1891.
81. *Ibid.*, December 20, 1891.
82. *Ibid.*, March 15, 1891.
83. *Boston Beacon*, October 4, 1884. My italics.
84. *Ibid.*, November 10, 1894.
85. Alexandre Dumas, *The Count of Monte Cristo*. The manuscript promptbook, marked "Property of J. B. Studley," is complete with musical score for piano, clarinet, two violins, viola, bass, trombone, flute, cornet, and tambour. Studley, who had been associated with the production of this play for a number of years, played Danglars for Charles Fechter on April 28, 1873, at the Grand Opera House, New York, and undoubtedly used the same book when he played Dantès at the Mount Morris Theatre,

— *259* —

New York, in 1884. HTC, call number TS 3436.700.

86. *New York Times*, September 9, 1898. My italics.

87. Stage directions in the J. B. Studley promptbook. See note 85.

88. *Boston Globe*, September 18, 1900.

89. *Boston Herald*, September 19, 1900. The following three quotations are from this review. My italics.

90. *New York Sun*, October 22, 1896.

91. *Boston Globe*, November 3, 1896.

92. *Ibid.*, December 28, 1897.

93. Review of *The Clansman* dated January 8, 1906 (HTC).

94. Letter from Thomas Dixon to the *Boston Herald*, published November 11, 1905.

95. W. P. Eaton, "The Canned Drama," *American Magazine*, LXVIII, 506 (September 1909).

96. Lewis Jacobs, *The Rise of the American Film; a Critical History* (New York: Harcourt, Brace, and Company, 1939), p. 35.

CHAPTER THREE

1. Nicoll, *Early Nineteenth Century Drama*, I, 39.

2. Thomas Dibdin, *Reminiscences* (2 vols.; London, 1827), II, 179.

3. W. W. Burridge, "Development of Scenic Art and its Relation to the Drama," reprinted from *The Coming Age* (Boston and St. Louis, June, 1900), vol. III no. 6, p. 558.

4. Joseph Harker, *Studio and Stage* (London, 1924), p. 197.

5. Joseph Knight, *Theatrical Notes* (London, 1893), p. 216.

6. Alfred Tennyson, *Enoch Arden*. A manuscript promptscript for dramatic production, marked "Felix A. Vincent," has complete music cue sheet and full productional annotation, costume plot, scene plot, and so forth. HTC, call number TS 3198.300. Another manuscript dramatization of the same poem in three acts and six tableaux, marked "Property of L. P. Barrett, Esq.," and entitled *Under the Palm*, is also on file (TS 3696.146).

7. Review of *Enoch Arden* which appeared in a Boston newspaper (HTC).

8. *Chicago Times*, July 9, 1889.

9. *Chicago News*, July 9, 1889.

10. *Ibid.*

11. *Chicago Herald*, July 7, 1889.

12. *New York Dramatic Mirror*, July 13, 1889.

13. Knight, *Theatrical Notes*, p. 27.

14. *Ibid.*, p. 27.

15. Quoted in Harker, *Studio and Stage*, p. 198.

16. Harker, *Studio and Stage*, p. 103.

17. *Ibid.*, p. 105.

18. *Ibid.*, p. 51.

19. *Boston Traveler*, November 9, 1865.

20. Harker, *Studio and Stage*, p. 106.

21. *Ibid.*, p. 108.

22. *Ibid.*, p. 68.

23. *New York Dramatic Mirror*, March 16, 1889.

24. *London Daily News*, June 7, 1897.

25. *The Stage* (London), April 15, 1897.

26. *Boston Transcript*, September 4, 1891.

27. *Boston Journal*, September 5, 1891.

28. *New York Dramatic Mirror*, March 16, 1889.

29. *New York Sun*, April 15, 1900. The following three quotations are also from this review.

30. *The Era* (London), May 29, 1900.

31. *London Daily Telegraph*, May 7, 1900.

32. *The Era* (London), May 7, 1900.

33. An original program for the production at the Broadway Theatre is in the Harvard Theatre Collection. The scenes listed are from this bill.

34. *Boston Herald*, January 16, 1907. My italics.

35. Described by Hillary Bell in the *New York Herald*, December 3, 1899.

36. W. W. Ellsworth, "Behind the Scenes at Ben Hur," *The Critic* (March 1900), p. 245.

37. *Boston Transcript*, March 18, 1902.

38. *New York Herald*, November 30, 1899.

39. Hillary Bell, in the *New York Herald*, December 3, 1899.

40. *Ibid.*

41. Ellsworth, "Behind the Scenes at Ben Hur," p. 245.

42. *Boston Transcript*, December 21, 1900.

43. *Ibid.*

44. *Boston Herald*, October 20, 1903.

45. Review of *The Light that Failed* (HTC).

46. *Boston Herald*, October 20, 1903.

47. Review of *The Light that Failed* (HTC).

48. Review of *Ramona* dated March 21, 1905 (HTC).

49. *New York Evening Post*, April 6, 1916.

50. *San Francisco Examiner*, January 7, 1906.

51. *Boston Transcript*, October 14, 1904.

52. *San Francisco Call*, January 7, 1906. My italics.

53. *Boston Transcript*, October 14, 1904.

54. *San Francisco Examiner*, January 7, 1906.

55. Thomas Bailey Aldrich, *Judith of Bethulia*. A printed promptbook inscribed "Miss Nance O'Neill's own copy of her play from her friend Thomas Bailey Aldrich, December 5, 1904." Stage directions have been added by Miss O'Neill. HTC call number Thr 865.2/15*.

56. *New York Dramatic Mirror*, January, 1906.

57. *Ibid.*

58. *New York Evening Post*, January 13, 1906.

59. *Ibid.*, March 4, 1915.

60. Review of *Brewster's Millions* (HTC).

61. From an article entitled "A Masterpiece of Stage Effect," dated July 7, 1907, and describing *Brewster's Millions* (HTC).

62. *New York Dramatic Mirror*, January 12, 1907.

63. *Boston Transcript*, February 11, 1908.

64. From "A Masterpiece of Stage Effect." See note 61.

65. Eaton, "The Canned Drama," p. 498.

66. *New York Tribune*, December 3, 1915.

67. *New York Times*, December 26, 1915.

68. *New York Dramatic Mirror*, December 11, 1915.

69. *New York Tribune*, December 3, 1915.

CHAPTER FOUR

1. Quoted in F. Rahill, "Melodrama," *Theatre Arts*, VIII, 291 (April 1932).

2. T. W. Stevens, *The Theatre from Athens to Broadway* (New York: D. Appleton and Company, 1932), pp. 167-68.

3. *Ellen Terry's Memoirs*, with Preface, Notes, and Additional Biographical Chapters by Edith Craig and Christopher St. John (London: V. Gollancz Ltd., 1933), p. 235.

4. From an original letter by Boucicault included in the "Irving" volume of *Actors and Actresses of Great Britain and the United States*, ed. Brander Matthews and Laurence Hutton (5 vols.; New York, 1886), vol. V, no. 8, pts. 1 and 2.

5. *Chicago Inter-Ocean*, March 6, 1896.

6. From review of *The Bells* dated February 27, 1884 (HTC).

7. Knight, *Theatrical Notes*, p. 189.

8. *Ibid.*, p. 226.

9. Dutton Cook, *A Book of the Play* (2 vols.; London, 1876), I, 365.

10. Bram Stoker, *Personal Reminiscences of Henry Irving* (2 vols.; New York: The Macmillan Company, 1906), I, 55. Quoted by permission of The Macmillan Company.

11. *Ibid.*, II, 21n.

12. *Ibid.*, I, 156-158.

13. *Ellen Terry's Memoirs*, p. 138.

14. Stoker, *Henry Irving*, I, 159-160.

15. *Ibid.*, I, 160-61. My italics, except for the word *salt*.

16. Knight, *Theatrical Notes*, p. 148.

17. William Winter, *Henry Irving* (New York, 1885), p. 100.

18. *New York Mail and Express*, October 22, 1901.

19. From a review by H. T. Parker in the *Boston Evening Transcript*, October 22, 1901. The same opinion was expressed by H. H. Clapp in the *Boston Evening Record*, February 18, 1902.

20. Stoker, *Henry Irving*, I, 139. My italics.

21. Cook, *Book of the Play*, I, 158.

22. *Boston Transcript*, February 18, 1902.

23. *Boston Evening Record*, February 18, 1902.

24. *New York Times*, December 5, 1883.

25. Stoker, *Henry Irving*, I, 76.

26. *Chicago Inter-Ocean*, October 3, 1893.

27. *Boston Advertiser*, March 1, 1884.

28. *Boston Evening Transcript*, December 13, 1883.

29. *New York Commercial Advertiser*, May 11, 1896.

30. *Ibid.*

31. *London News*, February 19, 1898.

32. Knight, *Theatrical Notes*, p. 101.

33. Cook, *Book of the Play*, I, 307.

34. *Ibid.*, I, 307.

35. Stoker, *Henry Irving*, I, 205.

36. *Ibid.*, I, 206.

37. *Ibid.*, I, 94.

38. *Ibid.*

39. *The Era* (London), December 7, 1907.

40. Stoker, *Henry Irving*, I, 98-99.

41. *The Era* (London), December 7, 1907.

42. *Boston Beacon*, November 8, 1884.

43. Stoker, *Henry Irving*, II, 66, 67.

44. *Ibid.*, I, 176.

45. *Ibid.*, I, 178.

46. *Ibid.*

47. *Ibid.*, I, 180.

48. *London Evening Post*, December 31, 1888.

49. Stoker, *Henry Irving*, I, 24.

50. *The Times* (London), December 31, 1888.

51. *London Morning Post*, December 31, 1888.

52. *London Daily Chronicle*, December 31, 1888.

53. *London Daily Telegraph*, December 31, 1888. My italics.

54. *London Daily Chronicle*, December 31, 1888.

55. *London Daily Telegraph*, December 31, 1888.

56. *The Times* (London), December 31, 1888.

57. *London Daily Telegraph*, December 31, 1888.

58. *Ibid.*

59. *London Evening Post*, December 31, 1888. My italics.

60. *Ibid.*

61. *London Star*, December 31, 1888.

62. *London Daily Telegraph*, December 31, 1888.

63. *London Standard*, December 31, 1888.

64. *London Daily News*, December 31, 1888.

65. *The Times* (London), December 31, 1888.

66. *London Star*, December 31, 1888.

67. Stoker, *Henry Irving*, I, 113.

68. *Ibid.*

69. *Ibid.*, I, 114.

70. *Ibid.*, I, 115.

71. From a letter to Irving quoted in Stoker, *Henry Irving*, I, 116.

72. From the same letter.

73. *Boston Herald*, October 2, 1895.

74. *Boston Globe*, October 2, 1895.

75. *Ibid.*

76. *Boston Home Journal*, October 5, 1895, p. 10.

77. *Boston Globe*, October 2, 1895.

78. *Boston Herald*, September 20, 1895.

79. *New York Times*, November 5, 1895.

80. *Boston Herald*, October 2, 1895.

81. *Boston Globe*, October 2, 1895.

82. Stoker, *Henry Irving*, II, 85.

83. Michael Orme (Mrs. A. A. Grein), *Reminiscences* (n.p., n.d.,), p. 221.

84. Stoker, *Henry Irving*, I, 272.

85. Winter, *Belasco*, II, 455.

86. N. Vachel Lindsay, *The Art of the Moving Picture* (copyright, 1915, by The

Macmillan Company; copyright, 1943, by Mrs. Elisabeth C. Lindsay), p. 108. Quoted by permission of Mrs. Lindsay.

87. Winter, *Belasco*, I, 108.

88. Quoted, *ibid.*, I, 109.

89. From a review in the *San Francisco Evening Bulletin* quoted in Winter, *Belasco*, I, 110.

90. Winter, *Belasco*, I, 117.

91. *Ibid.*, I, 119.

92. *Ibid.*, I, 119.

93. *Ibid.*, I, 123.

94. Quoted, *ibid.*, I, 124.

95. *Ibid.*, I, 124-25.

96. *Ibid.*, I, 118.

97. *Ibid.*, I, 250.

98. *Ibid.*, I, 250-51.

99. *Boston Advertiser*, November 27, 1888.

100. *Ibid.*

101. *New York Mirror*, December 3, 1887.

102. *Ibid.*

103. Winter, *Belasco*, II, 3.

104. *New York Tribune*, February 6, 1901.

105. The Byron photographs of *Under Two Flags* are in the Harvard Theatre Collection.

106. From a review of *Under Two Flags* (HTC).

107. *New York Sun*, February 10, 1901.

108. *New York Times*, February 6, 1901.

109. *New York Sun*, February 6, 1901.

110. *New York Times*, February 6, 1901.

111. *New York Sun*, February 6, 1901.

112. Winter, *Belasco*, I, 482-483.

113. From a review of *Madame Butterfly* dated March 6, 1900 (HTC).

114. *Boston Herald*, October 8, 1907.

115. *New York World*, February 17, 1901.

116. *Ibid.*

117. Winter, *Belasco*, II, 248.

118. *Boston Transcript*, December 26, 1901.

119. *New York World*, December 26, 1901.

120. See note 105, above.

121. *Boston Transcript*, December 26, 1901.

122. *New York Commercial Advertiser*, December 26, 1901.

123. *Boston Transcript*, December 26, 1901.

124. *Ibid.*

125. From a review of *Madame Du Barry* dated December 27, 1901 (HTC).

126. *Harper's Weekly* (New York), January 18, 1902.

127. Winter, *Belasco*, II, 56.

128. *Boston Transcript*, November 18, 1903.

129. Winter, *Belasco*, II, 85.

130. *New York Sun*, December 4, 1902.

131. Winter, *Belasco*, II, 73.

132. *New York Sun*, December 4, 1902.

133. *Ibid.*

134. *Boston Transcript*, November 18, 1903.

135. *New York Herald*, December 4, 1902.

136. *New York Dramatic Mirror*, December, 1902.

137. *Boston Transcript*, December 4, 1902.

138. *New York Sun*, December 4, 1902.

139. Winter, *Belasco*, II, 97.

140. *Ibid.*, II, 147.

141. *Ibid.*, II, 139.

142. *Ibid.*, II, 226.

143. *Ibid.*, II, 226.

144. Quoted, *ibid.*, II, 234.

145. *Ibid.*, II, 261.

146. *Ibid.*, II, 265. It is of particular interest to note that Cecil B. De Mille worked with Belasco in this and other productions in a variety of capacities, even to the co-authorship of the highly successful *The Return of Peter Grimm*. This was corroborated by a letter to me from Mr. Donald Hayne of Paramount Pictures dated June 24, 1949. Needless to say, these preliminaries have found significant expansion in Mr. De Mille's subsequent achievements in the film.

147. *Ibid.*, II, 349.

148. *Ibid.*, I, 202, 205.

149. *Boston Globe*, January 25, 1898.

150. *London News*, November 2, 1897.

151. *New York Herald*, October 6, 1897.

152. *New York Journal*, October 6, 1897.

153. *Philadelphia Ledger*, November 16, 1897.

154. *Boston Advertiser*, January 25, 1898.

155. Winter, *Belasco*, I, 258.

156. Quoted, *ibid.*, I, 257.

157. *Ibid.*, I, 409.

158. *Boston Journal*, November 23, 1893.

159. *Boston Post*, Janaury 29, 1895.

160. *Boston Herald*, January 29, 1895.

161. From a review of *The Girl I Left Behind Me* (HTC).

162. *Boston Advertiser*, November 14, 1893.

163. From a review of *The Heart of Maryland* dated November 29, 1896 (HTC).

164. *New York Dramatic Mirror*, March 28, 1896.

165. *Ibid.*

166. Winter, *Belasco*, I, 443.

167. *New York Dramatic Mirror*, March 28, 1896.

168. *Ibid.*

169. *Ibid.*

170. *New York Herald*, October 27, 1895.

171. *Chicago Daily Tribune*, April 28, 1906.

172. *Ibid.*

173. *Ibid.*

174. *Ibid.*

175. Winter, *Belasco*, II, 202-203.

176. *Chicago Daily Tribune*, April 28, 1906.

177. Winter, *Belasco*, II, 205-207.

178. *Boston Herald*, October 21, 1884.

179. *Boston Journal*, October 21, 1884.

180. *New York Telegram*, November 2, 1887.

181. *Boston Home Journal*, October 6, 1888.

182. *Ibid.*, November 12, 1887.

183. *New York Times*, November 4, 1887.

184. Lindsay, *Art of the Moving Picture*, p. 21.

185. Winter, *Belasco*, I, 461.

186. *New York Sun*, January 4, 1899.

187. *New York Times*, September 24, 1901.

188. The three quotations in this paragraph describing the play are from a review in the *Boston Herald*, September 9, 1902.

189. *New York World*, September 24, 1901.

190. *Boston Herald*, September 9, 1902.

191. *New York Dramatic Mirror*, October 19, 1901.

192. Winter, *Belasco*, II, 119.

193. *New York Globe and Commercial Advertiser*, October 17, 1907.

194. *Boston Transcript*, April 20, 1909.

195. *Washington Post*, October 19, 1907.

196. *Boston Transcript*, April 20, 1909.

197. Winter, *Belasco*, II, 270.

198. Quoted, *ibid.*, II, 379.

199. For an excellent treatment of this naturalistic "touches" method of acting, see E. J. West, "Histrionic Methods on the London Stage, 1870-1890" (dissertation, Yale University, 1941).

200. From a review of *Rose Michel* by Nym Crinkle dated January 18, 1876 (HTC).

201. From a review of *Rose Michel* which appeared in the *New York Graphic* (HTC).

202. *Ibid.*

203. *Ibid.*

204. *New York Times*, November 24, 1875.

205. From a review of *Rose Michel* dated November 24, 1875 (HTC).

206. *New York Dramatic Mirror*, April 12, 1890.

207. From a review of *Money Mad* dated December 25, 1888 (HTC).

208. *New York World*, April 8, 1890.

209. *Boston Transcript*, September 30, 1890.

210. Quoted in MacKaye, *Epoch*, II, 242.

211. *New York Sun*, April 8, 1890.

212. Robert G. Ingersoll, quoted in MacKaye, *Epoch*, II, 151.

213. Quoted, *ibid.*, II, 158. Italics probably MacKaye's.

214. *New York Dramatic Mirror*, December 31, 1887.

215. *Boston Herald*, December 11, 1888.

216. Quoted in MacKaye, *Epoch*, II, 158.

217. *Philadelphia Times,* January 6, 1889.

218. *New York Star,* January 2, 1888.

219. MacKaye, *Epoch,* II, 153.

220. *Ibid.,* II, 145-46.

221. *New York Sun,* December 25, 1887. My italics.

222. *New York Despatch,* January 8, 1888.

223. Quoted in MacKaye, *Epoch,* II, 146-47.

224. *Buffalo Express,* May 31, 1887.

225. From a review of *Paul Kauvar* (HTC).

226. Quoted from an interview May 23, 1881, in MacKaye, *Epoch,* I, 410.

227. Patent applied for September 9, 1879.

228. From a published interview of November, 1879 quoted in MacKaye, *Epoch,* I, 323.

229. Quoted from a contemporary review, *ibid.,* II, 11.

230. Patent application no. 434,297, filed May 25, 1892; quoted *ibid.,* II, addenda, lxxxii.

231. Patent application no. 434,291, filed May 25, 1892; quoted *ibid.,* II, addenda, lxxxiv.

232. Patent application no. 434,293, filed May 25, 1892; quoted *ibid.,* II, addenda, xci.

233. Patent application no. 434,296, filed May 25, 1892; quoted *ibid.,* II, addenda, xciv.

234. Patent application no. 434,295, filed May 25, 1892; quoted *ibid.,* II, addenda, lxxiv.

235. Patent application no. 434,289, filed May 25, 1892; quoted *ibid.,* II, addenda, lxxvii.

236. Patent application no. 434,290, filed May 25, 1892; quoted *ibid.,* II, addenda, xcvii.

237. *Boston Courier,* December 16, 1888.

238. Louis E. Cooke, "Reminiscences of a Showman," *Newark Evening Star,* July 1, 1915.

239. From a press report quoted in MacKaye, *Epoch,* II, 83.

240. From a press report quoted *ibid.,* II, 85.

241. The American painter, Robert Reid, quoted, *ibid.,* II, 331.

242. *Chicago Times,* August 24, 1892.

243. Quoted from a statement by Steele MacKaye, delivered at the opening of his Scenitorium in Chicago, February 5, 1894—three weeks before his death (MacKaye, *Epoch,* II, 346-47). MacKaye's italics.

244. *Chicago Sunday Advertiser,* March 26, 1893.

245. Frank Russell Green, quoted in MacKaye, *Epoch,* II, 323.

246. *New York Daily News,* March 13, 1893.

247. From a press notice quoted in MacKaye, *Epoch,* II, 345.

248. *Ibid.,* II, 353.

249. *Chicago Inter-Ocean,* February 1893.

250. *Chicago News,* February 9, 1894.

251. *Chicago Times,* February 6, 1894.

252. *Ibid.*

253. *Chicago Inter-Ocean,* February 6, 1894.

254. Quoted in MacKaye, *Epoch,* I, xx. My italics.

CHAPTER FIVE

1. Seven portfolios of clippings, playbills, and other theatrical miscellanea, collected by Charles Durang and entitled "Philadelphia Stage," is in the Harvard Theatre Collection (call number TS 275.5). The review in which this quotation appears is in chapter 42.

2. Charles Durang, *The Sleeping Beauty.* This manuscript promptbook is dated 1825. Durang at that time was serving as an actor at the Chestnut Street Theatre, Philadelphia. A cast of the production at the Park Theatre, New York, is written in on the title page, and this book was probably used for a presentation there on January 18, 1828. There is also the likelihood that an 1825 production was given at the Chestnut Street, although no record of this early showing exists in Odell, Du-

rang, T. A. Brown, or the Harvard playbills. HTC, call number TS 3624.75.

3. Felix A. Vincent, *Aladdin*. The manuscript promptbook is marked "Property of Felix A. Vincent" (HTC, call number TS 3024.26). Vincent, according to the Harvard playbills for the Cleveland Theatre, Bank Street, played Kasrac there on November 7, 1855. A playbill of G. H. Gilbert's production at Wood's Theatre, May 16, 1862, is pasted into the back of this promptbook. Included in the same hand as that of the manuscript itself (which can be identified from letters on file at the Harvard Theatre Collection as that of Vincent) is a cast list which names Vincent as Kasrac and Loie Fuller as Zobedie. This cast cannot be placed as to theatre, but since Loie Fuller was born in 1870 and began her career very young, it can be safely assumed that the script was used by Vincent in the middle and late eighties.

4. *New York Mirror*, January 18, 1879.

5. *Ibid.*

6. Review of *Arabian Nights* (HTC).

7. Boston Record, January 10, 1888.

8. Review of *Arabian Nights* (HTC).

9. *The Era* (London), February 19, 1887.

10. Review of *Cinderella* dated December 31, 1896 (HTC).

11. Unsigned article entitled "London Theatres," in *The Stage*, December 31, 1896.

12. *Ibid.*

13. *London News*, December 28, 1896.

14. *Ibid.*

15. Jacobs, *Rise of the American Film*, p. 30.

16. "London Theatres," *The Stage*, December 31, 1896.

17. *Saturday Review* (London), January 23, 1897.

18. *Boston Sunday Herald*, January 14, 1894.

19. *Illustrated Sporting and Dramatic News*, January 20, 1894.

20. *Ibid.*

21. *Boston Sunday Herald*, January 14, 1894.

22. *The Era* (London), December 28, 1895. My italics.

23. *London News*, December 28, 1896.

24. *The Stage* (London), December 31, 1896.

25. *London Standard*, December 26, 1899.

26. *The Era* (London), December 28, 1895.

27. *The Stage* (London), December 10, 1896.

28. *London Telegraph*, December 28, 1899.

29. *London Daily Mail*, December 17, 1899.

30. *Ibid.*

31. *New York Sun*, November 5, 1901.

32. *Boston Transcript*, February 3, 1903.

33. *Boston Globe*, February 2, 1903.

34. *New York Dramatic Mirror*, November 8, 1901.

35. *Boston Globe*, February 2, 1903.

36. Undated cliping from *The Era* (London). See under *The Sleeping Beauty* (HTC).

CHAPTER SIX

1. Jacobs, *Rise of the American Film*, pp. 57-58. In an interview I had with Mr. F. J. Marion of Kalem Pictures on October 12, 1941, Mr. Marion told me that a system of artificial lighting was set up for the filming of the Jeffries-Sharkey championship boxing match in 1899, but this was by no means practical for daily filming.

2. *Boston Herald*, May 19, 1896.

3. *Ibid.*

4. From an early motion-picture review entitled "A Wonderful Invention." See under *Arrival of the Paris Express* (HTC).

5. *Biograph Catalogue* (New York, 1902), p. 123. The volume I consulted was in the library of Mr. F. J. Marion in Stamford, Connecticut.

6. *Ibid.*, p. 125.

7. M. Jackson-Wrigley and Eric Leyland, *The Cinema* (London: Grafton and Company, 1939), p. 191.

8. *Biograph Catalogue* (1902), p. 247.

9. *Ibid.*, p. 156.
10. *Ibid.*
11. *Ibid.*, p. 240.
12. *Ibid.*, p. 244.
13. *Ibid.*, p. 9.
14. *Ibid.*
15. The quotations in this paragraph describing the scenes from *The Downward Path* are from the *Biograph Catalogue* (1902), pp. 242-43.
16. *Edison Catalogue* (dated about 1900-1903 by the Museum of Modern Art Film Library), film 5735.
17. *Ibid.*
18. Described to me by Mr. F. J. Marion, author of the film and one of the founders of Kalem Pictures, in our interview October 12, 1941.
19. *Biograph Catalogue* (1902), p. 34.
20. *Ibid.*, p. 67.
21. *Ibid.*, p. 241.
22. *Ibid.*, p. 50.

CHAPTER SEVEN

1. Jacobs, *Rise of the American Film*, p. 23.
2. *Star Films, Méliès Catalogue* (Paris, New York, 1900-01), p. 18. This passage is also cited by Lewis Jacobs *(Rise of the American Film*, p. 24).
3. Terry Ramsaye, *A Million and One Nights; a History of the Motion Picture* (2 vols.; New York, 1926), I, 394.
4. Jacobs, *Rise of the American Film*, p. 26.
5. *Bioscope and Warwick Catalogue* (London, September 5, 1900), pp. 62-64, film 4264.
6. Ibid.
7. *Star Films, Méliès Catalogue*, Supplement 11 (Paris, New York, 1904), films 527-535; and *Star Films, General Catalogue* (1905), p. 37.
8. *Star Films, Méliès Catalogue*, Supplement 5 (Paris, New York, 1903), p. 1, films 484-498; and *Star Films, General Catalogue*, p. 26.
9. Both quotations in this paragraph are from Jacobs, *Rise of the American Film*, pp. 30-31.
10. *Star Films, Méliès Catalogue*, Supplement 29 (Paris, New York, 1905), pp. 1-8, films 740-749; and *Star Films, General Catalogue*, pp. 82-87.
11. *New York Morning Telegraph*, June 13, 1905.
12. *Star Films, Méliès Catalogue*, Supplement 33 (Paris, New York, 1906), pp. 3-8, films 824-838; and *Star Films, General Catalogue*, pp. 100-105.

CHAPTER EIGHT

1. The quotations in this paragraph can be found in the *Edison Catalogue* (dated 1900-1903 by the Museum of Modern Art Film Library), p. 89.
2. E. W. Sargent, *The Technique of the Photoplay* (New York, 1913), p. 8.
3. *Edison Catalogue* (1906). A full and elaborate description of *The Train Wreckers*, film 6222, appears on pp. 67-68 of the *Edison Catalogue* (c. 1900-1903) in the Museum of Modern Art Film Library. This volume also includes, on pp. 9-11, a scene-by-scene summary of *The Great Train Robbery*.
4. *Edison Catalogue* (1906). This film is also listed as number 6116 in the 1900-1903 *Edison Catalogue* (pp. 55-56).
5. Edison Catalogue (1906). This film is also listed as number 6098 in the 1900-1903 *Edison Catalogue* (pp. 54-55).
6. *New York Sun*, August 15, 1905.
7. Eaton, "The Canned Drama," p. 500.
8. *Ibid.*, p. 498.
9. M. J. Moses, *The American Dramatist* (2d ed., rev.; Boston, 1917), pt. IV, p. 305.
10. B. B. Hampton, *A History of the Movies* (New York: Covici-Friede, 1931), p. 41.
11. *Ibid.*
12. Interview with Mr. Marion, October 12, 1941.
13. Cf. page 171.
14. From an article by E. H. Lacon entitled "The Silent Stage," in the *London Daily Telegraph*; reprinted in the *Boston Transcript*, May 11, 1925.

15. Linda A. (Mrs. D. W.) Griffith, *When the Movies Were Young* (New York: E. P. Dutton and Co., Inc., 1925), pp. 37-40. Quoted by permission of E. P. Dutton and Co., Inc.

16. See Gene Fowler, *Father Goose: The Story of Mack Sennett* (New York: Covici-Friede, 1934).

17. An interesting analysis of his work appears in Joyce Kilmer's "In Memoriam: John Bunny," in *The Circus and Other Essays* (New York, 1916), p. 116. See also John Palmer, "Mr. Bunny," *Saturday Review* (London), CXVII, 466-67 (April 1914).

18. *Vitagraph Bulletin*, III, 7 (October 1, 1913).

19. *Edison Catalogue* (1904), p. 50.

20. *Bioscope and Urban Catalogue* (1903), p. 31.

21. *Ibid.*

22. *Biograph Catalogue*, Bulletin 108 (1907).

23. *Ibid.*

24. *Bioscope and Urban Catalogue* (1903), p. 111, film 3551.

25. *Ibid.*, p. 133. *A Christmas Dream* is here listed as a Bioscope reissue of an original Méliès production.

26. From a lecture by Frank Woods entitled "Growth and Development," delivered February 27, 1929, at the University of Southern California; included in the unpublished "Introduction to Photoplay" (Academy of Motion Picture Arts and Sciences: Los Angeles, 1929).

27. Talbot, *Moving Pictures*, p. 171.

28. Lindsay, *Art of the Moving Picture*, pp. 74-76.

29. *Moving Picture World*, VIII, 463 (March 4, 1911).

30. *Ibid.*, XVI, 165 (April 12, 1913).

31. Grau, *Theatre of Science*, p. 132.

CHAPTER NINE

1. Jacobs, *Rise of the American Film*, p. 96.

2. Griffith, *When the Movies Were Young*, p. 65.

3. *Biograph Catalogue*, Bulletin 151 (July 14, 1908), film 3454.

4. *New York Times*, October 10, 1909.

5. Lindsay, *Art of the Moving Picture*, pp. 43-44.

6. *Biograph Catalogue*, Bulletin 261 (July 29, 1909), film 3598.

7. *Ibid.*, Bulletin 263 (August 5, 1909), film 3601.

8. *Ibid.*, *Bulletin* (August 29, 1912), film 3994.

9. Jacobs, *Rise of the American Film*, p. 97.

10. *The Biograph Weekly*, vol. I, no. 2 (New York, September 12, 1914), p. 11.

11. From a contemporary review (unidentified) quoted in Lindsay, *Art of the Moving Picture*, p. 59.

12. Lindsay, *Art of the Moving Picture*, p. 60.

13. Griffith, *When Movies Were Young*, p. 225.

14. Lindsay, *Art of the Moving Picture*, p. 62.

15. *Ibid.*, p. 64.

16. Clarence E. Sinn, "Music for Pictures," *Motion Picture World*, vol. XX, no. 1 (April 4, 1914), p. 50.

CHAPTER TEN

1. Eaton, "The Canned Drama," p. 500.

2. *Moving Picture World*, XVII, 527 (August 2, 1913).

3. Talbot, *Moving Pictures*, p. 169. Talbot has hit upon the three basic qualities of early cinema: "gorgeous mounting," "melodramatic episodes," and "realism."

4. *New York Sun*, April 22, 1913.

5. Grau, *Theatre of Science*, p. 271.

6. *Ibid.*

7. *Scientific American*, CX, 489 (June 13, 1914).

8. W. P. Eaton, "The Theatre; a New Epoch in the Movies," *American Magazine*, LXXVIII, 95 (October 1914).

9. Lindsay, *Art of the Moving Picture,* p. 57.

10. *Ibid.,* pp. 55-56.

11. Eaton, "The Theatre," p. 97.

12. Jacobs, *Rise of the American Film,* p. 168.

13. Lindsay, *Art of the Moving Picture,* pp. 152-156.

14. *Ibid.,* p. 154.

15. *Ibid.,* p. 155.

16. *Ibid.,* p. 156.

17. P. Whitney, "Expressing Movie Emotion," *Vanity Fair,* October 1919.

18. W. P. Eaton, "Wanted—Moving Picture Authors," *American Magazine,* LXXXI, 69 (March 1916).

19. *Ibid.,* p. 68.

20. Lindsay, *Art of the Moving Picture,* p. 11.

21. Hugo Münsterberg, *The Photoplay; a Psychological Study* (New York, 1916), p. 218.

22. *The Biograph Weekly,* vol. I, no. 10 (New York, November 7, 1914), p. 10.

23. *Ibid.,* vol. I, no. 11 (November 14, 1914), pp. 10-11.

24. *Ibid.,* vol. I, no. 46 (July 17, 1915), pp. 6-7; and no. 47 (July 24, 1915), pp. 13-14. *Under Two Flags* was billed at that time as the first three-reel Biograph film.

25. W. C. De Mille, *Hollywood Saga* (New York: E. P. Dutton and Company, 1939), pp. 105-06.

26. *Ibid.,* pp. 105-06.

27. Iris Barry, *D. W. Griffith, American Film Master* (New York: The Museum of Modern Art, 1940), p. 29.

28. Richard Barthelmess, quoted in A. B. Paine, *Life and Lillian Gish* (New York: The Macmillan Company, 1932), p. 158.

29. Jacobs, *Rise of the American Film,* p. 336.

30. Eaton, "Wanted—Moving Picture Authors," p. 69.

31. Lindsay, *Art of the Moving Picture,* pp. 41-43.

32. *New York Times,* June 6, 1915.

33. Woods, "Growth and Development," pp. 25-26.

34. *New York Sun,* March 4, 1915.

35. *Ibid.*

36. *Ibid.*

37. Ramsaye, *A Million and One Nights,* p. 643.

38. *New York Evening Post,* March 4, 1915.

39. *New York American,* March 5, 1915.

40. *Ibid.*

41. Both quotations are from Julian Johnson's review, "The Shadow Stage," in *Photoplay,* X, 77, 81 (December 1916).

42. *Boston Evening Transcript,* April 27, 1920.

43. *New York Herald,* August 20, 1922.

44. *Ibid.,* August 15, 1922.

45. *Christian Science Monitor* (Boston), February 17, 1926.

46. *Boston Herald,* February 23, 1926. My italics.

47. *Boston Transcript,* February 23, 1926.

48. *Ibid.*

49. *Ibid.* My italics.

50. Iris Barry, "The Cinema," *The Spectator* (London), CXXXVII, 898 (November 28, 1926).

51. *Ibid.*

52. Review of *Ben Hur* (HTC).

53. *Boston Globe,* February 23, 1926.

54. Hampton, *History of the Movies,* p. 305.

55. Eaton, "The Theatre," p. 97.

CHAPTER ELEVEN

1. See S. M. Eisenstein, *The Film Sense,* translated and edited by Jay Leyda (New York: Harcourt, Brace, and Company, 1942), chap. i.

INDEX

INDEX

— 273 —

INDEX

INDEX

Titles of Related Interest —